COUNTY
IT
SNYDERS ADDITION
PARK CITY
SILVER CREEK
ONTARIO SPUR
DEER VALLEY
MEADOW
ONTARIO MILL
SEC. COR.
ONTARIO - DALY
TUNNEL
DRAIN
CONSTELLATION
MINING CO.
HANNEYR McHENRY MINING CO.
AVONDALE MINING CO.
HOMESTAKE MINING CO.
ONTARIO
BUG GROUP
SILVER
MINING DISTRICT
DISTRICT
T. 2 S. R. 4 E.
LEDGE
GROUP
MINING COMPANY
SNAKE CREEK
CONSOLIDATED
MINING CO.
MINING DISTRICT
T. 3 S. R. 4 E.
COUNTY
ATCH
MONTREAL SILVER MINING CO.
TOWNSHIP
36
1
SEC. 24
COR. 25

Park City at the turn of the century.

TREASURE MOUNTAIN HOME

PARK CITY REVISITED

Books by
George A. Thompson
Published by
Dream Garden Press

SOME DREAMS DIE
Utah's Ghost Towns & Lost Treasures

THROW DOWN THE BOX
Treasure Tales From Gilmer & Salisbury,
The Western Stagecoach King

FADED FOOTPRINTS
The Lost Rhoads Mines and Other
Hidden Treasures of Utah's Killer Mountains

TREASURE MOUNTAIN HOME
Park City Revisited

Treasure Mountain Home

Park City Revisited

By

George A. Thompson

and

Fraser Buck

Dream Garden Press
– Salt Lake City, Utah –

Library of Congress Catalog Card No. 68-8569

Paperback Edition ISBN: 0-942688-89-9
Hardbound Limited Edition ISBN: 0-942688-90-2

New Revised Edition 1993

10 9 8 7 6 5 4 3 2 1

Design & Production: Tor Anderson
Creative Direction: Ken Sanders

Published by:
Dream Garden Press
P.O. Box 27076
Salt Lake City, Utah 84127

Front and back cover illustrations by J.E. Coyle

*Framed prints of J.E. Coyle's illustrations
can be purchased at fine stores
throughout Park City, Utah*

FOREWARD

INTRODUCING PARK CITY

There is hardly a mining camp in the west whose story has not been told, either because they became well publicized ghost towns on the tourist circuit or like the camps of Nevada's Comstock and California's mother lode country they were immortalized by famous writers like Mark Twain and Bret Harte. Volumes have been written about camps whose chief claim to fame was one outstanding mine or perhaps some colorful character or favorite son. Most of them bloomed for only a day and then, like the delicate Sego Lily, faded and died. Park City, Utah, never achieved the doubtful honor of ghost town status nor did it have a press agent of either Twain or Harte stature. But its record as a mineral producer is far greater than the more famed El Dorados and Golcondas and it can boast multi-million dollar mines and great citizens without equal. Though reduced to ashes and subjected to the worst of depressions, labor troubles, and panics, it hung on and kept going while Ophirs and Treasure City's too numerous to list fell victim to time and the seasons and were forgotten.

Dr. E.P. LeCompte. He was long a familiar figure in old Park City.

In these pages we have tried to tell the real story of Park City, resorting to cold statistics and facts where necessary, but mostly just trying to give the reader an accurate and interesting account of those remarkable pioneers who turned an unknown canyon in Utah's rugged Wasatch Range into one of the richest and best known mining camps in the world. It is the story of those exciting days of discovery when mine names like the Flagstaff, Ontario, McHenry, Crescent, and Silver King stirred men's spirits and men like R.C. Chambers, John Daly, John Judge, Thomas Kearns, David Keith, and Sam Raddon lived history every day it was being made. The saga of Park City's first 100 years is the story of strong men and brave women who made a home in a rough land and endured all of the hard times and the Lips and downs that only a mining camp can know. And they lived through it all to build a city known throughout the west as the treasure chest of the Wasatch.

Today the prospectors' camp fires have long since turned to ashes and their trails have grown dim. The whistles of the Marsac, Union, and Mackintosh mills are silent and it has been a half century and more since the steam engines of the Glen Allen, Hawkeye, and Roaring Lion mines have turned a wheel. Hardly a man today can remember the Jones-Bonanza or Revelator mines, the Sampson or the Little Bell. In once busy canyons where great ore wagons raised clouds of dust, deer now slip quietly among the quaking aspens. Where thundering stamp mills pounded out millions of dollars in silver ore only crumbling rock foundations and sagging buildings remain. Only a hint of what was Chinatown can be found and the little camp on Lake Flat where it all began has vanished without a trace. In modern theatres built upon the ruins of once magnificent opera houses today's actors play the parts of "Little Nell" and "The Drunkard" while the ghosts of Maggie Mitchell and John L. Sullivan and "Buffalo Bill" Cody keep silent watch from the shadows.

Tourists pause momentarily in their endless rush to take photos of shafts and tunnels where fortunes in silver were dug from the earth's depths by the muddy booted argonauts of yesteryear and then hurry away to the cool retreat of a gay 90s saloon where cold-eyed dealers dealt Faro or 21 and where miners feeling their oats shot it out with men who had been their drinking partners only minutes earlier. They wonder how miners lived in the rough cabins that in places still cling to the sidehills and line the narrow canyons but don't know that some of those same pick and shovel prospectors owned the finest mansions along Salt Lake City's "Millionaire's Row" and built the capitol city's tallest skyscrapers. If our history succeeds in telling them the fantastic story of Park City and its wonderful pioneers then the labors spent in writing it will have been more than repaid.

To all those fine people who helped so greatly in the preparation of this history we give our sincere thanks. To those great old-timers who took time to recall tales and memories from the past and to everyone who made available old photos, personal reminiscences, and other historical information we are indebted. Much of the information contained in this work was drawn from personal interviews and from a lifetime of watching the town's history being made while libraries, mining journals, and reference works of all kinds and descriptions added unexpected bits and pieces of fascinating nostalgia. With information from so many different sources over so long a period of time it is possible that errors have crept in unnoticed. We hope that they are few and embarrass no one. There were so many wonderful people who contributed to Park City's history that if someone who should have been mentioned was not included the oversight was not an intentional one.

Special thanks is due Mrs. Maie Raddon who generously allowed the use of her treasury of old Park Records in which Park City's history was recorded week by week. No more accurate record of any mining camp can be found than that recorded by its pioneer newsmen and Sam Raddon, who guided the Record through its early years, was among the most accomplished of those early editors. We are also indebted to Kendall Webb of the Valley Studio for preparing many of the photos used and also to the Utah State Historical Society, the United Park City Mining Company, and the Utah State Mining Association for permission to use photos from their files. To Wm. James Mortimer for his efforts and guidance from the time the book was a dream until it became a reality we express our deep appreciation. To everyone who aided in this work we give our thanks for without them this volume could not have been written. And although many hours were spent and much midnight oil burned before the last lines were written it was not all work for it has been a labor of love. So come join us now, as we visit in memory once more, our Treasure Mountain Home.

Fraser Buck
George A. Thompson

A delivery wagon climbing the steep grade past the Ontario boarding house.

CONTENTS

INTRODUCTION

1969, Park City's centennial year, has long since come and gone. Some changes we hoped for then have happened, but some we hoped wouldn't happen have. Miners are working at the Ontario again, but some other businesses have disappeared. Historic ginger-bread buildings and colorful old homes have been razed, replaced by rows of condominiums that can only be described as ugly. New-comers are delighted with the new Park City but old-timers are appalled by it. But whether they love it or hate it, everyone agrees that Park City's new image is here to stay.

For most of Park City's residents, and for nearly every tourist, the big news today is skiing and ski resorts. Most old-timers don't even talk about runs and lifts, or cross-country and powder. For men who were yesteryear's miners, a lift is still a mine cage and powder is still dynamite. But they can't ignore the resort complex they disdainfully refer to as "the recreation", for it won't go away.

Thomas Kearns. In ten years he turned ten cents into a million dollars.

The ski resort business has boomed, even more than its most hopeful promoters could ever have dreamed of a few years ago. Where once it was hoped that some day Park City might compete with Aspen and Vail, or Sun Valley, now the only question seems to be, will they be able to keep up with it?

New ski runs and tourist hotels seem to be everywhere while talk of new areas like Deer Valley, Lake Flat and the old New Park property make what has already been built seem like only a drop in the bucket compared to what is yet to come. Perhaps it would be good to pause a moment and look back to see how it all happened.

In 1970 the Royal Street Company obtained an option to purchase the old Treasure Mountain Resort, and exercised that option in February, 1971. The new owners appropriately named their new organization the Greater Park City Company. 1972 saw many new ski areas developed, including chairlifts at Payday, Crescent and Lost Prospector, while work was started on the Thaynes Canyon runs. A big boost was given Park City when the official U.S. Ski Team was headquartered here, at the old Silver King Mine.

In 1974 rumors were heard that the Greater Park City Company was having financial troubles, and the following year they were confirmed when the resort complex was sold to Alpine Meadows of Lake Tahoe, Nevada. The change in management was professional, with winter sports oriented people in charge. Long range plans were developed and the future looked better than ever. In the words of company president, Warren King, "We are not a short term, fast buck company. We are here to stay!"

Meanwhile the picture was not so bright at Ski West. Several years of light snowfall combined with large financial losses from dozens of unsold condominiums built at high interest rates forced the company into bankruptcy. In May, 1975 the Park Record reported that the last four employees at Ski West had walked off the job because their wages hadn't been paid.

Ski West was sold at a foreclosure sale to Halbet Inc. of Orem, Utah for $333,000, only a fraction of the investment made at that resort. To recover more than $4,000,000 owed them for money loaned to build the Ski-West Condominiums, the Ford Motor Company purchased the condos at a sheriff's sale for $1,800,000, losing more than $2,000,000 on the deal.

There was a bright side, however, for Ford resold the condos at below market cost, selling every one in only a week's time, providing an unexpected opportunity for purchasers and giving a real boost to the Park City economy. And with new owners at the resort, Ski West was on its way to becoming a first class ski area once more.

But the real headline story at Park City was the comeback of the Ontario Mine. Skiing and winter sports are well enough for skiers and tourists, but the real history of Park City is silver, not snow, and the saga of silver is the Ontario. Both started out together. In July, 1872 Herman Buden and Rector Steen recorded the Ontario claim and on the 4th of July that same year Park City was given its name. More than 100 years later both names are synonymous, it's hard to think of one without the other.

When Royal Street took over the resort operation early in 1971, the companies mining properties became known as Park City Ventures, under the direction of Niles Andrus. A long hard look was taken at all the old diggings, from the Silver King to the Daly-West and the Park Utah, but the camp's mining future and fortunes were found in the depths of the old Ontario. Extensive long hole drilling confirmed that great silver ore bodies were still there, hidden under hundreds of feet of icy cold water. Getting to the ore proved to be a real problem.

No mining company anywhere worked harder or spent more search of success than did Park City Ventures. With money advanced by Anaconda Copper and American Smelting & Refining a complete modernization of the old Ontario was started. The #3 shaft was reopened and concreted at a cost of millions, and a huge new 900 horsepower double-drum hoist was installed in a brand new hoisting house and surface plant. To save the cost of shipping ore, a modern $17,000,000 mill was built to process ore not even yet mined.

Hauling ore before diesel trucks. Ore was hauled from the mine ore bin to the railroad.

The old wagon road up Ontario Canyon was paved all the way to the mine, a luxury old-timers who had lived in the canyon could never have dreamed of, and by 1974, except for Main Street it was the busiest street in town. Salt Lake City newspapers proclaimed that "Park City Mining Flourishes Again", and in March, 1975 they announced operational tests of the new 750 ton per day mill, designed to operate 24 hours a day, 7 days a week.

$30,000,000 had been invested in the Ontario by Park City Ventures, and optimism was high. More than $5,000,000 worth of concentrates were sold by 1976, but a lot of money was still owed before the Ontario would be out of debt. And then without warning it all fell apart. The old story of declining silver prices, always as fickle as a dancehall girl, made mining headlines, and black ones at that. The price of silver dropped daily, and the Ontario's black ledger entries turned into red ones.

Because of depressed prices the mine had been operating at a loss, and to top it all off, costs of pumping water soared to $45,000 a month.

With no warning, on February 15th, 1978, Park City Ventures closed the Ontario Mine. Everyone was stunned. General Manager Bill Norem reported the decision was made at a hastily called meeting, while Miner's Union President Blackie Sorenson said that in view of the company's losses he had expected something, "but not quite this drastic!" Park City Mayor Jack Green was "completely surprised!"

Overview of Park City, Utah in 1950.

For the first time in its history, Park City was without an operating mine. Even during the panics of 1873 and 1893, and the depressions of 1907 and the 1930s some miners were kept working, but now there was no one. And the irony of it all was that the silver was still there, huge bodies of it, but so was the 10,000 gallon a minute underground river of water, the Ontario's historic nemesis. R.C. Chambers must have rolled over in his grave!

Miners' spirits were at an all time low when stories were heard that some large out-of-state mining company was looking at the Ontario. And then rumors became fact when the giant Noranda Mining Company of Canada took over the multi-million dollar development started by Park City Ventures.

The Noranda was a miner's mining company, one which treated mining as a profession, not just a job. With operations worldwide, they knew how to do the job, and lost no time doing it. Almost overnight men were back on the job. Not only was the Ontario working again, but this time everyone knew it was for keeps. The Noranda Company meant business. As one old-timer put it, "They're a real cracker-jack outfit!"

All of the Noranda staff are professionals, from Superintendent Koos Schippers to Engineers Chuck Stone and Richard LaPrairie, including shift bosses, miners and mill men. With more than 800 miles of underground tunnels, drifts, stopes, winzes and raises, all subject to instant flooding should the pumps fail, and with 350 miners working on a $50,000,000 investment, they have to be professional. Rest easy, Mr. Chambers, the Ontario is in good hands again.

But while things were booming at the Ontario, the outlook wasn't so rosy at the New Park Mine. Back in the 60s when uranium millionaire Charles Steen became president of the New Park Company, Parkites hoped that some of his midas touch would rub off on Park City, but Steen proved to be a better uranium prospector than he was a silver miner. Experienced mining personnel like W.H.H. Cranmer and Fraser Buck were replaced with people unfamiliar with the New Park's deep, hot workings, and their loss combined with declining metal prices and labor troubles sounded the death knell for one of the district's most promising properties. Born during the great depression, the New Park was used to hard times, but it couldn't survive poor management, and plunged from the nation's sixth largest gold producer to a closed property of locked gates and silent buildings.

Most of Park City's old mines slowly rotted away once they were abandoned, but not the New Park, for in August, 1972 everything went on the auction block. Hoists, mucking machines, mine cars, pumps, drill steel and locomotives, everything; even the 500 ton mill, was put up for sale, everything to be sold in only two days, cash or check, no refunds!

Nothing was left, not even the buildings. Except for the waste dump and scars left on the mountain side the mine site didn't look much different than it had fifty years earlier when it was called the Glen Allen.. But $100,000,000 had been produced during that time, and that's some difference!

Surface rights at the New Park were sold to Ed Vetter and associates of Salt Lake City for $1,205,000 with tentative plans to use the property, which includes the 10 000 foot slopes of Bald Mountain and McHenry Canyon for a proposed new ski resort. The Silver King and Park Utah properties had been turned in to a ski resort, so why couldn't the New Park.

If a former resident were to return to Park City after a long absence, he wouldn t recognize the old camp. New subdivisions of look-alike condominiums have sprung up in such unlikely places as the Pacific Bridge sand flats and atop rocky and barren Quarry Hill. Hundreds, if not thousands of people have purchased high priced victorian style houses in places with names like Prospector Square, but they are not Parkites. The few natives left still live in Empire Canyon, on Rossie Hill, in Deer Valley or high on the back streets of Treasure Mountain in hundred-year-old houses. And more than a few have moved to Heber and Coalville, or to Salt Lake City.

Hugh Steel's old Cozy Saloon is gone, replaced by something called the Carbide Lamp, while the old hole-in-the-wall-size Club is now shiny and spotless, without any cobwebs hanging from the ceiling, something Heinie Hernan wouldn't even recognize. John Aimo's City Cash Market is a beauty salon now and the old camp even has its own radio station, KPCW. About the only things that isn't new is Mayor Jack Green, and although not old, he is an old-timer. So long as he's mayor, Park City will always seem a little more like home.

It seems like only a few years ago when people were amazed and few even amused, that the late Bob Murphy was urging them to renovate and reopen Park City's historic old Main Street buildings. It was Bob who remodeled the old Orange Blossom building into Car 19, reopened the long vacant Independent Telephone Company building, now the Alamo, kept Davitch's Saloon (the Handlebar) in business and was remodeling Sullivan's Boarding House when heart trouble struck him. There are a lot of people now who wish they had had his foresight.

Besides Bob Murphy, a lot of other old-timers have crossed the divide since Park City's centennial year including Fraser Buck, businessman, mining director and editor of the original edition of Treasure Mountain Home. Ken Webb, owner of the Valley Studio for 29 years, Boy Scout leader and friend to all has also passed on. Eric Joffs, long time foreman at the Judge loading station is gone also. For that matter, so is the loading station, familiar landmark for more than 70 years. And two of Park City's best loved lawmen have passed on, George Fisher, County Sheriff for over 30 years, longer than any sheriff in Utah history, and Chuck Thomas, City Marshal and policeman for about as long as anyone can remember. Tom Costas, Miner's Union President, City Mayor at a dollar-a-year salary, mining engineer and self-made millionaire is also gone. Another who is now missed from our streets is white bearded Santa Claus-look alike Sam Lowry, life long resident of Jordonelle and frequent visitor to Park City.

Parade making its way up Main Street, typical of the parades Park City used to have.

The future looks bright for Park City, its people, the Ontario and for what will soon be the biggest and best winter sports area in the country. The Park City Resort company's new Deer Valley development alone almost staggers the imagination. $50,000,000 will turn 5,000 acres of prime ski area into four new resort communities, boasting 2,000 housing units with an estimated population of 8,000. There will be ski villages at Deer Valley, Lake Flat, atop Bald Eagle Mountain and at the American Flag Village in Constellation Gulch off the head of Main Street. They will feature more than 20 new lifts and gondolas, a dozen tennis courts and a convention center with an eighteen hole golf course. The size of it all boggles the mind.

Nearly deserted Main Street in winter.

And that's not even counting proposed new resort developments at the old Park Con and Queen Ester mine properties, or the soon to be seen resort planned at the New Park Mine; all of which will add more than 2,000 additional acres of prime ski area. Stockholders of Park Con and Queen Ester, who a few years ago couldn't sell or give their stock away, might just make their fortune in snow instead of silver. How many can remember old Pete Cunningham saying, "Hold on to your Park Con stock boys, it'll make you rich someday!"

But though the future is bright, lets not forget our historical past. Our heritage is built on silver, not snow, and besides, a little reminiscing and nostalgia are good for the soul. Let's not forget the pioneers who built our town. No matter that it is now shiny and new, Park City will always be remembered as a mining camp. Let's not forget the argonauts of 1869 who built the camp we call Treasure Mountain today. Let's honor all the old-timers as we recall those good old days, the days of sixty-nine.

THE DAYS OF SIXTY NINE

I well remember those old times,
The days of sixty-nine, sir,
When miners gaily singing went
Into each silver mine, sir.
When buckskin coats and patched up pants,
Were fashions of the day, sir,
And when a mining claim would yield, The biggest kind of pay, sir.

Those highly interesting times,
When miners used to think, sir,
That whiskey straight was very cheap, At fifty cents a drink, sir.
When miners made an ounce a day, In any kind of dirt, sir,
And often times would freely pay,
Ten dollars for a shirt, sir.

Those highly interesting times,
When never would a man, sir,
Think claims were good unless they paid, $5 to the pan, sir.
When merchants always
got the dust, For what they had to sell, sir,
But never were afraid to trust,
Men paid them up so well, sir.

I do respect those good old times, For men were honest then, sir,
The diggin's paid, men wouldn't stop, To cheat their fellow men, sir.
This salting and this jumping claims, Was not considered fair, sir,
You'd ask a man where you might work, He'd tell you anywhere, sir.

And anywhere you went to work, A fortune could be made, sir,
With nothing but a rocker, a pan, A bucket or a spade, sir.
And sometimes with only a hand pick,
You'd work a little while, sir,
And ere you knew what you had done,
You'd made a bully pile, sir.

If one was found a rascal then,
Men took his case in hand, sir, And made him go to pulling hemp,
Or drove him from the land, sir.
But men are more enlightened now,
And stringent laws we'll make, sir,
And officers enforce the same, To raise a poker stake, sir.

But now, alas, those times have flown,
We never shall see them more, sir,
But let us do the best we can, And dig for silver ore, sir.
And if we strike a decent lead, Let's work and not repine, sir,
But take things easy as they did, In good old sixty nine, sir.

Ontario #3 shaft house. Man on the left is George Murray.
Note the flat cable used on the hoist.

CHAPTER 1

SOLDIER-PROSPECTORS

The Great American Desert was what they called it, the Utah Territory of the 1850s, a place of hostile Indians and wild animals, and according to Horace Greeley, "Not worth a tinker's dam!" Greeley had taken his own advice by going west and in the dispatches sent back to his newspaper he said of the Salt Lake Valley that "If Uncle Sam should ever sell this ground for 1¢ an acre he will swindle the purchaser outrageously!" But there were some who saw more to the new territory than its outward appearance of desolation. In 1847 Brigham Young and his Mormons followed the wagon tracks of the Donner party down Echo Canyon and over the backbone of the Wasatch. As their wagons approached the last steep grades leading to the head of Emigration Canyon the pioneers passed by a high mountain meadow, knee deep with lush green grass and carpeted with acres of wildflowers. How welcome that cool valley with its sparkling streams and timbered hills must have been to that little band after crossing a thousand miles and more of wilderness. Surely this was the promised land their prophet had led them to, and indeed, when the view of the Salt Lake Valley unfolded before them, Brigham Young rose from his wagon sick bed and said, "It is enough, this is the place!"

Brigham Young. He discouraged mining, fearing the gentile invasion it would bring.

In their forced migration the Mormons were looking for a place where they could live far from their persecutors and build a society apart from them. Of necessity that society had to be an agricultural one for there were no railroads or supply points closer than the east they had been driven from or the Spanish settlements on the far away Pacific. For 15 years they built their farms and grew their orchards and although they were well aware that in the nearby mountain canyons where they cut timber for their homes and quarried great blocks of granite for their temple there were minerals in abundance they made no effort to mine them. As a matter of fact, their leader had forbidden them to search for precious metal, knowing full well the influx of Gentiles, or non-Mormons, that would result if finds of gold or silver were reported.

Referring to the stampede of gentiles a gold rush would bring, Young said, "I can stand in my door and see where there are untold millions in rich treasures of the earth, both gold and silver. But the time has not come for the Saints to dig gold. It is our duty first to develop the agricultural resources of this country. As for gold and silver and other rich minerals of the earth, there is no country that equals this, but let them alone, let others seek them, and we will cultivate the soil, for if the mines are opened first, the people would rush in here in such great numbers that they would breed a famine, and we would be overwhelmed."

On another occasion Young admonished the Saints, "Do not go to the gold fields. I can take fifty of the wealthiest who did, and fifty who stayed, and the fifty who went cannot buy out the fifty who stayed. The wealthiest man I know of from the mines is old Father Rhoades (of Lost Rhoades Mine fame), who brought back $17,000 and he cannot buy what I have gained in one year! And look at the widows that have been made, and see the bones that lie bleaching and scattered over the prairies!"

The Mormon prophet ridiculed prospectors who would be millionaires, saying, "Whenever I see a man going along with an old mule that can hardly stand up, with a frying pan and an old quilt, I say to myself, there goes a millionaire in prospect! These millionaires are all over the country, they are in the mountains, on our roads and in the streets, and they haven't a six-pence between them!"

But even in its isolation their valley was visited by passing traders, trappers, and gold seekers enroute to California and once more because of their practice of polygamy, or plural marriage, the Mormons were again feeling the persecution they had fled the East to avoid. On orders to "Restrain the unruly Mormons" General Johnston's army had been sent into the valley in 1858, finally settling at Camp Floyd, some 50 miles south of the "City of the Saints." An uneasy truce continued between the soldiers and the "Saints" until 1861 when the troops were called back to the East because of the outbreak of the Civil War.

The Mormons were not to be left entirely alone, however, for in October, 1862, Col. Patrick E. Connor leading a small band of 300 California and Nevada volunteers marched into the valley and organized Fort Douglas, named for Lincoln's secretary of war, on a bench land overlooking the city. Col. Connor's arrival marked the birth of Utah's mining industry for while Brigham Young had forbidden mining Col. Connor did everything he could to encourage it. Col. Connor's reason for sending his troops to prospect the mountains was two-fold. He realized that with the discovery of valuable ores increasing numbers of prospectors and miners would enter the territory, diluting the Mormons' political and economic grip on the area, and also because both he and most of his men were old-time California miners who were anxious to prospect the virgin land. Col. Connor was also concerned because "his troops were engaged in eating the bread of idleness" so in the spring following his arrival in the valley he issued orders "Allowing troops to prospect the country in the vicinity of their posts and to furnish facilities for the discovery and opening of mines of gold, silver, and other minerals" and perhaps as a warning to the "Saints" he added "that miners and prospectors will be provided with the fullest protection of the military." That his troops were good prospectors is evidenced by his report to his commander at summer's end when he reported "the results so far have exceeded my most hopeful expectations." It was evident that Col. Connor fully intended to make President Lincoln's prophecy come true, "That Utah will yet become the treasure house of the nation."

A group of surveyors getting ready to go underground at the Anchor Mine.

The first mining claim filed in Utah was the West Jordan located in Bingham Canyon on Sept. 17, 1863, followed soon afterwards by several rich finds near Stockton in the Tooele district. In 1864 the first discovery of silver in the Wasatch Range was made by Col. Connor himself. It was made at the head of Little Cottonwood Canyon near the claim which a few years later would become the world famous Emma silver mine at Alta. There was little work done on the Cottonwood Canyon claims for several years because Utah was still without transportation other than wagon and team. The territory's isolation would soon end however for the rails of the Union Pacific being laid from the east and those of the Central Pacific from the west were drawing closer together. On May 10,1869, the golden spike linking the east with the west was driven at Promontory Point. The coming of the railroad meant much to both Utah and Col. Connor for it marked the start of the mining industry in the west. While the railroad broke down Utah's isolation once and for all even more importantly it provided a means of transportation for the haulage of heavy ores from its mines. Almost overnight prospectors began flocking to the deserts and mountains of the Great Basin. They came from everywhere and soon the remote and secret places of the Wasatch Range heard the ring of prospectors picks and saw the muddy tracks of booted miners where once there had been only the cry of the mountain lion and moccasin print of the Indian.

Some of the first arrivals made their way to the head of Little Cottonwood Canyon where Col. Connor had made his discovery five years earlier and a few went even further, crossing Big Cottonwood Canyon and the high divide beyond. Finally they stopped at the crest of the high windswept ridges that tumble down from Clayton Peak and Scott Hill and looked down on Pioneer Ridge and across the Bonanza Flats to the unknown canyons beyond. In the distance they saw the green mountain meadows seen by Brigham Young and his little band 22 years before. Although they didn't know it then other prospectors were making their way from those same meadows into the foothills and canyons between them. Almost simultaneously the discoveries that would give birth to the West's best-known mining camp as well as one of its richest were about to be made. The year was 1868 and the camp was Park City, the treasure house of the Wasatch.

Underground in the Daly Mines. - *Utah State Historical Society* -

Not long after their arrival in 1847 a handful of "Saints" followed their steps back to that green mountain meadow they had gazed on with such delight. Parley P. Pratt, one of the Church's apostles, began grazing a few head of livestock there and it wasn't long before the meadows were being called Parley's Park. The meadows must have seemed like a park to the weary Saints compared to the harsh desert of the valley below. In 1853 Samuel Snyder purchased "squatter's rights" in the park from Pratt for a yoke of oxen and a few years later built a small sawmill where he cut timber for the growing city in the valley below. Parley Pratt built a toll road into the Salt Lake Valley and in the year 1850 collected $1,500 from gold seekers enroute to the great California gold rush at Sutters Mill. Heber C. Kimball and J.M. Grant, who were also grazing cattle in the park, continued the toll road to the Kamas Prairie a few miles further east. A tiny community named Snyderville grew up around Snyder's sawmill but life even in such picturesque surroundings wasn't always easy, for records show that on July 17th, 1853, two of Snyder's sawmill workers were killed by Indians.

Although Snyderville was only a few miles from the future site of Park City and its fabulous ore deposits, apparently there was little actual exploration of the area until the late 1860s. In 1868 the tiny population of Snyderville was augmented by the arrival of a group of prospectors who made their camp nearby while prospecting in the foothills and canyons beyond. The situation was an ideal one for the prospectors for supplies of milk, eggs and other farm produce could be obtained from the Parley's Park Saints as well as a few hand tools. Rector Steen, one of the first prospectors to arrive at Snyderville, later recalled prices, "As being very reasonable, with flour at $5 a sack and potatoes at 50¢ a bushel." Tools were more expensive with "picks selling for $5 each and shovels at $2.50."

So it happened that at the same time Col. Connor's soldier-prospectors were entering the district over the 10,000-foot-high passes to the south other prospectors were coming in from Parley's Park to the north. That both groups made discoveries of rich ore at about the same time is certain but just who made the first discovery is unknown. It is known however that the first claim filed in the new district was the Young America lode, recorded on Dec. 23, 1868, followed the next month by the Yellow Jacket and Green Monster claims. Because they were the first claims recorded doesn't necessarily mean they were the first located. The Walker and Webster claim discovered by Rufus Walker and the Pinion located by Ephraim Hanks were among the earliest discoveries.

On the east slope of Bald Mountain in McHenry and Glencoe Canyons several other rich and promising claims also had been located. The McHenry and Hawkeye shafts were being sunk in McHenry Canyon not far from the outlet of Lake Flat and in Glencoe Canyon the Glen Allen claim had been staked by Cook, Cupit, McCune, and Braun. An article which appeared in the New York Herald on July 17, 1872, reveals how McHenry Canyon received its name. "A body of mineral, said to be the greatest ever discovered, has recently been located by two men from Illinois named McHenry and Hughes in Utah's Wasatch Range about seven miles south of Kimball's stage station in Parley's Park. The ledge is 30' wide and numerous assays have shown values in silver from 250 to 1,000 ounces per ton and up to 54% lead. Visitors to the ledge estimate there are 25,000 tons of ore in sight with a value of over $5,000,000."

During the first year of discovery Col. Connor's men were busy also, in fact many credit them with the district's first discovery. The ridge which juts out from Clayton's Peak and separates Big Cottonwood Canyon from the Bonanza Flats is a high, rocky one. It was on a cold, stormy day late in the fall of 1868 when three of Col. Connor's troops wearily made their way over its jagged crest through the 10,000' high pass now known as Guardsman Pass, and started across the windswept flats below. The Bonanza Flats really aren't flats at all but are a high rolling plateau 10,000 feet above sea level and the gathering place of storms all year long. The tired soldier-prospectors must have given a sigh of relief when they finally reached shelter under the great towering outcrops of gray granite which mark the flat's northern end and separate them from Empire and Ontario Canyons below.

There, where the wind wasn't quite so strong, they made camp, and since they were prospectors, even though they wore uniforms, they checked the huge outcrops for minerals. Being experienced prospectors it was inevitable that they should find the glack galena and green copper that stained the rock. Later assays showed that their find contained 96 ounces of silver and averaged over 50% lead. Although they must have been elated with their find they soon learned Bonanza Flats was no place to camp, especially in the face of winter's first blizzard. Taking samples to show to Col. Connor they erected a dead pine pole with a bandana tied to its top as a flagstaff to mark their discovery and in so doing gave their find its name, the Flagstaff.

To the Flagstaff Mine goes the honor of making the district's first ore shipment. In 1871, 40 tons of galena ore were freighted by wagons to the new railroad at Echo City. That same year the Pinion claim owners reported finding a large ore body which assayed up to 250 ounces of silver per ton and made a contract to deliver 20 tons a day to a mill which was to be built at Ogden. Ore from the Walker & Webster claim was hauled to Godbe's Smelter in Rush Valley near Tooele, one of the pioneer mills built to process ores found in nearby Ophir and Dry Canyons. By the end of 1871 a number of promising claims had been located in the new district, including the Wild Bill, Rocky Bar, Buckeye, and several others. Rector Steen, the California prospector already mentioned, located the Pioneer claim and soon afterwards sold it for $6,000, which was probably the district's first claim to be sold. It wouldn't be the last for Steen.

CHAPTER 2

DISCOVERY

Rector Steen was a partner in, if not the discoverer of, Park City's greatest mine. It was the discovery of the Ontario claim in 1872 that started Park City on its way to becoming the West's greatest silver camp. For years miners argued loud and long in the camp saloons over who it was that actually made that most important and richest of all strikes. They all agree, however, that whoever it was he wasn't a very good businessman for he sold for only $27,000 a mine that produced over $50,000,000 and paid dividends in excess of $15,000,000!

It was in July, 1872, when the purple bluebells were still blooming in the shady places of Ontario Canyon, that four prospectors camped together at Steen's Spring excitedly passed a chunk of nearly pure silver from hand to hand. At that time there apparently was no question of who had made the discovery; that question never came up until 30 years later. The four men were Rector Steen, Herman Buden, James Kane, and Augustus Dawell. Many years later R.C. Chambers, then superintendent of the Ontario, claimed that Buden alone had made the discovery, and Buden, then living in California, confirmed the claim. In rebuttal, Steen wrote of his finding the ore. Possibly because he was a well-known prospector in many of the early camps of the west his version of the story is generally accepted as the correct one.

According to Buden's story, told years later in a letter written to the editor of the Park Record, he "drifted into Park City in 1872 from the White Pine District of Nevada." He had lost several good claims to crooked partners in the past, was deeply in debt, and couldn't get a grubstake. His only friend, the faithful horse he had ridden from the Nevada diggings, was taken away from him by a merchant to whom he owed money. Dejected, Buden said he had "decided to end it all, but with the pistol in my hand my mood changed and I decided to try it one more time." With his spirits low he was heedlessly climbing the east side of Ontario Canyon, idly swinging my pick at each outcrop as I went along," when he struck a rock that broke, exposing a shiny metallic surface to the sun.

Buden continued that he needed only a glance to know the rock was silver and, after building a discovery monument, hurried back to town to record his claim. He returned with an old friend, a blacksmith named Kane, and a miner named Dawell whom he had known in Nevada. Together they opened up the vein, exposing more of the rich silver ore as the hole grew deeper. Several weeks after his find Buden was approached by George Hearst, a mining promoter recently from Nevada's Comstock, who asked him what he wanted for the claim. "$75,000" was Buden's answer. "$75,000 for only three weeks work?" Hearst asked. "No," Buden replied, $75,000 for a silver mine!" The sale was finally made for $30,000 in cash, part of which Buden said he shared with his friends Kane and Dawell, no mention being made of Steen or any partnership.

Steen's account is much shorter and can be quoted in its entirety. "I camped in a brush shanty for six months at the branch just below the Ontario, waiting for the snow to melt off. I then went to what was called the Badger Mine; and on, or about, the 15th of June, 1872, we discovered the Ontario Mine. There stood right near this mine a pine tree, and nearby was a fine spring. When we discovered this mine we found a little knob sticking out of the ground about two inches. We had this rock assayed and it went from 100 to 400 ounces of silver to the ton. We sold the mine to Hearst on the 21st day of August, 1872, for $27,000. My partners were John Kane and Gus Dawell."

The original claim notice as well as the bill of sale to Hearst have been preserved so it would seem that only a simple examination of them would be needed to settle the question. But it's not that easy, as a matter of fact they only add to the confusion! It was common in those days, and still is for that matter, for a group of prospectors working together to each claim a portion of any claim staked, usually an equal portion if all shared equally in the discovery but sometimes one or two of the group receiving less than an equal part, usually because they did not share equally in the find or for some other reason agreed to by all. An examination of the original location notice reveals how the claim was divided. It is a hand-written document and reads as follows:

Underground at the Ontario long before the days of carbide or battery lamps.

NOTICE OF THE
ONTARIO LODE

We the undersigned claim for mining purposes (1500) fifteen hundred feet on this lead lode or deposit of mineral. We claim seven hundred and fifty feet north-westerly and seven hundred and fifty feet south-easterly from this notice and monument and one hundred feet on each side of the ledge with all the priviledges granted by the United States Mining laws and the local laws of the district. We claim all dips, spurs, angles, and variations situated on the Ontario hill about 'A of a mile from the lake opposite the Steen Spring, about 75 or 100 feet from the creek bed.

Easterly Uintah Mining District
Located July 15th, 1872
Herman Buden550 feet
James M. Kane550
Rector Steen200"
Augustus Dawell200"

Filed and recorded July 16th, 1872, at 15 minutes to 3 o'clock p.m. I have examined the above location and find that it does not infringe the rights of any previous location.

J.H. Black, District Recorder

It is strange that neither Buden or Steen mentioned the other in their accounts of the discovery yet the names of each appear on the claim notice! It doesn't seem reasonable that if Buden had made the discovery by himself as he claimed that the claim would have been divided four ways. Neither is it reasonable that if Steen had made the find he would have gotten the smaller share. Steen was an old-time prospector and it is doubtful that he would have let anyone beat him out of any deserved share. If any of the four were more responsible for the discovery than any of the others it would appear to be Buden and Kane because they received the largest shares. Of course it is possible that there was some reason now unknown for the unequal division of ownership. Also unexplained is why in Steen's account he placed the discovery on or "about the 15th of June" while the claim notice is dated one month later, on July 15th.

Perhaps the most plausible explanation is that Buden made the discovery as claimed and took his friend Kane and Dawell in as partners. They camped with Steen who was at Steen's Spring and gave him a share for help received on development work. Buden took the larger share, giving his friend Kane the same amount, and divided the remainder between Dawell and Steen. The bill of sale to Hearst shows all four of their names and the amount received as $27,000 as reported by Steen, not $30,000 as claimed by Buden. Like so many old-time, one-blanket prospectors they sold their claim for a pittance and moved on, leaving unanswered questions for today. And so the argument goes on with nothing really decided one way or the other and tonight, as on a thousand nights past, Park City's old-timers will meet again in the camp's saloons and argue it all once more. About the only thing for sure is they'll have a good time doing it!

Prospectors and miners are usually thought of as being brothers of the same fraternity but this is a misconception. Prospectors belong to a rare breed apart, a special clan. Never can they be tied down for long for their hearts are in the wild and unknown country, not in some mining camp or noisy town. Buden, Steen, and their partners in the Ontario were prospectors of the old school and like those old-time prospectors they were interested in finding mines, not in working in them. True, when circumstances like 'being broke' demanded it, the prospector would become a miner, but his heart was never far from the unspoiled ridges and canyons and just as soon as he could get a grubstake he would be off roaming the unknown deserts and mountains again. Steen, as already noted, was an old-time prospector who had sold several good claims, including the Pioneer just the year before, and he was in favor of selling the Ontario. Buden, who had just about had his fill of prospecting and partnerships, probably agreed. What Kane and Dawell felt about it isn't known but the partners dilemma was about to find its solution with the arrival of George Hearst, a mining man, not a prospector.

George Hearst grew up in the exciting mining world of the gold rush California of the 1850s. As a young man he made money in San Francisco real estate when the discovery at Sutter's Mill sent land values booming. When silver was discovered at Nevada's Comstock in 1859 Hearst knew enough about mining and land values that he lost no time getting to the new diggings. He made and lost money at the Comstock but he learned a lesson that stayed with him, always be first at a new strike!

In 1863 when rumors were heard of a rich, new silver strike in central Nevada's Toiyabe Range, Hearst hurried there. The new strike became the boom camp of Cortez, and Hearst, with his partner, Samuel Wenban, got in on the ground floor with their Cortez Consolidated Mining Company. For the next few years he was content to develop his Cortez holdings and watch his bank account grow but then in the early '70s there were rumors that another rich strike had been made in the Wasatch Range in the Utah Territory. His Cortez holdings were beginning to lose their luster, for milling problems were taking all the profits. So leaving his partner to "watch the store" he went off again in search of the Leprechaun's treasure and by a lucky chance arrived at the fledgling little camp of Park City in July, 1872, only a few days after the discovery of the Ontario.

In the winter sleighs replaced wagons. George Street hauling ore, Main Street.

Even at that early date promoters had arrived at the new camp, lured by the siren call of silver. Among those whom Hearst met was Marcus Daly, later of Anaconda Copper fame at Butte, Montana, who had come from the rich surface diggings of Ophir Canyon in the Oquirrh Range. Daly told Hearst about several promising claims in McHenry Canyon, a deep, pine-choked gulch that drained Lake Flat on the shores of the sparkling mountain lake of the same name. By the time the Flagstaff Mine made the district's first shipment of 40 tons in 1871 a small town was already growing up around the shores of Lake Flat. Its location was an ideal townsite compared to the depths of McHenry Canyon where the sun seldom shone and snow drifts stayed past mid-summer. Building lots had been laid out and sold and many of the miners who worked at the McHenry and Hawkeye mines in the canyon below, as well as at the Lady of The Lake at the water's edge and at claims being staked every day in the upper reaches of Ontario Canyon, were making their homes there. The line of log cabins circling the water, along with several large, log boarding houses at the forest's edge, gave it the appearance of a permanent camp.

Hearst continued past Lake Flat and rode into McHenry Canyon where he stopped to examine the McHenry Mine. The McHenry tunnel was in 90 feet and had assays showing up to $200 in silver while boasting similar values from its 400-foot shaft.

The McHenry workings were all being driven into a terrific flow of underground water and in its shaft the flow was so strong that miners were hard pressed to make headway. Although the ore carried high silver and lead values, Hearst was discouraged at the prospects of an ever-increasing water problem and decided against buying the property.

Possibly discouraged by Hearst's decision the owner gave up sinking the shaft deeper soon afterwards. Good ore was mined from the tunnel for some time until the property passed into the hands of a German syndicate which allowed it to sit idle for many years. Abandoning the shaft was not a very good decision on either Hearst's or the owners part for years later another company, known as the Park Utah, ran a tunnel under the McHenry not far below the level of the shaft when Hearst examined it and encountered a great body of silver ore from which $15,000,000 was mined.

George Hearst didn't miss his chance at fortune that day, however, for after he left the McHenry he rode back onto Lake Flat where he again met Daly who was also looking for mining property. Daly told him about another prospect just over the ridge in Ontario Canyon and suggested that Hearst look into it. As Hearst crossed the low ridge that divides Lake Flat from Ontario Canyon he noticed a group of men at work in a prospect hole. Although it was then late afternoon he stopped to visit with them. The men were Buden, Kane, Steen, and Dawell. They were busy digging an open-cut trench to expose the ore vein they had discovered.

Hearst knew silver when he saw it and he liked what he saw at the Ontario but to his dismay he learned that a 30-day bond on the property had been given to James Berry and Al Guiwitz for $30,000. Buden explained that the 30 days were about up and he hadn't heard from the bondholders.

Taking a saddlebag of samples with him Hearst returned to Park City where he had assays made which showed values of $200 a ton. He asked his new friend, Daly, to keep an eye on the property for him and when the 30-day bond expired without the holders buying the property Daly took a 10-day bond in Hearst's name for the same amount, $30,000. On Aug. 23, 1872, only a few days before the bond ran out, Hearst purchased the Ontario for $27,000, which makes it one of the best bargains of all time, for the mine went on to produce $50,000,000 and is still going strong.

Hearst had to borrow the money he purchased the Ontario Claim with from a mystery man whose maneuverings could be found behind nearly all western mining camps, but whose face was seldom if ever seen in any of them. That man was James Ben Ali Haggin, a wealthy California lawyer of Turkish descent, who looked and played the part of an eastern sultan or potentate. Haggin had backed Hearst's earlier mining ventures in California and Nevada, but the Ontario proved to be their most lucrative investment.

Haggin and Hearst religiously followed two rules in their mining partnership, never buy into any claim they couldn't purchase the majority of stock or controlling interest in, and never pay more than the value of ore in sight. If a claim owner argued that there was more ore than could be seen, Hearst would reply that that was the reason he was willing to buy the claim at the price offered, that he was willing to gamble that there was more ore on which he could make a profit, but he would only pay for what he could see, and would not invest on any other terms.

The question of whether the price paid was $27,000 or $30,000 appears to have been answered in a comment Hearst made years later, when he said that he paid Buden (not Steen) $27,000 and paid $3,000 more to a man named Stanley who claimed some unexplained ownership in the property. At either price, it was a bargain.

Although Hearst made money from his Nevada holdings it was the Ontario that made him wealthy and was the basis of the great Hearst fortune which eventually included the famed Homestake Mine in South Dakota, the Cerro de Pasco Mine in Peru, the famous Hearst castle in San Simeon, the great Hearst newspaper chain continued by his son, William Randolph Hearst, and which made him U.S. Senator from California.

Young Hearst was an occasional visitor to the Ontario and the story is told that when he graduated from Harvard he and a friend stopped in Park City to tour his father's famous mine. While they were being lowered down the shaft a clutch failed to hold on the hoist engine and they were dropped 60 feet before the brakes could be set and their flashing descent brought to a sudden stop. The white-faced cage tender and frightened engineer both expected to be fired but neither young Hearst nor his companion were hurt and they both laughed the thrilling experience off as a real lark, even forgetting to tell Hearst's father about it!

CHAPTER 3

A CAMP IS BORN

While Lake Flat was growing into a mountain hamlet and the Ontario was changing hands, new claims like the Walker and Buckeye on Pinion Ridge, and the Woodside, Tenderfoot, and Northland on Treasure Hill were being located. The new strikes were attracting many more people to the new district, a few settling near Snyderville in Parley's Park but most living near the prospect holes and mines in the canyons above.

Quite a number of the newcomers located their tents and brush-covered dug-outs along Silver Creek near where it forked at Deer Valley. A small camp began to take shape as brush shanties and tents made way for log cabins and rough board shacks. The camp grew rapidly for lumber was easily obtained from Snyder's sawmill while farm produce and fresh meat could be purchased from the farmers in Parley's Park.

The site of the camp was in a grove of quivering, whitebarked aspens. A deeply rutted muddy wagon road twisted its way around the largest trees and past the deepest mud holes to make its way to the Ontario and other claims near Lake Flat. A cold, clear, sparkling brook named Silver Creek tumbled and splashed its way over the bed of polished stones. Mountain ferns and wild roses crowded its banks where sage hens, grouse, and songbirds came to drink. Willows lined the creek bottom and wax-green Kinikinic made a jungle of the sidehills while here and there an occasional giant cottonwood towered over all. A check of Utah's 1870 census shows a total of 164 persons living at Parley's Park, which included the few prospectors then camped in the shadow of the Treasure Mountains.

James Ben Ali Haggen, mysterious mining financier. His money bought the Ontario Mine.

On the 4th of July, 1872, the miners, prospectors, and farmers from Parley's Park all gathered together at the little camp for a celebration and while there decided to take a vote to determine what the new camp's name should be. Several good names were suggested but Parley's Park City was the most popular and it was chosen. However the Mormon apostle's name was soon dropped making the camp's name just plain Park City.

No one had a flag but since it was Independence Day several of the women got together and made one from strips of colored cloth, and the miners proudly raised it to the top of a newly cut pine pole. As more people moved in and the camp grew larger it became apparent that the narrow, winding road that twisted its way through the trees couldn't handle the large ore and freighting wagons being used by the growing mines. A straight cut was made through the trees from where Ontario, Empire, and Woodside Canyons joined to where the

Deer Valley road angled away from the main canyon.

An eight-horse team dragged a stone-filled sled back and forth until all the underbrush, roots, and rocks were torn loose and an open roadway made. At first wagons sank hub deep in the loose black soil and after rain storms or in the spring the new road became a quagmire. Wagon loads of rocks were hauled from the hillsides and from nearby mine dumps to fill the holes and it wasn't long before the rough mountain road began to look like a town street.

When horsepower meant horses. G.W. Gulliver's team hauling a mine boiler up Main Street.

Numerous springs bubbled to the surface along the new roadway with one of the largest located on the street's upper west side where it kept a long wooden watering trough filled to overflowing. Later on, when one of the new camp's leading stores was built on the same spot, the spring's run-off was carried away through a wooden flume. Years later puzzled customers of Welch, Driscoll and Buck's general store would stop to listen when they heard the spring water gurgling under the store's floor. Before the Treasure Mountains were denuded of timber and deep mine shafts lowered the ground water table, springs and sparkling streams were found in nearly every gulch and draw. A few old-timers can still recall when almost every house and cabin in the canyons above town had its own spring.

It wasn't long after the new road was finished before log cabins and whip-sawed board houses lined the street, with stores, shops and saloons standing side-by-side with miner's cabins.

George Snyder built the camp's first house only weeks before the large log building that housed W.J. Montgomery's General Store and the Post Office made its appearance where the Kimball Art Center now stands.

Young Charles Streets, who had driven a herd of cattle from Montana to sell at the Salt Lake City markets, came to the new camp and opened a butcher shop in a log building which he built near the present city's business center. In short order a blacksmith shop and livery stable were started and J.A. Nelson opened a boarding house. An express office was opened in the building that housed Montgomery's store and each day bars of bullion from the mines were brought from the camp's assay office and kept there to await shipment.

Every passing week saw new businesses springing up along the narrow street with saloons out-numbering all the others. It wasn't long before the sound of the honky-tonks broke the silence where once the loudest sound heard had been the sigh of the wind in the pines, and wagon wheels turned where deer had slipped quietly through the aspens only months before.

While 1872 had been a year for making bonanza ore discoveries, 1873 was a year that forecast much of the new camp's future. Men who were destined to be its leaders and developers for years to come arrived in great numbers that year. Foremost among these was R.C. Chambers, an experienced miner and friend of George Hearst. As a young man Chambers joined the gold rush to California where he learned the secrets of wrestling wealth from the earth. Evidently he was well liked for he was elected sheriff of Pano County in 1862 and was a successful merchant until 1868, as well as operating his mining claims.

He was prospecting around Camp Floyd when Hearst brought him to Park City and installed him as superintendent of the Ontario, a position he held until his death in 1901.

The story of Park City's first 15 years is the story of the Ontario Silver Mining Company and the story of the Ontario is Chambers' story. To say that Chambers was an unusual man or even a peculiar one would be generous. For years he was the subject of controversy, his name associated with law-suits, scandals, and high-handedness. But if he was a nemesis to his enemies he was always faithful to Hearst and the Ontario and it was his guidance that made it the camp's leading producer.

Just as soon as Chambers took over the Ontario he began its development. The ore vein found by Steen, or Buden, or whoever it was, was opened for 700 feet along the surface and three discovery shafts were sunk over 100 feet each, all in good ore and promising even better below. From the start the Ontario was plagued with the same water problems already experienced by the mines in McHenry Canyon. A tunnel was started from the canyon floor and driven below the discovery ledge, boasting $250-a-ton ore all the way. Chambers chose a site for what he called the No. 1 shaft and a crew of men was set to work sinking it. Wages then being paid averaged $3 a day and they worked 10 hour days, 7 days a week. The new shaft was in ore all the time and values increased with every foot of depth. When it reached 500 feet an immense body of ore was struck, its value being modestly estimated at $1,000,000.

The old original log boarding house at the Ontario #2, the Empire Mine at top center.
- Utah State Historical Society -

It soon became apparent that the No. 1 shaft would have to be abandoned. In the first place, it had been sunk right into the orebody, making mining the ore hazardous at best. Also the wet, heavy ground couldn't be held. Timbers snapped under the weight from above allowing cave-ins to rain rocks into the shaft and block the tunnels. Underground pressures were so great that heavy shaft timbers were crushed like matchsticks and steel rails twisted and buckled. About a quarter of a mile down the canyon the No. 2 shaft was started, eventually reaching 1,500 feet in depth. A year after Chambers took over the Ontario its production reached $14,000 a week, not bad considering the entire camp's weekly production was then about $20,000.

It was also in 1873 that there arrived in Park City several other men whose names would always be associated with the town's development. As the fame of the new El Dorado spread, miners, businessmen, and investors from as far away as the eastern states hurried to stake their claims on its future. Among these newcomers was a group from Grand Haven, Mich., which included E.P. Ferry, D.C. McLaughlin, J.W. Mason, and F.A. Nims. Later Col. William Ferry, E.P. Ferry's brother, also moved to the new camp. They were all men with foresight and, probably even more important, men with money.

As already described the Flagstaff, discovered by Col. Connor's troops, was one of the first claims located but because of the coming winter and its isolation high on Bonanza Flat it was not developed until the following year.

When summer returned to the high country the soldiers who made the discovery returned to explore it further and were busily engaged in opening the vein they had found when they were approached by James M. Kennedy. After examining the open trench the soldiers had cut, Kennedy offered them $5,000 for the property, which they quickly accepted. It was Kennedy who started development of the Flagstaff and made the district's first ore shipment in July, 1871. Not long after the arrival of the 'Michigan bunch' E.P. Ferry purchased the Flagstaff for $50,000, making a tidy profit for Kennedy.

Ferry immediately began building a new mill which he named the Marsac to process ore from the Flagstaff. It was a 20-stamp mill costing nearly $50,000 and was built at the foot of Rossie Hill on Silver Creek, just east of where the city hall now stands. At the same time the Marsac Mill was being built the McHenry Company was erecting an almost identical 20-stamp mill in Deer Valley, about a half mile to the east.

Both the Marsac and McHenry Mills were located a long way from the mines where their ore came from. Ore from the Flagstaff was hauled down what was known as the Utah grade, a steep and narrow road that followed the ridge crest separating Empire and Ontario Canyons. The road between the McHenry Mine and its mill climbed up out of McHenry Canyon, snaked its way across Lake Flat and around the head of Constellation Gulch, and then dropped sharply down into Deer Valley.

Partly due to technical problems in reducing the complex ores in the crude stamp mills but mostly because of the distance the ore had to be hauled across rough country with deep winter snows, neither mill operated very steadily or satisfactorily.

The Ontario's problem with its ore was that there was just too much of it! The Ontario had been shipping its ore by wagon to the smelters in the Salt Lake Valley but in 1877 the company built a huge 40-stamp mill below the mine near the mouth of Ontario Canyon. It cost $325,000 and was considered to be one of the finest mills in the West. While the McHenry was having water problems its mill was often idle so, while the Ontario Mill was being built, Chambers leased it and also Ferry's Marsac Mill to reduce Ontario ore. Still, both mills together couldn't handle the great stream of silver wealth coming from Ontario and some of the mine's first class ore was shipped all the way to Liverpool, England.

It is almost impossible now to imagine the hardships the old-time miners had getting their ore to a smelter before the trans-continental railroad was completed. After digging and hoisting the heavy ore from a dark, deep, wet shaft, they had to get it to a wagon road. Often the ore was sewn inside cow hides and skidded into the canyons below the mine portal. There it was sacked and loaded onto pack horses or mules to be packed to the Salt Lake Valley, where it was loaded onto heavy wagons for the long haul across the Nevada deserts and over the Sierra Nevadas to San Francisco. Then, almost unbelievably, the ore was loaded aboard sailing ships, usually as ballast, bound for the long ocean voyage around the tip of South America and half-way around the world to the smelters at Cornwall.

And believe it or not, those same sailing ships returned to San Francisco carrying hard quartz cobblestones from the coast of Wales. Those cobblestones were hauled by team and wagon to the mines at Park City where they were used as balls in early day ore grinding ball mills. Until recently many of those quartz "balls" could be found near the old mill at the Keystone Mine.

The Ontario Mill. Note that nearly all the timber on the mountain front has been cut.

Although Ferry's newly acquired Flagstaff Mine wasn't turning out to be the bonanza he had hoped for his day would soon come. Meanwhile his Michigan partners, Mason, Nims, and McLaughlin, weren't letting any grass grow under their feet.

Although a name had been chosen for the new camp and homes and business houses were being built the townsite had never been surveyed or properly obtained from the government. McLaughlin made a survey while Nims made formal application to the government for a townsite, including the ground on which many miners and businessmen already were living. Mason's job appears to have been to discourage new people from settling on the proposed townsite until he and his partners obtained title to it and trying to get rid of the "squatters who were already there. His efforts were something short of successful for the miners couldn't see how they could be forced out of the homes they had built. Delays were soon encountered, partly because the application hadn't been properly made, and also because J.L. Streets, whose pioneer butcher shop had been one of the camp's first businesses, started a law-suit to stop the townsite application.

Hard feeling began to grow between the townsite faction led by Nims and the residents and businessmen who had been on the scene before his arrival, the latter group led by Streets. The people already living there had built the camp's Main street, had their homes on ground they had cleared, and couldn't see why they should apply to a townsite company for what they already had.

By that time Chambers was the town's wealthiest and most important citizen. Yet he always stood aloof and apart from the town, never trying to gain public favor and at times even seeming to work against the town's interests. It came as something of a surprise then when Chambers came out publicly against the townsite company's plans. But the people hardly had time to change their opinion of him when to their further surprise he reversed himself and advised the people not to oppose the townsite company but to pay them for their land. The townsite application was approved soon afterwards and the entire community area sold to Nims. Streets, who owned the large log building which housed his butcher shop as well as four other lots, lost his law-suit and was forced to surrender his property. It was later learned that Chambers received title to the Ontario Millsite, located within the townsite boundaries. Some claimed he received the property for the aid he gave the townsite people. How easy it would have been for him to have taken a civic interest and won the people's friendship by helping them, but his interests were always those of the Ontario and he cared little for the people's problems.

Miners at an underground winze hoist, waiting for photographer's signal, Ontario Mine.

The town continued to grow despite Chambers and the townsite company. Soon after the townsite was obtained a waterworks company was started by Col. William Ferry and Nims began advertising for new businesses to settle in the town. Boardwalks were built, side streets were surveyed, and still more people poured in. New cabins were built along Silver Creek, one of the first erected by Henry Cunningham near where Ontario Canyon and Empire Canyon creeks came together. Cunningham made charcoal for the mines and had a small coke oven near the mouth of Woodside Gulch in Empire Canyon.

As in many early mining camps of the Great Basin, Park City's population was a mixture of Irish, Cornish, English, Scots, Chinese, and Scandinavians. The completion of the transcontinental railroad in 1869 found thousands of "Cousin Jacks" "Micks", and "Celestials" foot-loose and unemployed and many of them found places to settle in camps like Park City. The Cornishmen and Irishmen were natural enemies while the Scots considered themselves above both. Fights in the camp's saloons were common and cries of "Ye bloody Mick, you!" and "Ye damned Cousin Jack!" were often heard coming from behind the swinging doors. The Scots were clannish and lived apart, many of them settling at Lake Flat where the high mountains and sparkling little lake reminded them of the "bonnie highlands" they had left behind.

The setting was one of unsurpassed beauty, with its whitebarked aspens mirrored on the tiny mountain lake, all outlined by stands of forest green pines and carpeted with acres of crimson Indian Paintbrush and nodding white Columbines. Little wonder the miners who lived there called it The Robin's Nest Of The Wasatch.

The Cornishmen were the world's best miners. While still only children they were sent into the deep, wet mines of Cornwall where they held a candle for their father or brother until they were big enough to begin working.

Like the coal miners and craftsmen of Scotland their working conditions were almost intolerable and men from both countries left their homes to come to America. In Ireland, potato famines left much of the population near starvation, the worst occurring in 1847.

In the next ten years nearly two million Irish immigrated to America, many of them finding work on the trans-continental railroad and in the metal mines of the West. The Swedes and the Finns, although fewer in number, came first to find work in the sawmills, cutting railroad ties and mine props, and gradually found their way into the mines.

All of the old-country miners were superstitious, and many were the strange tales they told. Some claimed to have seen the man in the yellow slicker, a ghostly apparition who haunted the deep, wet drifts. Any who saw him would run for their lives, for he was supposed to be the ghost of a miner killed in a cave-in, and whoever talked to him would be the next to die!

Others told tales of a white mule that wandered the miles of old abandoned tunnels, according to them the only survivor of some long ago underground explosion, set off by a spark from a miner's candle. If an Irish miner's candle went out, he would say that the white mule kicked it out. Still others reported seeing a beautiful long-haired woman riding an all white horse in the depths of the Zev Shaft, forever looking for her dead husband, lost somewhere in that icy shaft.

The Cornishmen would never go into a working where a woman had been, but their greatest fear was of the Tommy Knockers, tiny leprechaun-like ghosts of miners killed in the mines. Once they heard the ghostly tap-tap of a Knocker's pick, nothing could ever get them to go back into those haunted workings again. Their superstition is described in an old Cornish ballad.

- TOMMY KNOCKERS -

'ave you 'erd of the Tommy Knockers
In the deep dark mines of the West,
Which all Cornish miners can 'ear An it is no bloody jest.
For I'm a Cornish miner
An I'll tell you of it today,

Of the tap tap of a tiny pick
As we work in the rock and clay.

A view of the engine on the great Cornish Pump, Ontario Mine.
- Courtesy Utah Mining Association -

We go down in the shafts with our buckets
With 'earts which nothing fazes,
Each man with a candle to light the way
Through the drifts an' winzes an' raises.
An' the stale air smells of powder
An' the mine is full of sound,
But 'tis only the tap of a Knocker
That makes our 'earts rebound.

It's their tap, tap, tap Like sounds of tiny liners,
Just a tap, tap, tap From souls of dead miners.
For they're locked in the rock wall
Those who found death down there,
An' 'tis the tap tap of tiny picks
Which makes on end stand our 'air.

So we'll leave the 'aunted place
For we won't work where they be,
An' wherever we 'ear their knockin'
We sure will always flee.
For it means whoever 'ears it
Will be the next in line,
For the tap, tap, tap of the Knockers Is a last an' awful sign!

Like all western mining camps Park City had its Chinese population and soon a Chinatown began to grow up behind the camp's Main Street under the brow of Rossie Hill. Rossie Hill got its name because so many people who settled on its flanks came from Rossie, N.Y. Most of Rossie Hill's residents were Englishmen or "Cousin Jacks" and they looked down with dislike at Chinatown below them but through which they had to pass to get to town. Years later, in 1886, their problem was solved when a long, narrow footbridge called the "China Bridge" was built from just off Main Street, passed high over the Chinatown below, and connected with Rossie Hill beyond.

It was painted bright red and was wide and strong enough for a horseman to ride across. For years it was a reminder of Park City's turbulent past and though built to avoid the Chinese it became a memorial to them until it was burned in the great fire of 1898.

After the fire it was replaced with a far less imposing bridge which served for over a half century before it was torn down after being declared unsafe. There was hardly a boy who passed over the old bridge who didn't carry a pocket full of rocks to throw down on the tin roofs of the long suffering "Celestials." Then they'd run for their lives from the mad, fist-shaking Orientals below.

Many of the Chinese raised fine gardens and peddled their produce from house to house in great baskets which hung suspended from long poles they carried across their shoulders. Whenever a sale was made the peddler would make a mark in mysterious Oriental characters by the side of each customer's doorway showing the amount owed and would return to collect his pay when payday came to the mines. Although Park City's population figures seldom showed more than two to three hundred Chinese every mine boarding house employed a dozen or more as cooks, waiters, and gardeners and many of them were never included in the population figures.

Cold and wet inside the Ontario mine on a cross-drift at the 1,300' level .
- Utah State Historical Society -

The Chinese wore loose-fitting, formless clothes while working but had very colorful and fancy costumes to wear while celebrating. On Chinese New Year they would parade through the streets, some concealed beneath a great fire-breathing dragon while others passed out trinkets and strange nuts and candies to the spectators. A Chinese funeral was a spectacular event, especially when the camp's Oriental population numbered several hundred. A parade of mourners in strange costumes would make its way through the city streets to the cemetery, accompanied by weird music and the popping of fire-crackers. Colored bits of paper would be dropped along the way to mis-lead evil spirits and great quantities of rich and fancy foods would be left at the grave to feed the departed on his unknown journey.

A Record article described a Chinese funeral in which an important woman member of the Chinese community had died. She was dressed in the finest silks and jewelry and was laid out in a fine white casket. Friends of the family rode in or walked with the hearse which was decorated with gay streamers and burned punk and joss sticks as the procession made its way to the cemetery. Small pieces of paper, each punched with nine holes, were thrown from the hearse as it moved along.

When the burial was complete a chicken and several pieces of pork were placed at the head of the grave to sustain her on the way to her final reward. A flask of aged whiskey was sprinkled over the grave with much kowtowing from the mourners and no doubt regret from the thirsty miners who were watching. When the funeral was over all of the departed's clothing, bedding, and other personal items were thrown into a great fire and burned.

No one knows how many Chinese were buried at Park City for at intervals their bones would be dug up and shipped to China to be buried along-side their ancestors. This custom was followed in all of the old mining camps and although some China towns had thousands of residents it is a rare thing to find a Chinese grave. Though their customs were strange to the miners they were good people, loyal, hard working and thrifty. Many of them operated the town's best restaurants and laundries. They were well liked and respected by all who knew them.

J.A. Nelson, who had a home near where the hospital now stands, ran a boarding house but his great love was prospecting. One day during the summer of 1873 he climbed up Woodside Gulch not far from his cabin home and discovered rich float ore. He followed the pieces of float to a ledge where he staked the Woodside and Tenderfoot claims. Nelson, like many of the other old-time prospectors, was content to prospect and leave the mining to others; the following year he sold his undeveloped claims to E.P. Ferry. Although Ferry and his associates sunk a shaft at the Woodside and had considerable development work done at both claims they decided the return didn't warrant the expense and leased their property. For several years the Woodside and Tenderfoot were worked by leasors, and then only in the most random and haphazard way. But the gods of fate, fickle as a dance-hall girl, were hiding the fortune of Treasure Hill for just a little while longer, waiting for the coming of men who would be legends in their own time.

While the secret of Treasure Hill lay hidden other claims in adjoining canyons and gulches were being located. The names of some would soar to the heights, like a meteor reaching its zenith, while others would fade in the brighter lights of the stars. Among them were the Apex, Climax, Roaring Lion, Jupiter, Keystone, Rebellion, and Woodhine to name but a few. The work being done at the new claims and the increased activity at older ones were bringing ever more people to Park City. The narrow canyon floor was nearly cleared of trees to make way for new streets where rows of houses and business buildings quickly took their places. Talk of a railroad was even being heard. The sleeping giant was awakening.

Ontario #1 in the foreground, #2 on the right, and #3 on the left.
- Utah State Historical Society -

CHAPTER 4

BIG PUMPS & NARROW RAILROADS

In December, 1876, the Ontario Silver Mining Company was incorporated with $10,000,000 in stock. Already it was the territory's richest producer and was only beginning to flex its muscles. The following year its new 40-stamp mill was completed and began reducing the rich silver ore, the lease on the Marsac and McHenry mills then being allowed to expire. The No. 2 shaft was rapidly being sunk while across the canyon about a thousand feet away preparations were under way to start the new No. 3 shaft, now used by the Noranda Company miners.

It soon became apparent, however, that if the mine was to be sunk to the richest ore something would have to be done about the heavy flows of underground water being encountered. Since the primitive pumps then in use couldn't raise the water more than a few hundred feet a drain tunnel seemed to the only solution. A tunnel was started from near the mouth of Ontario Canyon, just below the mill, and driven to intersect with the shaft at its 600 foot level. Much of the best ore had been mined-out above that depth and the great volume of water below that point stopped deeper operations. In 1877 the company paid its first dividend of $50,000. If they were to continue it would be necessary to complete the new drain tunnel as quickly as possible.

To speed up work on the drain tunnel a fourth shaft known as the No. 4 was sunk between the tunnel's portal and its destination. When it reached the depth at which the drain tunnel would run, miners began working both ways, toward the tunnel being driven from the shaft and toward the one being driven from the surface. With the tunnel being driven from four different faces at once work went rapidly and it was completed in 1881. A flume carried water from the tunnel down Ontario Canyon to where it was used in the milling process at the Marsac Mill. Not only did the new drain tunnel empty the deeply flooded workings and allow the shaft to be sunk deeper, it also provided an entrance to the mine from the canyon mouth. This allowed the miners to live at Park City where the variety of business houses and easier winters, at more than a thousand-feet lower elevation, made life a lot easier than living in the steep, narrow canyon near the mine. The new tunnel also marked the beginning of the end for the little Scottish settlement on Lake Flat.

During the time the 600-foot drain tunnel was being driven Chambers had another problem. The way he handled it gives another insight into the man. A United States Marshall named Shaughnessy had acquired several mining properties adjacent to the Ontario, including the Last Chance and Henrietta claims, and began mining underground ore which Chambers claimed belonged to the Ontario.

Threats and accusations were exchanged between the two men. Eventually the argument erupted into underground fights between the men of the companies in the tunnels which interconnected the properties. There was a natural flow of underground air from the Ontario workings through the Union Tunnel and into the Shaughnessy property. Chambers had his men carry barrels of tar, oil, sulphur, blasting powder, and other foul and disagreeable substances into the connecting Union Tunnel where they were set on fire.

Clouds of dense and sickening smoke soon filled the Shaughnessy workings sending the miners reeling to the surface, sick and gasping for air. When they finally got their breath back they went down into the mine again and closed the tunnel with a hastily built door of boards and wet blankets and with the use of a powerful fan changed the direction of the air flow forcing the sickening fumes back into the Ontario. The underground battle had almost reached a state of armed war when Hearst heard about it and invited Shaughnessy to San Francisco where a settlement was made, Hearst buying the Shaughnessy property and adding it to his already extensive holdings, which is probably what Chambers wanted all along.

At about the same time another incident, involving murder, was attributed to the Ontario's Superintendent. It was claimed that Jack Smith, who owned a claim which adjoined the Ontario had been accused of tunneling into Ontario ground and taking high grade ore out. Apparently threats failed to stop Smith. A tough named Jim Moray was hired by the Ontario and a few nights later he met Smith at Pape & Bowman's Saloon, where he accused Smith of moving Ontario claim stakes. An argument flared up and Moray shot and killed Smith. Unfortunately for Moray, Smith was unarmed. Miners cried murder, and Moray fled, but was later found hiding at the Flagstaff Mine and was tried for the murder of Smith. Moray was convicted, but the Ontario Company hired attorneys who got Moray released from prison 18 months later. Incidents like that didn't do much to endear R.C. Chambers to Parkites.

Editor Raddon had something to say about it also, when he wrote, "A few years ago we thought vigilante committees a curse, but a couple of years at Park City will give anyone ample reason for changing their mind. In only two years seven men have been sent to their graves by their fellow men, and the only punishment meted out to any of them was a short term in the penitentiary, where they fared better than they would have at home. We are anxious to see the law of the land prevail, but when that fails, then let the people act! It is time we are up and doing!"

Even while the Ontario's drain tunnel was being dug Chambers realized that the solution would be at best a temporary one for the shaft could be sunk only a few hundred feet deeper before the pumps would again be taxed to their limit. The Ontario had been a California company right from the start and Hearst, who had moved back to the Golden State, put his mining associates to work on the mine's water problem. The solution was arrived at by W.R. Echart, a San Francisco mining engineer who designed what would be spoken of with wonder and awe for years to come, the world-famous Cornish Pump!

Ore train leaving Park Con Mine, Deer Valley. Later site of Snow Park Ski Lift in top center.

Echart had heard about a huge pump that had been built in Cornwall for the deep, wet, diamond mines of South Africa and knowing the Cornishmen were the world's master miners he studied their designs to come up with one of his own which he believed would solve the Ontario's water problems for years to come.

He convinced Hearst and Chambers that the great pump he proposed would do the job and as a result late in 1880 a contract to build it was given to J.P. Morris & Company of Philadelphia, Pa. Its building and installation was a tremendous undertaking. Some idea of its immensity can be realized just from the labor involved in its construction and assembly. Cornish artisans were hired and taken to Philadelphia to watch over its construction and when it was finally shipped piece by piece to the mine they accompanied it, helped install it, and some stayed to operate it. While its giant parts were being forged detailed planning and preparations for its arrival were under way at the mine.

The Ontario's No. 3 shaft, which was designed for the pump's installation, was rapidly being sunk to the

1,000-foot level. It was a three-compartment shaft, two of which were 4 1/2 by 5 feet for mining while the third was built 6 1/2 by 7 1/2 feet to accomodate the huge machine's underground parts. Excavations were started to house the surface works and engine which would power it. Edwin Kimball's freighting company received the contract to haul the heavy and awkward sections to the mine. When parts began arriving late in 1881, Kimball found it necessary to purchase more teams as well as build a large livery barn and a new boarding house, called the Utah House, to take care of the added teamsters he would have to hire.

Two men are dwarfed by the great Cornish Pump. Note the flags, occasion unknown.

Chambers needed a capable man to supervise the pump's installation and for that important and exacting job he chose a miner who both he and Hearst had known back in the days of the Comstock. In the fall of 1881, David Keith, a shrewd, sharpminded miner with a keen understanding of geology and engineering, arrived from Virginia City. That he was competent in installing the huge machine is a matter of record, but even more important, a giant had arrived on the scene. Within only a few short years the names of David Keith and Park City would become almost synonymous.

Some of the weights of the pump sections hauled by Kimball's teams are as follows: the pump body and straps weighed 40 tons, the main beam 72 tons, the cylinders (there were two of them) 45 tons, and the pillow-block bearing 35 tons. When all the sections and parts finally arrived at the No. 3 shaft they totaled nearly 500 tons! The pump's great size is hard to comprehend, even today. The pump itself, with its two 20-inch pistons, was located at the shaft's 1,000-foot level while the engines which powered it were on the surface! The connecting rod between the pump and the engine was 1,060 feet long, made of Oregon pine 16 inches square in sections 70 feet long, with the sections joined together with three-quarter inch iron plates 10 inches wide and 35 feet long. The entire connecting rod hung suspended in the shaft and was connected on the surface to a flywheel 30 feet in diameter that alone weighed 70 tons!

The pump's two 20-inch pistons had 10-foot strokes that pumped water from the shaft's 1,000-foot level up to the 600-foot drain tunnel level at the rate of 320 gallons with each stroke of the piston. That was 2,560 gallons every minute, 153,600 gallons every hour, or nearly 4,000,000 gallons a day!

It is said that so great was the power of the steam engines which turned the pump that the ground would tremble with each turn of the great flywheel. The Cornish Pump allowed the Ontario to mine to depths once thought impossible and many great and rich ore bodies once inaccessible were opened because of it, adding millions to the company's treasury and added jobs and stability to Park City.

The story is told that one day the great pump quit running and none of the mechanics on duty could get it started again. Water was beginning to rise in the shaft and finally, in desperation, Chambers called for a Cornish mechanic from a nearby mine to do what he could.

Upon his arrival the Cornishman carefully looked the giant pump over and then climbed high on its huge fly-wheel where after several minutes deliberation he struck it a mighty blow with a double-jack sledge hammer. At once the engine gave a great shudder and then slowly began to turn again.

Greatly pleased that the pump was running once more Chambers thanked the mechanic warmly, but thanks wasn't enough, for the mechanic wanted cash! When he told Chambers his fee was $100 the superintendent was outraged. He cursed and then threatened but the fee remained the same. Finally Chambers demanded an itemized bill for the mechanic's services and the little Cornishman quickly wrote one out on a scrap of paper and handed it to him.

After staring at the bill in amazement for several minutes Chambers ordered it paid for he couldn't argue with the truth of it. The undaunted little Cornishman had written: "For hitting the flywheel with a hammer, 50¢; for knowing where to hit it, $99.50!"

An early photo of the Ontario looking up canyon.
Note how the hills have been denuded of timber.

When the Cornish pump was installed gasoline and electric power were almost unheard of and engines like those on large pumps and hoisting engines were steam powered. The rows of huge boilers which furnished the steam to run them had voracious appetites, consuming unbelievable quantities of fuel. Wood was the only fuel easily obtainable and Park City had what at first appeared to be an unending supply. It is hard to believe without looking at old photos or reading early accounts of the region, just how heavily forested the mountains and canyons were then. Along the streams which came out of every canyon were dense growths of willow and aspen dwarfed by towering cottonwoods while the sidehills and ridges above were covered with thick stands of pine and cedar.

Almost every early mining claim that amounted to anything had a steam-powered hoist or engine of some description that required a constant supply of fuel and the timber abounding in the district provided that supply. Huge surface plants like the one at the Ontario quickly consumed all the nearby timber and when even larger boilers like those on the Cornish pump were installed the fuel supply quickly became critical. Often the large mines had as many men cutting and hauling wood as they had working in the mine. In only a few short years all the nearby canyons and mountain sides were so denuded that wood for fuel and mine timber was being freighted in from other areas. Sawmills were set up as far away as the Kamas and Heber Valleys and even in the Strawberry Valley, 40 miles to the east. Old-timers can still recall cordwood piled higher than a man's head all the way from the mouth of Ontario Canyon to the mine, a distance of more than a mile.

Margaret Murray, one of the camp's early settlers, recalled cooking for a camp of timber cutters in the Strawberry Valley, her young husband among them. It was late in the season and snow had started to fall when they decided to leave the mountain camp.

Her husband, George, hitched up their team and with the help of a young man who intended to accompany them prepared to leave for the lower valley. Their young friend had planned to leave the high country before being snowed in for the winter but for some unknown reason changed his mind at the last minute and stayed behind.

Quickly leaving the high camp before winter's first snow got any deeper the Murrays forgot all about their expected passenger until the following spring when one of the timber cutters came into town and asked how far they had traveled before their young friend caught up with them. It was only then they learned that about an hour after they left the timber camp the young man had changed his mind again and followed after them.

He had drawn his summer wages and since he had no horse he started out on foot to catch the Murray's wagon, assuring his companions of the past summer that he would easily catch the slow-moving team in only a couple of miles. When they explained they had not seen the young man after leaving the sawmill a search party was organized, expecting to find his body in some brush filled gulch or ravine. Although several searches were made that summer no trace was ever found nor did his parents in Heber Valley ever hear from him again. Whether he was lost in some unknown canyon or whether someone followed him from the sawmill to rob and hide his body was never learned but their young friend's strange disappearance was a mystery the Murrays never forgot.

Union Pacific Railway Depot, Park City, Utah.

Early in 1880 the Utah Eastern Railroad hired a crew of 200 men with 70 teams and began building a railroad grade from Echo City to Park City. In November, 1881, its narrow gauge rails were laid into town and 15 days later the first passenger train arrived with Billie Chatterton at the throttle.

At last Park City had rail transportation and before long trains carrying coal replaced wagons hauling cordwood. Coal had been discovered in the early days at Grass Creek near Coalville, 30 miles to the north, where a narrow gauge known as the Summit County Railroad was built from the rails of the Utah Eastern to the mines, where a small coal camp named Grass Creek soon blossomed forth. When the railroad was completed the Ontario Company purchased control of a coal mine there and began mining it for their own use. The huge amount of cordwood the engines of the Cornish Pump consumed can be imagined for records show that when the engines were converted to use coal for fuel they consumed 100 tons per day!

Soon after the Utah Eastern began operation the Ontario Company obtained control by loaning its builders $100,000 to insure a steady delivery of coal to the mine. Three rails were laid up the grade into Grass Creek so both the narrow gauge Utah Eastern and the standard gauge Union Pacific could use it. A few years later the Utah Eastern was sold to the Union Pacific when that company agreed to deliver coal cheaper than the Ontario's cost of operating the narrow gauge line.

The Union Pacific wouldn't have its monopoly for long, for Park City was soon to have another railroad. A race began in 1881 between the Salt Lake & Eastern Railroad and the Salt Lake & Fort Douglas Railroad to see which could build a grade up the steep rocky sides of Parleys Canyon first. It was to take nearly 10 years of the hardest work, financial loss, and heartbreak before the first engines finally puffed into town in May, 1890.

By then both lines had merged with the Utah Western to become the Utah Central. Parley's Canyon was, as one old timer put it, "A helluva place for a railroad!" It was narrow, brush-choked and rocky, and the upper section had almost prohibitive grades.

The steep grades were finally conquered by the use of switchbacks. As the engine passed Lamb's Canyon it pulled its load of cars up a long grade past a switch which was turned after the last car passed. Then the train was backed across the canyon and high up the opposite slope. There another switch was turned and the train went forward again until it was almost to the summit where it turned west through a narrow pass that led to the mountain's opposite side and the steep downgrades leading to the make believe city of Gorgoza.

From the start the Salt Lake & Eastern Railroad had been the brainchild of John W. Young, son of the Mormon prophet and leader, Brigham Young, and was known as "John W's railroad." He had dreamed of a railroad to connect the rich mines of Park City with the Mormon capital but his dreams hadn't included the high costs, great labors and delays the builders would encounter.

With bankruptcy facing him Young went to New York where he tried unsuccessfully to raise enough money to save his tottering company. While in New

York, Young, who wasn't always as honest as his more famous father, heard of a wealthy Spanish nobleman who had made investments in the American west. In hopes of getting the Spaniard to invest in his railroad he took the next ship to Europe. A meeting was arranged in France where Young met the Spaniard, Rodriguez Velasquez de la Gorgozada. However, the wealthy noblemen didn't appear to be impressed with Young's scheme. Another meeting was scheduled and in desperation Young and his associates feverishly plotted a make-believe city on the maps they would present to Senor Gorgozada. Streets were laid out with buildings, parks, and business sites all marked and named.

Site of the make-believe city was at the edge of Parley's Park where Kimball's Creek meets the small snow water creeks coming down from Parley's Summit. At the meeting all of the site's advantages were pointed out to Senor Gorgozada and as a final inducement to get his investment, Young had named the city Gorgoza in his honor. Senor Gorgozada was impressed to the tune of $1,000,000, which he invested in Young's railroad to the non-existent city.

The investment made completion of the railroad into Park City possible and eventually allowed it to continue to the banks of the Provo River in Heber Valley. When it was finally completed Senor Gorgozada visited America and rode the new railroad but he found no city named Gorgoza and though he threatened all sorts of actions against Young's company he was never repaid nor, as far as anyone knows, did he ever receive any dividends from his million-dollar investment.

After the railroad was completed a tunnel was driven under the summit and a high shaky trestle built across Lamb's Canyon. Women passengers so feared the ride across the high trestle that they preferred to take Kimball's stages to Salt Lake City. An item which later appeared in the Park Record makes one wonder whether the new railroad was any improvement over the stage coach for passengers complained that the cars were cold, with windows broken, and that there were no fires in the car stoves on cold mornings. The railroad company must have taken notice of the complaints for soon two new upholstered coach cars were added to the line.

The Utah Central was narrow-gauge like the Utah Eastern and like the Eastern it too was finally swallowed up by a standard gauge, the Rio Grande Western. But Park City had a lot of growing to do before that happened. After the Cornish pump made it possible to go to ever greater depths for the gleaming silver treasure, growth wasn't long in coming.

The Crescent Narrow Gauge Railway.

CHAPTER 5

RADDON OF THE RECORD

Any history of Park City must be the history of the Park Record, but even more, the story of Sam Raddon. All three grew up together, and all three shared the good times and the bad, the rich and the poor, the highs and the lows and the ups and the downs.

The Park Record had its birth in 1880. Sam Raddon guided it for sixty-five years, but few today can recall the old Park Record as he published it. In those long gone days before out-of-town newspapers were easily available, a town's own newspaper was a thing of pride. It not only reported everyday happenings at home, but also kept folks aware of what was going on at other camps. Often there was a real rivalry between the editors of rival camp newspapers, which sometimes led to personal feuds between them. The old Park Record was such a paper, and Sam Raddon was known as a fighting editor.

The Park Mining Record first made its appearance on February 7th, 1880 under the guidance of James Schupback as publisher, but by June, 1881 its masthead announced that Harry White had become publisher, Schupbach having moved to greener pastures in Butte, Montana. In July, 1881 a small back page item reported that Mr. Sam Raddon of the Salt Lake Tribune had been a visitor at the Record office. There was probably more to that inconspicuous entry than met the eye, for later events revealed that Raddon had more than just a passing interest in the Record.

In 1883 the Record again reported that Raddon had been a visitor at Park City. The following year J.J. Buser succeeded White as the fledgling paper's publisher, while another entry reported that Raddon was "visiting" the Record office again. That his interest was more than casual was proven in November, 1884 when the Record announced that Mr. Sam Raddon, formerly of the Salt Lake Tribune, was now on the staff of the Park City paper. Only a month later the Record's masthead listed the Record's owners as Buser & Raddon. The following July Buser was replaced by L. E. Camomile. The masthead then read Raddon & Camomile, but shortly afterwards Mr. Camomile's name was dropped, leaving Sam Raddon as editor and publisher, something which would remain unchanged for more that half a century.

From the very start of Raddon's association with the Record he was controversial, both he and his paper often outspoken and critical. Like many other small and penny-pinched newspapers of pioneer Utah, the Record was anti-everything, including anti-Mormon, anti-Chinese, and anti-Indian. This didn't necessarily mean that Raddon was anti-anything, it only meant that was a good way to sell newspapers, especially in a gentile mining camp where Chinese weren't welcome, and where Indians were about as popular as smallpox.

Early issues of the Record are filled with acid-tongue editorials. An April, 1882 issue commented on the death of a fellow mining camp newspaper, the Silver Reef Miner, after it fell into Mormon hands. "The Silver Reef Miner had got itself mired so deep in the sand that the new owners could not dig it up again. When we heard that it had fallen into Mormon hands we felt that it was doomed to death!"

Another issue reported the death of a Park City Chinaman. "He had been ailing for some time, and looked as though he was living only to save funeral expenses. He was buried by his fellow Chinks, and with his hat on, so he wouldn't catch cold on his way to the happy hunting grounds!"

Raddon's anti-Mormon editorials became so vitriolic that they finally drew fire from other editors. In November, 1887 the Provo Territorial Enquirer goaded Raddon with the following editorial. "The Park Record has got the Mormon rabies bad, and is proving itself a complete ass. Poor thing, it is a financial fizzle, and thinks it may make a living catering to the tastes of the anti-Mormons. Will someone please knock it in the head and end its miserable existence!"

Editors like Sam Raddon seldom missed a chance to editorialize in the most caustic terms against their fellow editors, for readers waited from week to week to follow those verbal feuds on paper, and they did sell newspapers when there was little real news to report. In February, 1891 Raddon commented on a running feud between the Herald and the Bugler, both of Brigham City. "The Herald and the Bugler are engaged in a life and death struggle, but the Herald is edited by a lady, so it seems to have the best of the argument!"

Another tongue-in-cheek comment was directed against the editor of the Times at Frisco, an especially dry Utah desert mining camp. "Whenever the gentle raindrops visit Frisco, the editor of the Times and other smart boys there hunt up a mud hole to take a bath!" But not all of Raddon's acid comments were directed against editors, for he never spared even the high and the mighty. When the great John L. Sullivan, the famed prize fighter, appeared in a stage play at Park City's Grand Opera House, Raddon wrote, "He is a far better fighter than he is an actor!"

Raddon printed the truth as he saw it, but his editorials directed against the camp's elite or the "400" sometimes resulted in threats against him. He didn't seem to worry about personal attacks, although he certainly recognized there was a real danger, for it was a time when editors were challenged to duels, or run out of town on a rail. Many such incidents hit close to home, to friends of his, and the Record reported them.

One such attack occurred right next door at Heber City, when Wasatch Wave Editor Glanville was "licked right in his own barn, the first licking ever given a Wave editor for printing the news." Publishers of the Wave weren't scared off though, for the next issue carried the following ad. "Wanted: A fighting editor, at this office. One who stands six feet eleven inches in his stocking feet and tips the beam at 197 pounds fighting weight, who can handle his fists, feet, a gun or a club!"

Raddon also observed an attack on fellow editor Charles King of the Morning Rustler at Ogden. "About midnight a party of masked ruffians entered King's office, abused him, dragged him out into the darkness, tarred and feathered him, and fled the scene!"

The Big Store, Blyth-Fargo's in wintertime.

Violence against outspoken editors hit even closer to home September, 1897 when Editor J.J. Flahiff of the Utah Patriot, of Raddon's rival papers at Park City was assaulted Raddon observed, "This job of licking editors has become fashionable the last to come to our notice was a few days ago when Editor Flahiff of the Patriot and Matt Connelly, Foreman at the Ontario, came forcibly together." Raddon then added some good advice to Flahiff, saying, "We would suggest that editors who live in belligerent communities such as this make a breast plate of old boiler plate iron and wear it under their shirts!"

The Utah Patriot was only one of several Park City newspapers that tried to run the Record out of business. The first to try was the Park City Call, which first appeared in January 1887 under direction of Publisher E.H. Buchanan. Like the Record, the Call started out as an anti-Mormon weekly, but it lasted only a year and a half. In August, 1888 Raddon purchased that failing paper and added its press to the Record's plant.

Next to appear was the Park City Miner, in

September 1890, with C.S. Austin listed as "proprietor, publisher, editor and manager." Other Utah editors welcomed it, among them the Brigham Bugler, whose editor wrote, "The initial number of the Park City Miner strutted up and gave us a hearty handshake. It is a live, clean paper with good sense backed by sinewy legs. Put 'er there boys, put 'er there!"

But the Miner failed to catch on, and had trouble attracting paying advertisers. Raddon noted "a bad odor," about the Miner and called it "A particularly obnoxious publication", noting that Col. Trewick of the Wabash Mine was suing its editor for libel. The Miner tried to publish on a daily basis, but as Raddon dryly noted, "There isn't enough oxygen at this altitude for a daily!" The Miner reverted to a weekly and finally died from lack of oxygen in August, 1892.

As already noted, another paper which tried to best the Record was the Utah Patriot, under the guiding hand of J.J. Flahiff. After Editor Falhiff's losing fight with Matt Connelly of the Ontario, the paper changed hands. On December 3rd, 1897 the Wasatch Wave noted, "J.J. Flahiff, the fat man from Arkansas, has gone north to the Klondike." Its new editor, J.T. Camp, tried to make the Patriot a daily, but the Wave editor noted, "Being a daily was obviously too fast a rate for the machinery, and its bearings wore out, or else the editor lost his bearings, for it got to running wild and died!" And that was the last real competition the Record ever had.

The grocery section of Welsh, Driscoll & Buck's old general store.

The hard times which plagued the competition often nagged the Record too, and sometimes Raddon had to take in his belt a notch. During the silver panic depression of 1893 Raddon wrote, "Hard times are tough on everyone and during such times people should help one another. Our business is slack, so please, advertise! And subscribe to the Record, now!" His appeal worked, for new subscriptions came in and the presses kept rolling.

During hard times editors sometimes pined for palmier days, such as some years earlier when Raddon wrote, "There is altogether too much promiscuous shooting on the streets at night!" Once Raddon's longing for better days was expressed in an editorial which recalled happier times at Silver Reef, "When that camp used to dish up a man or two once a week for breakfast. Ah, those were the palmy days!"

Without doubt the Record's darkest days were right after the great fire of '98. Its newly completed printing plant was completely destroyed, and all equipment and records burned; still, to its credit, not an issue was missed. The first few issues after the great fire were printed by the Herald Republican at Salt Lake City, but even before the ashes were cool, Raddon was operating out of a borrowed tent.

The Payson Header probably best described the courage of the Record staff. "No neighbor, not an an issue was missed. It was a bad blow. When the ashes cooled, the staff stood dazed, but for only a moment. In only a few hours after the fire, a tent was pitched, and for several weeks the Record was issued from that borrowed tent."

Sam Raddon was damn mad about that fire which nearly destroyed his town, and he left no doubt what would happen to any arsonist caught at Park City. "Should anyone be caught in the act of setting fire to a building, his life would not be worth a straw. Murder may be committed and the law allowed to take its course, but the line is drawn on the firebug. God help the man who is caught! A short rope and a long drop will be his portion, just as sure as hell!"

Where the town which burned to the ground in 1898 had been a rough and ready shoot-em-up mining camp, the phoenix which grew up on its ashes was a city, but even so, it retained a frontier flavor and some wild and wooly ways. The Reverend French Oliver visited the new Park City in 1901, but it was a little too wild and wooly for him, for he wrote, "Salt Lake City is the wickedest city in America, while Park City is only 40 rods from hell, and the editor of the Park Record is the ring leader of the whole dirty business!"

But in spite of Reverend Oliver's opinion, Park City had moved into the twentieth century, and even Sam Raddon had mellowed. He still called a spade a spade, but in a little milder language. He never lost this touch completely though, as seen when he exposed the editor of the Eastern Utah Advocate at Price as an arsonist. Raddon wrote, "It seems his greed was attracted by the big Democratic campaign fund, and he planned to get a snug portion of it. He set his office on fire to cover his tracks, but the scheme was exploded, and instead of getting a cash assist, he got run in for arson!"

He had an even lower opinion of Editor C.W. Snyder of the Sevier County Times at Elsinore, for he wrote, "That petty paper seems to be in a peck of trouble. It is owned by C.W. Snyder, who is neither a printer nor an editor. Mr. Camp, sort of an adventurer, has had charge and has been doing the scribbling, but he and Snyder had a falling out, and Camp decamped!"

The Record weathered the panic of 1907 and grew during the prosperity of the 1920s, it outlasted the depression of the '30s and reported war battles from Havana Harbor to Vietnam. It survived the near ghost town status of the 1940s and 50s when town kids purchased a handful of papers for 2 1/2¢ each and sold them door to door for a nickel.

Raddon's Record witnessed the tough times and the good times. It reported the birth of weeklies all over the state, and it outlasted them all to become Utah's oldest weekly newspaper.

For more than 100 years the Park Record faithfully reported the life and times of Utah's leading mining camp. Frisco and Kimberly, Mercur and Ophir, Silver Reef and Gold Hill and dozens of other camps, with their dozens of mining camp papers have all come and gone, but Park City and the Park Record are still going strong, both well into their second century. They are inseparable.

Men ready for work at the Ontario, rubber boots, yellow slickers and all. Note the election posters for Roosevelt and McKinley, also the company sign which states, "All employees of the Ontario Mine not having families here are required to board at the mine boarding house."

CHAPTER 6

GROWING PAINS

The 1870s saw an unknown, brush-choked canyon in Utah's Wasatch Range explode into a bustling mining camp of 3,000 sweating, cursing miners. The next decade would see that rough camp of board shacks and shanties grow into a city of 5,000 boasting the finest of dressed stone buildings and comfortable homes. And along with its new-found wealth and prominent citizens came its share of "hard times" and "tough-nuts." Park City wasn't a wild camp like Frisco or Pioche and never wanted to be but it did have its share of ruffians. One particularly brutal murder occurred during the 4th of July celebration in 1880.

Two young fellows name Fred Hopt and John Turner rode into town on the afternoon of the 3rd, not to join the celebrating miners but to start on a prospecting trip, at least that's what young Turner thought. Hopt and Turner had been boyhood friends and grew up together in the Provo Valley, Turner as the the son of the Utah County sheriff and Hopt the son of a poor farmer.

John Judge. He became a millionaire, but lost his life to miners' consumption.

As a boy Hopt was always in and out of trouble and often had to be counseled or picked up by Turner's father. One day it became young Turner's unwanted duty to help his father arrest his friend. While Hopt was in jail he brooded over what he considered an injustice and began to blame his friend for all his troubles.

When he was released he approached young Turner, acting as if nothing had changed between them, and reminded him of a proposed prospecting trip they had planned together.

After some coaxing Turner agreed to the trip, even borrowing two of his father's wagons and teams to carry supplies and equipment. Together they traveled to Park City where they were met by a dull-witted friend of Hopt's named Jack Emmerson. The 4th of July celebration was in progress when they arrived in the mining camp and, although they hadn't intended to celebrate, the high spirits of the miners proved infectious and before long they found themselves "whooping it up" in the camp's saloons.

Emmerson soon passed out and by midnight Turner returned to their camp where he quickly fell asleep. During the small hours of the morning of the 4th Hopt staggered into a saloon, his shirt front covered with blood, his hands shaking. After brooding over his drink for a few minutes he startled the bartender by asking if he had ever killed a man. At the bartender's negative reply, Hopt said he had killed someone, that he had killed an innocent boy! The bartender passed Hopt's words off as just the ramblings of another drunk but several days later he would have good cause to remember them.

Early the next morning Emmerson joined Hopt at the camp and helped him finish loading the wagons. When he asked where Turner was Hopt answered that he had gone on ahead. Late that afternoon Emmerson stopped the wagon he was driving and lifted its canvas cover to find his canteen. Underneath was Turner, his head split open and a bloody axe by his side. Emmerson would have fled in terror but Hopt stopped him and persuaded him to help bury Turner, giving him the money Turner had in his pockets and promising to share half of whatever they could get from the sale of his wagons and teams. Emmerson finally agreed and after burying Turner in a shallow grave at the edge of a rock-slide they continued on to Piedmont, Wyo., where they sold the first wagon and team. When Emmerson saw how little his share of the money was he argued with Hopt and they parted company. Hopt continued to Green River where he sold the second outfit. While Hopt and Emmerson were travelling northward an old prospector named Len Phillips discovered the hastily covered grave of Turner near the mouth of Echo Canyon. He notified Sheriff William Allison at Park City who, with Sheriff Turner, the victim's broken-hearted father, quickly took the trail of the murderer.

On July 24, 1880, City Marshall T.J. Carr of Cheyenne identified Hopt from a wanted flyer which had been sent to all local officers and arrested him. When Sheriff Turner arrived in Cheyenne the sight of his son's murderer was too much for him and he had to be held to keep from killing him.

Hopt confessed the killing without emotion and was returned to Park City, then moved to Salt Lake City for trial which was held on February 18,1881.

He was quickly found guilty but a long series of delaying actions taken by his attorney kept postponing the sentence. In the meantime Emmerson surrendered and was held for stealing Turner's livestock but Sheriff Turner dropped the charges when Emmerson told about his part in the crime. After turning state's evidence he was released, never to be seen again in Park City.

On Aug. 11th, 1887, Hopt sat alone and blindfolded in the morning sun, tied to a chair in the yard of the territorial prison. At a signal six rifles echoed as one and he paid the price for "killing an innocent boy."

A busy street scene, the old Utah Power office and Blyth-Fargo's on the right.

From a rough camp of brush shanties and muddy wagon trails, Park City was growing into a town of frame houses with graveled streets. The Park Record described some of the changes made during the early 1880s.

"A year ago a team and empty wagon found it hard to reach the head of Main Street, today it is a passable thoroughfare for loaded teams. Pedestrians were compelled to walk in single file, and with a hop-skip-and-a-jump evade mud holes or else walk through them, now we have sidewalks the entire length of the street. Drunkeness and rowdyism have modified to a great extent, and the firing of pistols in the dead of night is a rare occurrence now. Even the heathen Chinese are regulated in their opium habits. The sanitary condition is fully 100% better than in former years, and the great piles of ashes which adorned the street in front of every business house are no longer visible, nor are there one quarter as many cases of diptheria as there were in years gone by."

The early 80s saw a whole host of new Park City businesses open up. The Rocky Mountain-Bell Telephone Company began operations in 1881 with 60 subscribers, making Park City the third city in the state to have telephone service, the rate being $3.00 a month when miner's wages were $2.50 a day. Among the other new business houses were the Park City Bank, the Dexter Stables, a corner grocery owned by Charley Shields, and a fine brick and stone general store built by M.S. Aschiem. The big Aschiem store was a well-known landmark for many years. It was a two-story building with iron window shutters and one of the first fireproof metal roofs in town. Ground was broken for a new City Hall in 1885 and a new cemetery was started to replace the old one in Deer Valley where the town's pioneers were buried.

Dr. E.P. LeCompte, Park City's favorite son, famed pioneer and cavalryman.

The old cemetery was located on the dry sage covered hill just to the left, northeast, of where the present dirt road now forks towards the old outdoor rifle range in Deer Valley. According to obituaries in early issues of the Record, some 19 people were buried there and in another small plot on a hill north of Snyderville, near where the State Road sheds are now located.

George G. Snyder had grazed his livestock where the new cemetery is located, and for years whenever someone died or was killed, miners would say that they had been planted in Gidley's pasture! It had a real name though, which has been forgotten today, the Mountain View Cemetery. The Glenwood Cemetery, now nearly forgotten and hidden among condominiums was started by several lodges of the day as a burial place for their members.

A straight-away race track was built under the shadow of Mt. Neff in Deer Valley where the sports wagered on their favorite racers with many a gold piece changing hands. In the first race held there, the Record reported that Col. Wall's grey beat A.M. Smith's racer. A circular track was later built below town about a mile east of the present cemetery.

Races with horse-drawn carts were a popular sport with Dr. E.P. LeCompte and Ed Berry being two of the regular contestants. Dr. LeCompte was a fine physician who had served with Col. George Custer's 7th Cavalry right up to the time of the Little Big Horn Battle in 1876.

In addition to Dr. LeCompte there were a number of other fine doctors in town, among them Dr. McFalls, Dr. Gregor, Dr. Mantor, and Dr. C.M. Wilson. Dr. McFalls was once accused of not having been schooled as a doctor but later it was proven he had been an army surgeon for a long period. He left Park City and was succeeded by Dr. Gregor in July, 1883. Dr. Gregor and Dr. Wilson were brothers-in-law and formed a partnership in which they proved themselves capable, efficient, and well-liked.

New hotels and rooming houses were being built on every street, the Salt Lake House in the center of town being one of the most popular while the Park City Hotel owned by a Mr. Fischel and the Park Hotel operated by L.A. Simmons considered among the finest. On June 23, 1883, Burt and Robert Kimball took over the Park City & Salt Lake Stage Line and installed the best Concord coaches available. They had four relay stations along the route where stops were made and teams changed. By 1885 business was so good that local stables were being called upon to furnish wagons to handle the added business. The Kimballs were among the first settlers in Parley's Park, operating a stage station and ranch there for many years. In June, 1885, W.H. Kimball, known as "Old Stager," visited Park City and invited all his friends to the ranch to celebrate the success of the stage line. He offered drinks on the house for everyone, the "drinks" being buttermilk! The Kimballs erected a boarding house for their employees, which was a landmark known for many years as the Utah House, located across Park Avenue from the old Utah Central Depot.

On Dec. 2, 1882, a disastrous fire started in room No. 14 in Fisher's Hotel and soon swept through Wiseman & Clark's Jewelry, the Park City Bank building, and the Theriot Building, but the fast work of the volunteer fire department stopped its advance just short of a row of frame houses. On Aug. 22,1885, the American Hotel and Dr. Snyder's office were destroyed by another fire which would have been a disaster if Henry Newell's meat market hadn't been nearly torn down to slow its advance. These were only the first of a long series of fires which plagued the town for many years.

The original Park City Hotel, site of the present-day Claimjumper Hotel.

Since early in 1882 Park City had tried to get a charter of incorporation. But the state kept refusing until 1884 when it could no longer ignore the camp with its population in excess of 4,000. Finally on Mar. 8, 1884, the charter was granted. An election was soon held and F.W. Hayt, the camp's postmaster, was chosen for Mayor over Edward P. Ferry by a vote of 304 to 92, at the magnificent salary of one dollar a year! Now officially incorporated, Park City began to take on class. One of the first ordinances passed by the city fathers forebade Chinese laundries on Main Street!

Many of the popular lodges of the day began to open branches in town, including the Ancient Order of United Workmen and the Independent Order of Odd-Fellows. Dances were held at Dudler's Hall, Lawrence Hall, and sometimes at the Ontario boarding house. In 1883 the Society Hall was built by subscription by the various lodges and for years was considered to be one of the finest show houses in the west. It was equipped with a large orchestra pit, elaborate stage scenery, and a fancy lobby and seating area. The Record advertised such prominent stage plays as "The Twelve Temptations," "Light Of The Moon," and "The Avenger." Many great stars of the day appeared there including Maggie Mitchell, America's Favorite, in "The Little Maverick," and Goodrich, Elitch, and Schillings Minstrels, as well as Zinlock the Magician, and William F. (Buffalo Bill) Cody.

Early issues of the Record were filled with stories of shootings and murders that shocked the camp. Some of them, though, contained a touch of humor. An 1883 article reported that while "Plum-Bob" Walker was working in his yard near the foot of Main Street someone concealed in a log barn across the street fired a gun through a crack in the logs and killed him. The story added that he was survived by "two wifes and 31 children" and "that murder is definitely suspected!" "Plumb-bob" got his name because he used a sort of plumb bob, really a Spanish dip-needle, to locate ore bodies. He was 68 years old and was considered to be a harmless old character. Not quite so funny was the killing of Zeke Durnall, who was shot by Tex Wilson in April, 1882 over a three dollar debt.

Another story of Park City "justice" was related by the Wasatch Wave on October 12, 1889. "Last Saturday a man approaching Park City saw the hind wheels of a wagon, and some quilts and trappings at the foot of a dugway, and looking about he saw a dead man lying near the roadway. He ran into town to report what he had found. The Judge there summoned a coroner's jury, and taking several bottles of whiskey and some cigars they returned to the place where they found the body. From appearances it seemed the team had run away, throwing the man out and running over him. The judge and jury members decided what to do over one bottle of whiskey, and two of them took hold of the corpse to lift it into the wagon when the dead man opened his eyes and said, "What's the matter, can't you let a fellow sleep?" One of the jurors took another drink and asked, "Ain't you dead?" "Not by a damn sight!" the corpse replied! But the Judge didn't propose to be fooled in any such way as that, and took him to town where he was locked up until he sobered up. Next morning he was fined for something or other. The Judge wanted him to pay the expenses of the inquest, for whiskey and cigars are expensive, but the corpse demurred, saying it was bad enough for a man to pay for an inquest when he was dead, but he sure as hell wasn't going to pay for one when he wasn't!

Kimball's Stables, later site of the Kimball Garage, now the Kimball Art Center.

Early day judges often had no legal training, although their decisions usually insured that justice was done, but not always. A story is told that one morning the body of a transient miner was found behind one of the "bucket of blood" saloons. There was no identification, but a Derringer pistol and seven dollars was found in a trouser pocket. The judge-coroner deliberated for a moment, and then gave his decision: "I find the deceased came to death from causes unknown, and I fine him $7 for carrying a concealed weapon!"

An even more exciting shooting took place in August of that year. Two miners named Matt Brennen and E.M. Wheeler hired two surveyors, Will Gorlinski and J. M. Chapman, to survey their claims in Iron Canyon.

As they were riding through the brushy canyon bottom to the claims Brennen was shot from his horse. Just before he died he told the others that it had been "Black Jack" Murphy who had done him in. Although no one had seen who fired the shot a call was made at Murphy's shack which was nearby. When Gorlinski peeked into the window he faced the muzzle of a six-shooter. Gorlinski jumped back and a minute later Murphy walked out of the cabin, the gun still in his hand, and rode away.

The other men were all unarmed and made no attempt to stop him. As soon as they got back to town they learned that Murphy had ridden into town and surrendered to the sheriff. Later testimony was given that the six-shooter had been loaned to Murphy by a friend and that when he surrendered one bullet had been fired.

Feelings were running so high that Murphy was hustled out of town and taken to the Coalville jail for safe-keeping. The jailer at Coalville was so sure that a lynch mob would try to take his prisoner that he took him out of jail at night and made him sleep in an open hay field nearby, his leg tied to a stake driven into the ground. After several days the jailer decided that any danger from a lynch mob had passed and returned his prisoner to the jail at night.

Unknown to him, however, there was a vigilante group in Park City with other ideas. During the night the vigilantes captured Engineer Thomas of the Utah Eastern as well as Fireman George Acuff and Trainmaster George Hughes. They were forced to fire up the engine, hitch on a caboose, and head for Coalville.

It was long after dark when they arrived in Coalville and before anyone knew what was happening they marched to the jail, took Murphy without a fight, returned to the train, and headed back for Park City. As soon as they arrived in town a quick trial was held by the side of the tracks while a noose was adjusted from a pole nearby.

The following morning early risers were greeted by the sight of "Black Jack" Murphy's body slowly swinging in the breeze. Park City had its toughs all right, and the people knew how to deal with them, too.

One of the first buildings built after the great fire, a temporary Post Office
- Courtesy of Ken Webb -

CHAPTER 7

THE ONTARIO GETS COMPETITION

While the Park Record was reporting the building of churches and the hanging of outlaws, its editor never overlooked happenings at the mines. At Lake Flat the Walker Brothers of Salt Lake City banking prominence had spent over $100,000 on their Lowell shaft and the Parley's Park, owned by the Standard Oil Company of Ohio, had been sunk right next to the Ontario for over 800 feet with no ore in sight. The Empire and Little Bell mines in Empire Canyon had been located and in Ontario Canyon the Naildriver was making a name for itself.

New discoveries being made on Crescent Ridge were soon to result in the organization of one of Park City's pioneer mining companies. The Pinion and the Walker & Webster were both early day diggings that had shipped ore in the 70s. In the early 80s good silver showings were discovered at the nearby Climax and Rebellion claims while a high-grade ore body was uncovered in the Roaring Lion tunnel. At E.P. Ferry's Utah Mine a new steam hoist had been installed. The Walker and Buckeye claims were being worked on the same ore veins as the Climax and Rebellion claims and by 1882 most of the properties were tied up in litigation over apex rights, or just which property had the right to claim the ore.

David Keith, genius behind many early Park City mines. He installed the Cornish Pump and established the Silver King.

According to the mining laws of 1872 if ore outcropped or apexed on a claim the owners could follow the vein even though it dipped into an adjoining claim. The law of the apex kept lawyers busy for years and was the cause of many an argument ending in hot words and sometimes hotter lead. The Pinion, Climax, Walker, and Buckeye owners had all crossed their property lines into other claims, each claiming they had the apex of the ore and each suing the other.

Finally in 1882, Ferry, with the backing of his "Michigan bunch," was able to bring about the consolidation of the Pinion Ridge claims as the Crescent Mining Company with himself as company president.

The new Crescent Company almost immediately struck it rich. According to first reports it had one of the largest ore bodies in the district. The Rebellion tunnel was being driven into a face of ore 30 feet wide on one side of Pinion Ridge, while the Snowflake tunnel on the opposite side had the same size face of ore. There were 900 feet between the two tunnels and it was believed the same ore body connected both workings.

At the north end of camp Robert Mackintosh began building the Mackintosh Sampler to mill ore from the Crescent. In 1883 ground was broken for what was known as the Crescent Tramway. The tramway was not, as its name implies, an overhead tramway, but actually a narrow-guage railroad. It had a Sheatype engine which pulled a long line of ore cars up grades as steep as 12 per cent and across high trestles between the town and the mine.

The Crescent Company did not build the tramway but granted a contract to F.H. Dyer who agreed to build it, deliver 60 tons of ore a day to the sampler, and then, after it was proven, sell it to the company at the end of three years. Dyer named the tramway's first engine the Maud Withey in honor of the secretary's wife.

The Crescent Tram Depot was located at the bottom of Main Street where the drive-in is now. Its rails crossed in front of the Kimball Art Center and climbed the mountain front to the west, following the contour of the steep slope to the rocky point just above where the old High School "P" is located, and then wound around to the west side of the ridge, which it climbed to the Crescent Mine.

The Record of Aug. 4, 1883, reported the Crescent Tramway was hauling the 60 tons of ore per day that Dyer had contracted to deliver. Although the tramway worked well in the summer it was useless when winter snow drifted deep over its track. Then horses pulling great sleds with wide iron runners hauled the heavy ore from mine to mill.

Iron ore was necessary for flux at the sampler and smelter, and though it is hard to believe today, the heavy iron ore was hauled by wagon and team from the Dyer Mine in the high Uintah Mountains located some 50 miles north of Vernal, and then nearly 200 miles more across the Ute Reservation, through Strawberry Valley and past Heber City to the Mackintosh Mill, a long trip today for a modern diesel truck.

In 1880 Col. Ferry had located seven iron ore claims high on the Silver Meadows near Cold Springs, between Rhoades Valley and the Broadhead Meadows, not far from present day Trial Lake. It is said that the Indians knew of the red hematite ore long before white men came, using it for face paint. Ferry developed the claims and began shipping iron ore from them to the Marsac Mill, cutting the long haul from the Dyer Mine by more than half.

By October of 1883 profits were so high at the Crescent Mine that Ferry was able to purchase the nearby Walker & Webster Mine for $50,000. A record of the Crescent dividends only a few months after the company's organization indicates just how rich its ore was.

The Keith & Kearns Mine in Walker and Webster Gulch.

In May, August, and again in October, it paid monthly dividends of $60,000 and in November raised them to $150,000 and at the same time built a new surface plant at a cost of $148,000. Ferry would probably have been the first to agree that Grand Haven, Mich., had nothing on Park City, Utah.

And while Ferry was getting his Crescent Company in operation another mine, richer than any other except the Ontario, was being born. Its beginnings are obscured in the complex puzzle that was R.C. Chambers.

About 1881, John J. Daly was a miner at the Ontario. He was a quiet man but obviously one who understood mining, and he observed everything that went on around him. It is said that one day he met Chambers who was making a tour of the mine and asked him if the Ontario's ore did not extend to the west. "If it did I would have had it long ago," Chambers answered.

Apparently Daly didn't agree with Chambers' opinion for through discreet questions and investigation Daly learned that the ground to the west of the Ontario had not been claimed, mostly because it was not thought that the Ontario's ore extended that far and also because the water level was so close to the surface that sinking a shaft appeared to be next to impossible.

The Park City Consolidated Mine in Deer Valley, soon to be the site of the new ski area.

Daly was convinced the Ontario's ore bodies did extend to the west and by careful prospecting on his time off convinced himself that he was right. He quietly acquired 24 claims, some by locating, some by buying. Where Daly got the money to purchase the claims wasn't then known but it was later rumored that Chambers had furnished it. It is said that Daly would visit a claim owner to inquire about buying his claim and if the owner asked a high price it didn't seem to matter to Daly. If the owner showed any inclination at all to sell Daly would offer more than the claim was worth, often offering $10 a foot when most good claims sold for only half that much. If the owner then hesitated Daly would take out a great roll of five dollar bills and slowly count them out until he had the amount offered in a pile in front of him. Few poor claim holders could resist such a sight and Daly would then get the property.

When Daly finally got control of the 24 claims he wanted he started work on what was known as the Central Tunnel, located just below where Empire Canyon opens up into a small park-like basin.

In a short time he struck the ore fissure he knew he would find, an extension of the same ore veins originally discovered at the Ontario's "discovery hole." At the edge of the small mountain park just above the Central Tunnel Daly began sinking a shaft and almost immediately hit the same rich ore. Buildings were erected and the best of hoisting and mine machinery purchased. Production soon reached 800 tons per month, the ore being treated at the Marsac Mill where it was reduced to bullion bars. After Daly got his mine located and operating, he deeded a half interest to Chambers.

On 40 other claims Daly tried to persuade Chambers to form a corporation with him but Chambers refused, so Daly took his own half interest in the property and incorporated it as the Daly West Mining Company. The profits from his new company were so great that they soon repaid the entire cost of development and operation. From the time everything was paid for Daly deposited half of the profits in a special bank account which he held subject to final settlement of the property's ownership. After nearly ten years of litigation a settlement was agreed upon in which half of the property was deeded to the Chambers & Hearst interests.

The company's incorporation was raised from 75,000 to 150,000 shares of stock, valued at $3,000,000, and Chambers became president of the company while Daly was made vice president.

Why did Daly and Chambers resort to such devious tactics? Stories then told claimed that the great roll of bills Daly used to buy out claim holders actually came from the mysterious Ali Ben Haggin through the maneuverings of Chambers. The most logical explanation seems to be that Chambers' reputation had suffered when he told Daly there was no ore to the west of the Ontario, only to learn that there were bonanza lodes there, and to bolster his injured ego, he remained aloof in the background until the claims were secured and safely deeded to him. Such was the enigma of R.C. Chambers.

The Sampson Mine located on Crescent Ridge was another early producer which was later to distinguish itself. Within two years after its discovery the

Sampson went from an unknown claim to one of the camp's best producers. Galena ore was struck in its shaft at only 40 feet and overnight its stock soared but with another 40 feet of depth so much water was encountered that pumping costs reached $70 a day.

The cost of pumping water became so high that a loan from McCornick's bank was made but the company couldn't meet the loan payments and in 1888 the mine was sold at a sheriff's sale. The sale resulted in the Sampson Company coming under control of A. Hanauer as president and N. Trewick as vice president.

The new owners levied a $1 per share assessment against the company's stock and used the money raised to drive the Hanauer drain tunnel to the shaft's 400-foot level. Later the tunnel was extended into the Crescent Company's ground and drained that property also. In 1889 when Hanauer, Trewick, and John Daly started a deeper tunnel called the Alliance, the Sampson Mine was mined to even greater depths and its stock again went soaring to the heights.

Some of those old stock certificates had more gold on their gilted edges than their mines had in the ground! Park City never had scores of stock promoters like some camps but still a few of the unwary were taken. In the winter when claims couldn't be closely examined the game of stock trading reached its heights. Shares in some great magnificent ledge changed hands over polished bars or across poker tables on days when blizzards kept miners huddled around the pot-bellied stoves of the camp's saloons. And the more extravagant the stories became the easier they were to believe. "Why, this here stock is worth a fortune, but since you and me is friends, I'll just let you have it for ten bucks!" or "All I need is a grubstake, mister, why, just a few more feet and that shaft will be in the prettiest ore you ever laid eyes on!" And who could tell? Maybe it would! Or maybe Mark Twain was right after all. When old Mark was at the Comstock he said "All a mine is is a hole in the ground with a liar at the top!"

Mark Twain may have known what he was talking about when he described the mines of the Comstock but he wasn't talking about the discoveries being made at Park City. As early as the 1870's wonderfully rich ore, high in both silver and lead, was being mined at Ferry's Utah Mine on Pioneer Ridge as well as at the Jones-Bonanza on Bonanza Flat but work always had to be abandoned when the shafts reached 300 to 400 feet in depth because of unmanageable water problems.

The Creole Mine, owned by Jesse Knight, later merged with the Uintah-Treasure Hill property.

In 1883 another rich outcrop was discovered at the head of Empire Canyon not far above Daly's earlier finds. On Mar. 25, 1885, it was consolidated with the Utah and White Pine claims as the Anchor Mining Company with E.P. Ferry as manager.

A hoist was purchased, a boiler room and bunkhouse built, and a shaft was started with three shifts of 15 men each. Water was encountered almost immmediately and by the time the shaft reached 300 feet it was all the company's two large pumps could do to keep it free enough of water so that the miners could work. Each new foot of depth was achieved with only the greatest labor and expense until the shaft reached 600 feet and a near disaster struck.

An underground water course was hit that could only be called a flood. Icy water rose in the shaft almost as fast as the men could scramble ahead of it. When its rise was finally checked it was only 100 feet from the surface with the lower 500 feet of shaft and workings flooded. The company purchased two more large steam boilers to furnish an even greater head of steam for the pumps. Still the water could only be lowered to the

400-foot level. Even then it was a never-ending and costly operation.

In desperation company officials directed that a tunnel similar to the one at the Ontario be dug to drain the flooded workings. A contract was awarded to John Daly of the Daly Mine to run a 6,000-foot tunnel from near the mouth of Walker & Webster Gulch to connect with the bottom of the Anchor shaft at its proposed 1,200-foot level. An ingenious scheme, unheard of then in mining circles, was planned to connect the shaft's 600-foot bottom with the tunnel's 1,200-foot level.

On the long haul to the Crescent Mine, note the grade across the canyon.

On Oct. 12, 1886, Daly's men started work on the new Anchor tunnel and by the end of the first year it was driven more than 4,000 feet into the mountain's heart. In February, 1889, when the tunnel was 5,800 feet towards its goal the flow of water coming from its mouth was so great that progress was seriously slowed. Several bodies of good ore discovered in the tunnel helped off-set the high costs of mining and slow progress continued.

Finally, early in 1889, the tunnel reached a point directly under the flooded shaft above. In order to connect the flooded workings with the tunnel below a 6-inch churn drill was lowered into the icy water and a hole started from the shaft's bottom, the drill's engine being located on the surface. Rapid progress was made until the surface workings were first damaged by a snowslide and then destroyed by fire.

Drilling was resumed when the surface plant was rebuilt but had to be abandoned at 300 feet below the shaft's bottom when the drill bit was lost. The drill rig was then moved from the shaft and taken to the tunnel's end where drilling began again, this time aimed for the bottom of the shaft. There was a great danger that when the tunnel and shaft were connected by the bore hole the men in the tunnel below would be flooded. Therefore, when the hole reached 550 feet an explosive charge was pushed to its end and detonated. The explosion was not successful in tapping the water, so the hole was extended to 580 feet where the earlier hole drilled from the surface was hit and the shaft drained. The accuracy of hitting the shaft bottom with the primitive drilling equipment then in use is a tribute to John Daly's miners. Although the water flow was great, it was contained in a flume three feet wide and two feet deep. The Anchor Mine, later to be known as the Daly-Judge had been born.

While the bore hole was being drilled David Keith, foreman for Chambers at the Ontario, had been hired as superintendent at the Anchor, and it was he who supervised the project. A new and larger hoisting plant was installed and by 1892 the Anchor ranked with the Ontario and the Daly as the camp's biggest producers.

Park City had already survived one minor depression, a silver price drop in 1883, and in 1893 it witnessed a money panic. Most of the mines temporarily suspended operations but an indication of the Anchor's rich ore is shown by the fact that during the resulting depression it was the district's only mine still operating and shipping ore.

For a few years the Anchor's ore was milled by the Union Mill in Empire Canyon but soon the company built its own new and modern plant. No longer was Park City a one mine camp. The Ontario was now competing with both the Anchor and Daly, each producing millions from the steady stream of silver coming from their shafts, and even greater strikes were just ahead.

China Bridge connected Rossie Hill to Main Street over Chinatown.

CHAPTER 8

DEEP SNOW & DEEPER SHAFTS

While John Daly was driving the Anchor tunnel other companies were also deciding that tunnels were the only practical way to drain their mines. Although the cost of running the tunnels was high the cost of pumping water was higher yet. Water was always the curse of the Park City district and more money was spent in the early days for pumping water and digging drain tunnels than all other expenses combined.

On May 21 1889, John Judge, who had been foreman at the Daly Mine, obtained a contract to run the Alliance drain tunnel. It was started only a few hundred feet from the mouth of Ferry's Anchor tunnel but was driven westerly while the Anchor tunnel went to the south. The Alliance tunnel was driven 800 feet below the old Hanauer tunnel which had been dug to drain the Sampson Mine.

The Sampson had been a good producer a few years earlier but the company had gotten involved in financial difficulties when it couldn't pay $50,000 owed to W.S. McCornick who held a note against the property in that amount. The Sampson was reorganized on Feb. 16, 1889, as the Alliance Mining Company with A. Hanauer as president, N. Trewick as vice-president, and banker McCornick as a director.

By April, 1890, the Alliance tunnel was 3,200 feet under Walker & Webster Gulch and by June it had reached 4,200 feet from the portal. A body of ore had been struck in the tunnel's workings and was helping off-set the high cost of digging. In June of that year 30 tons of high grade and 100 tons of milling ore were shipped from the tunnel. The Alliance reached its goal, 4,576 feet from the portal, on Aug. 23, 1890. The tunnel had cost $80,000 but was effectively draining the Sampson ground as well as other nearby claims. Water flowing from its portal was carried by flumes to the city's new reservoir located just past the last house in Empire Canyon. The city had a contract to pay the Alliance Company $125 a month for the water but when a few years later the company threatened to stop the water unless the price was raised, E.P. Ferry said his Anchor Mine would supply it. The owners of the Alliance Company backed down in their demand but in later years the city's water would come from the Anchor Mine.

John Judge was a casualty of the Alliance tunnel but not one who would soon be forgotten. On Sept. 17, 1892, he died in a Salt Lake City hospital from the "miners' con". The "con" was the miners' name for Silicosis, a disease contracted by many miners.

In the early days holes were drilled into the hard quartz and granite rock with the use of hand steels. The miner held a short length of steel sharpened on one end and rotated it as he struck it repeatedly with a four-pound hammer called a single-jack. When deeper holes were drilled a longer steel was held and turned by one man while his partner hammered the steel at a trip-hammer pace with an eight pound hammer, known as a double-jack.

Whichever type drilling was done clouds of fine rock dust resulted and the miners breathed the dust into their lungs. The dust was made of minute particles of razor sharp quartz which penetrated the delicate lung tissues. Moisture in the lungs caused the tiny cuts to fester and filled the lungs with mucous, literally choking the victim to death. Often the miners' continual coughing to remove the mucous would bring on a fatal hemorrhage.

Some mines were worse to work in than others, depending on how wet the workings were and how much quartz or silica was in the rock. The infamous DeLamar Mine in Nevada, known as the "widow maker," often caused death in six months or less.

Many miners realized the danger and would pour water into the drill holes to cut the dust. In later years compressed air drills were made with hollow drill steel through which a stream of water was forced, greatly reducing the dust and its deadly danger.

In the early days many of the fraternal lodges at Park City raised money for widows of miners who died of the "con" but it was at best only a token gesture. When John Judge died he left his widow well fixed financially, having invested heavily in Park City mining stock.

Mary Judge, his widow, built the Judge Memorial Hospital in Salt Lake City for old and sick miners. For years victims of the "con" were treated there and after it had served its purpose as a hospital and better safety practices came into use at the mines it became the present Judge Memorial School. It was, and still is, a fitting memorial to John Judge, pioneer miner and mining man of Park City.

John Judge underground. He worked where his miners worked. - *Utah State Hist. Society* -

It is almost unbelievable today how fast those old-time miners could drill a hole into solid rock. Fortunately, the Park Record recorded the results of drilling contests engaged in for fun by those early-day miners.

In 1893 Charley Emery and Frank Ward argued themselves into a bet one night at a local saloon over which of them could drill the deepest hole in 15 minutes. A contest was proposed by the listeners and on June 14, 150 men gathered on the Bonanza Flats to back their favorite with hard-earned gold pieces. John Downey was Ward's drill turner while Mike Sullivan turned the steel for Emery.

Time keepers and judges were chosen and at the end of 15 minutes Emery had sunk his drill 12 inches but Ward won the purse with 17 1/2 inches! After that yearly contests were held on the 4th of July with the different mines competing against each other. In 1897 Mike Malia and Joe Tribley of the Daly won $100 by drilling a hole 24 inches deep in 15 minutes. Another good record was made in 1901 by Pat Hurley and John Witt of the Silver King with 25 inches. In 1904 Kelly & LeRoy of the Ontario made 18 1/2 inches in only 10 minutes when Harrington & O'Neil of the Silver King were forced to stop at 16½ inches with a broken drill.

While Daly was driving the Anchor Tunnel and Judge was pushing the Alliance ever deeper, R.C. Chambers of the Ontario was planning a new drain tunnel which would make them both insignificant by comparison. It was the new Ontario drain tunnel, 3 miles long to the mine's 1,500 foot level, 4½ miles to the Daly shaft, and later a mile beyond that. It was planned to cost $400,000 and would allow the Ontario to mine to the 1,500-foot level and deeper, opening up new and ever richer ore bodies. A site was chosen three miles east of the Ontario and named Camp Florence in honor of the daughter of Dan Robbins, the first woman to visit the site.

John Keetley was the man Chambers chose to supervise the great undertaking. A regular camp of mine buildings and bunkhouses was built and on Aug. 27, 1887, work was started with hand drills, the newly ordered compressed air drills not having arrived in time for the start. At the same time the first holes were drilled at Camp Florence work began in the Ontario shaft to drive a tunnel from that end to meet the one being started at the surface. It would be a test of underground surveying skill as well as a mining first.

The Record reported the surface tunnel at 4,000 feet in April, 1890, and by November it had reached 5,500 feet. That month the entire surface plans at Camp Florence burned, resulting in a delay of several months while new facilities were built. The fire could easily have been doused if the men had had the water encountered in the tunnel the following year. In November, 1891, the Record reported that "A flow of water so strong it tore out the planking between the mine rails was encountered. There are over 10,000 gallons per minute coming from the tunnel portal!"

After seven long, hard years the three-mile tunnel was finally completed when the tunnel driven from the surface met the shorter drift driven from the No 2 shaft. The date was Oct. 7, 1894. The tunnel was so straight that the two crews met almost "on the money" and a man standing at the shaft could see daylight from the portal at Camp Florence.

Mrs. Keetley was one of the first persons to crawl through the jagged opening that joined the two workings. It was not only an engineering, mining, and surveying triumph but also an achievement which gave the famous old Ontario a new lease on life, allowing it to go still deeper in search of silver treasure.

Although the men underground might face the dangers of cave-ins, floods, and the "miners con", at least they didn't have to worry about snowslides! If ever a mining camp suffered from snowslides in the early days it was Park City. When the first prospectors began working in the high canyons beyond Parley's Park the mountainsides were covered with timber which held the snow from sliding. As every available tree was cut for fuel and timber nothing remained to hold the snow on the steep slopes and many disastrous slides occurred.

Heavy winter snows frequently made automobiles useless.

In February, 1884, an avalanche raced down into Ontario Canyon smashing houses and burying everything in its path. Mrs. Harris was killed in her home while next door three children of the Reich family died under a suffocating blanket of white. The Johnson, Malia, and Welsh homes were badly damaged and snow filled the Clark residence completely.

Only a month later the same scene was repeated on the steep slopes above Lake Flat, demolishing the buildings at the Hawkeye Mine and some of those at the Lowell shaft. John Lawrence was on his way home from the Jupiter Mine the following month when he was carried a half mile by another slide but escaped unhurt. The Record reported many families living in the deep canyons were moving into town for safety.

In 1886 the worst storms ever seen hit the mountain camp with even the railroads unable to get through. In January a slide hurtled down into Empire canyon killing Mr. and Mrs. Peterson in their home and burying a Mr. Thorston who had been outside. On Jan 30, 1886, three ore wagons left the Crescent Mine wallowing in deep snow, and traveled only a few minutes when the first team driven by Sidney Nichols became bogged down. There were two men on each wagon and others went to help Nichols and his partner.

They were all near the first wagon when a huge slide thundered down on them. The men were swept from the steep mountainside and into the canyon below. J.C. Cleveland, who had been riding with the last wagon, was thrown into the top of a tall tree where he clung for dear life. When the slide came to a stop he was half buried but Nichols, who had been struck by only the edge of the slide, managed to dig him out. All four of the others were killed. They were William Sessions, Allonzo Gollard, William Backus, and Frank O'Hara. A rescue crew from the mine recovered the bodies and dug all of the horses out alive. The rescuers saved their own lives by going to the aid of their friends for within the next 30 minutes three more slides roared down off the mountain, burying the Crescent Mine buildings.

In 1888 snow started falling on the first day of January and didn't stop for a week. There was four feet of new snow on the level with even more in the mountains, and neither trains nor stages could get through to the lower valley. On Jan. 7, the snow stopped falling and slides began crashing down into the canyons. One slide buried C.P. Axtell and Scotty Hunter inside their cabin in Caribou Gulch and kept them prisoner most of the day while another nearby smashed the buildings at the Himalaya Mine.

Two miners, Bramberg and Johnson, were at work in the mine tunnel and had to dig their way out. After seeing their cabin and other buildings smashed beyond recognition they decided to move to town for the rest of the winter. While working outside at the Rochester Mine, Joe Baxter was carried away by a slide and his body wasn't found for ten days.

At three in the afternoon another slide carried the Anchor Mine bunkhouse and half of the boarding house into the canyon below. In one room a card game was abruptly interrupted when the room was torn in two and half the players were hurled down the slope with the shattered buildings.

Nine men had been in the room but only one, a miner named Frank James, was injured. At almost the same time another slide crashed into the engine room at the Daly Mine, nearly covering a man named Boss who was the hoisting engineer. Several Chinese cooks who were outside were knocked down, one of them suffering a broken shoulder.

Another bad year for slides was 1897. At 2 a.m. the night shift boss came out of the Silver King Mine and went into the warm boiler room to eat his lunch. The fireman, William Peterson, greeted him by saying "It would be a good night for a slide." The words were hardly out of his mouth when a giant slide tore into the building and buried both men under a mass of broken timbers and snow. The engineer sounded the mine whistle bringing all the surface workers on the run. It took 20 minutes to dig the two men out, more dead than alive, but they were saved. Only a few days later another slide demolished the Daly Mine bunkhouse. Four men were killed outright and five others were buried under the rubble but were saved by rescue crews. The same statistics, four killed and five rescued, were repeated a few days later when another slide roared down a nearby slope and hit the Quincy workings, located a little further up the canyon.

New-comers to Park City can't realize the difference in winters then as compared to now. Some say there is just as much snow now, but modern snow plows and paved streets only make it seem to be less. But old-timers know this isn't true, for they can easily remember their second story windows covered with snow, or garages completely covered over. And it was colder then, too. There are many records of people being lost in storms and later found frozen. One old fellow named Hanks who tried to walk to Salt Lake City wasn't found until spring, near the old Homer Ranch. A rusted pocket knife and a tiny pile of half burned wood shavings were found next to his body.

Another early day article reported that Dutch John, a stage driver, lost the trail in deep snow east of Kimball's Station, and realizing that he would freeze if he didn't keep moving, drove the stage in a circle all night, walking beside it. He saved his life and the four horses, but lost most of his feet to freezing.

A man named Norton and his twelve-year-old son left to walk to Coalville during bitter cold weather. After several miles the boy became exhausted, and his father carried him to just south of Atkinson, near where the present freeway junction divides to turn to Coalville. Believing his son was dead, and being exhausted himself, he laid the tiny body on the snow and continued on alone. Nearly frozen, Norton finally struggled into Wanship, from where the following morning a search party followed his tracks back to Atkinson. To their horror they found that the boy had revived and had crawled for nearly a half mile, following his father's trail before he finally fell from exhaustion and froze to death.

Perhaps Tommy St. Jeor, former City Marshal and long time Conoco service station operator described it best when he told a tourist how 40 years earlier snow used to cover the pines near the Spiro Tunnel just across from his station. The tourist reminded Tommy that the pines were a whole lot shorter then. Tommy reflected on that for a minute or so and then replied, "Well, maybe so, but it used to cover those telephone poles over there, and they ain't growed an inch!"

Although many slides claimed lives and caused great damage over the years they gradually became less frequent. Not only did winters become milder with much less snow but also the hills slowly regained their cover of brush and timber. Trees grew back on slopes that had been denuded by timber cutters and gradually snowslides became a novelty where once they had been the terror of families living in the deep steep-sided canyons.

But old-timers wouldn't soon forget the years when they had to go about their daily chores with one eye always on the slopes above.

CHAPTER 9

THE THREE Rs

Some of the editorial comments in the Record were humorous while others were dead serious. One comment in an 1887 issue stated "There is altogether too much promiscuous shooting in the streets at night!" while another observed that "Fennemores Mortuary purchased a new hearse for $800." At first glance the two items may not appear related but they were, for the shootings kept the new hearse busy.

On Aug. 6, 1887, G.J. Hughes was drinking with several friends at Cupit & Brennan's saloon when Neil Mulloy entered. Shortly after entering the saloon, Mulloy accused Hughes of being one of the vigilantes who took a Utah Eastern engine to Coalville and took "Black Jack" Murphy from the jail there and hanged him.

Hughes tried to explain that he had been one of the train crew who had been forced to go but Mulloy refused to listen and called him a liar. Hughes didn't want to fight and started to leave the saloon when Mulloy began waving a pistol which had been handed to him by J.T. Sweeney, a nearby spectator. Just as Hughes reached the saloon door and began to leave Mulloy fired a shot at him. At Mulloy's shot, Hughes fell dead into the arms of Jim Stevens who carried him back into the saloon. City Marshall Bennett was called and soon had both Mulloy and Sweeney under arrest. Mulloy was taken to Salt Lake City to prevent another lynching and Sweeney was held in jail without bail. Hughes was 41 years old when killed.

Col. E.T. Ferry, owner of the original Flagstaff Mine and associated with the Crescent, Anchor & Woodside mines.

How Bill Bennett happened to become city marshal is in itself a story. Bennett was a poor part-time miner who lived with his wife and six children in a small cabin with only a dirt floor that became a mud floor when it rained. At that time all of the canyons around Park City had streams coming from them and most had fish in them. In order to feed his large family Bennett would catch fish by setting dynamite blasts in the streams' deep holes.

Bennett was a large man with a mean temper, especially when drinking, and that was most of the time. Everyone was so afraid of him that the sheriff dreaded to arrest him and the judge feared to sentence him. Finally he convicted himself. One day while he was setting a dynamite charge something went wrong and he blasted his right arm off! The generous townspeople were more concerned with how he would take care of his family than they were that he had broken the law again. At that time it was almost impossible to keep a marshal but the judge had a bright idea. Why not make Bennett the town marshal?

After all most of the men were already scared of him. Donations were collected and a false arm with a wicked hook was purchased for Bennett. Armed with the sharp hook and equipped with a shiny new badge and six-gun, Marshal Bennett soon became the terror of the law breakers. He moved his family into a better home, quit drinking, and never blasted fish again. While he was marshall, justice was always swift and sure. He was afraid of no one and when he grabbed an offender with his hook there was no getting away.

Only a month after Hughes was killed "John Barleycorn" claimed another victim. C.P. Axtell and James Bowen, who with Scotty Hunter had a claim in Caribou Gulch, came into town for supplies. It seems that most of the supplies were of the liquid variety for when they started back to their diggin's neither was feeling any pain. They rented a packhorse from a livery stable and a boy accompanied them to bring the horse back to town.

While they were crossing Bonanza Flat about dusk the pack slipped and Bowen called Axtell a profane name since he was the one who had tied the pack. They began to quarrel and continued arguing until finally Bowen told Axtell to shut up or he would kill him.

The stable boy, no doubt scared by their arguing, claimed he wouldn't be able to find his way back to town in the dark and turned back. As they approached their cabin Axtell jumped from his horse and ran inside the cabin where he got their only gun and rushed back to the cabin door, all to the amazement of Hunter who was inside the cabin. As Ax tell went out of the door he saw Bowen standing in the shadows alongside the cabin with an axe raised over his head. Ax tell quickly turned and fired point blank, killing Bowen instantly.

Hunter was a witness to the killing but apparently nothing ever came of it for this was the same Axtell and Hunter who were buried in their cabin by a snowslide a year later.

Not all the deaths were quite so violent as that of Hughes and Bowen. In 1888 a smallpox epidemic claimed many lives. The Record of Aug. 4, 1888, reported that a "pesthouse" had been located in Empire Canyon where victims could be isolated. Later a diphtheria epidemic added still more crosses to the town's boothill.

It wasn't all killing and dying though for children were born and the town grew. In 1886 there were 1,600 registered voters and 433 houses within the limits of the Nims & McLaughlin townsite. The Record estimated the population at "Around 3,000 with a couple of thousand more in the hills!"

Episcopal Church, burned in fire of 1898.

James Ivers, a blacksmith at the Daly Mine, bought half interest in Wall & Gerrity's Stables for $4,000 and Kimball's was advertising an extra stage to accomodate the increasing number of passengers. Boyles Brothers of Ogden opened a fine furniture store on lower Main Street, a new fire department (with the same old equipment) had been organized, and the Record was making its perennial effort to have the county seat moved from Coalville to Park City.

Park City had good schools, right from the start. The Ontario Mine opened the camp's first school in 1875 for its miner's children in a one-room building just below the mine. It wasn't unusual in those days for the larger mines to build their own schools since the little mining camps were just getting started and their schools, if any existed, were too distant from the mines for the children to attend.

On St. Patrick's Day a dance was held to raise

funds to buy desks and other furnishings and continued to be a yearly get together until the little school closed years later. Agnes Gillespie was one of the first teachers followed by Eva Cairns and Miss McNally, and later by Dan B. Shields who became a prominent Salt Lake City attorney. Gertrude Woods was one of the last teachers before the little one-room school closed.

Park City's famed old Catholic Church, oldest in town and one of the oldest in Utah.

Among some of the families living in Ontario Canyon and at Lake Flat whose children attended the little mountain school were the Mitchells, Murrays, Hurleys, Kervans, Richardsons, Nimmos, and Groses. A few of the old-timers who learned the three Rs there still recall nature walks past the Ontario boardinghouse, where Chinese cooks passed out out strange cookies, and around Lake Flat into McHenry Canyon which were considered an important part of the schooling and certainly more fun than reading and writing.

In 1879 a free school was established and was soon followed by St. Mary's Catholic School and later by New West School and the Park City Academy. Ground was broken for a large finished stone building to be named the Washington School in 1885 and it was completed the following year. By 1887 there were 500 students enrolled at all the schools. A small three-room school known as the Jefferson was also built. It was located on upper Park Avenue and served until 1902 when it was torn down to make way for a fine three-story brick building, also named the Jefferson.

In 1896 the Lincoln School was built in the lower end of town as an elementary school. Later an addition was added but it was built on ground loose and wet from underground springs. It wasn't long before an ever widening crack appeared in the addition and it had to be declared unsafe and was abandoned.

Several new churches were also organized during the time the schools were being built, including the fine St. Lukes Episcopal building. The town's first branch of the LDS (Mormon) Church wasn't organized until 1887 and then meetings were held in Roy's grocery store and baptisms performed at Kilfoyles Ranch south of the city park until 1897 when the chapel on Park Avenue was finished.

Several months later, Raddon of the Record, always anti-Mormon wrote, "Last fall a branch of the Mormon Church was established here with Gad Davis and P.W. Timms at the helm of the rickety craft. Meetings were held in Erickson's cellar on Park Avenue or in the rear of Hop Chong's washee, but it no longer exists at Park City."

The old Catholic Church, built in 1881, still had by far the largest membership. A Masonic lodge had been started and held its first meeting on June 25, 1878, but there was some question concerning its organization and it never received a charter until 1880 when it became Uintah Lodge No. 7.

In a town boasting a new city hall and nearly a dozen schools and churches as well as all of the usual (and unusual) businesses of the day about the only thing lacking was one of those newfangled electric light plants like the big cities in the East had.

When it was decided the town would be one of the state's first to have electric lights no time was lost and before long there were three separate companies bidding to install the system. On Dec. 1, 1888, a group of Parkites raised $8,000 to back a local company and made a deal with Edison Electric to purchase 900 of their new incandescent bulbs. In January, 1889, the Park City Light, Heat, & Power Company was incorporated with M.H. Quick as president. Construction was started and a 65-horsepower steam engine installed to power the dynamos. The first business houses were wired by the new company in February and the first lights were turned on Mar. 22,1889. The Society Hall was equipped with the new system in April, and on May 17 the first street lights were turned on amid the cheers of the citizens.

Cost of the new service was 12 1/2¢ per candlepower with each customer being allowed to use up to 250 candlepower. Houses were wired for $6 each light installed with burned out globes to be replaced by the company. In 1881 Park City had been the third city in the state with telephone service and now it was one of the first with electric lights.

The Record estimated the city's population "at over 5,000" in 1889. The fame of its mines was spreading all over the west and their stocks were sold in London as well as on Wall Street. In April, 1889, the Ontario paid its 154th dividend for a total of $10,000,000 while the Daly Company was paying its 25th dividend for a total of $1,000,000. Several million more had also been paid out by the Anchor, Crescent, and other smaller companies.

Little wonder when the Record reported "The cry is more houses, there is no place to live!" Business was so good that in May, 1891, a new bank, the First National, was organized with the town's leading businessmen as directors. It featured a "chilled steel" vault with a modern time lock. The town's Opera House was showing "Little Lord Fauntleroy" and the great John L. Sullivan was scheduled to appear in "Honest Hearts & Willing Hands".

Another who old-timers recall appearing on stage was the reformed outlaw, Frank James, who performed fast draws and fancy pistol shooting. The Independent Order Of Odd Fellows paraded 100 strong in flashing new uniforms and the Record was still advocating moving the county seat from Coalville to Park City.

It was a bad year for fires in 1890. As already noted the Anchor Mine hoist and shops burned with a $75,000 loss to that company. At 4 a.m. on Sept. 13 a fire which broke out in the Lawrence Building near the head of Main Street gave the townspeople warning that only a thin line separated the town's safety from a disastrous conflagration. The fire was rapidly spreading to Kelly's Saloon and McDonough & Quinn's stables when the Marsac and Ontario mill whistles called all men to help fight the blaze.

The old Lincoln School, built on wet, springy ground, it soon cracked and was torn down.

The firemen were handicapped because their heavy, hand-drawn fire fighting equipment was located near the bottom of Main Street and had to be pulled up hill to the fire, taking a lot of valuable time. Finally the Marsac Mill closed down and its night crew was sent to help fight the fire and with their help a near disaster was averted.

Again the Record editor asked that better equipment be obtained and safety precautions be taken, such as moving the hose carts and steam pumper to high ground and requiring brick chimneys instead of the tin stove pipes most buildings had. The editor reminded his readers of other mining camps which had been burned to the ground but also predicted that just like them nothing would be done until it was too late. His was just a voice lost in the wilderness but it wouldn't be long until Parkites would have good cause to remember his words.

Only three days later the J. W. Savage home on Heber Avenue burned while Mr. Savage was at work. A neighbor found Mrs. Savage outside the house in her nightgown, throwing dirt on the fire with her bare hands, her hair and clothes burning. When the firemen arrived pulling their heavy pumper equipment the house was a blazing inferno, and Mrs. Savage was wailing for her two little boys who were cremated in the flames. Insurance companies were refusing to insure buildings at Park City, even at 10 per cent above normal rates. All these warnings were ignored however and tragedy was in the making. Meanwhile business boomed while millions in silver poured forth from every shaft and the town continued its mad, whirlwind pace.

Payday was the big day in Park City. The miners were paid in gold coin once a month and all of them, including those from the boarding-houses at the mines in the canyons above made a mad dash for the camp's two dozen saloons.

Park City's saloons were different in one respect from those in most other mining camps in that there were several where each nationality group gathered. There were saloons that catered only to the 'Cousin Jacks', the 'Micks', the 'Bohonks', the Swedes and the Finns.

As long as each group stayed in its own territory everything would be fine but after a few drinks someone would always want to pay a friendly visit to a saloon where his nationality wasn't wanted, and then the fun began! In minutes glasses, bottles, and chairs would be flying through the air and cries of "ya damn Mick, you!" or "ya big ugly Bohonk!" could be heard from behind the swinging doors.

Town marshals like Bill Bennett with his hook arm would come running and before long the merry-makers would be on their way to jail to sober up. The next morning they could be seen climbing back up the canyons to the mines, heads aching and here and there a black eye, and most promising to take the pledge, at least until the next payday came around.

The Ontario School, Park City's first. Located in Ontario Canyon just below the #3 mine.

In the early days there were no regular paydays, sometimes six weeks or more passing before the men were paid. Children who lived in Ontario Canyon then still recall the paymaster. He was a sour-faced old man dressed in funeral black and riding a white horse. Whenever he was seen riding up the canyon with his heavy money bags tied to the saddle children would hurry home to tell their mothers. Knowing that before the day was over there would be food in the house and a sack of hardtack candy for them. When the miners came home that evening they would be off to the stores to pay bills long overdue.

All of the stores operated on credit, allowing each family to run a bill until payday when the accounts would be squared and a new bill started. At least that's the way it was supposed to work if the housewife could get her miner husband to the store before he got to the saloon.

Dr. LeCompte, one of the town's pioneer doctors, had a unique system of keeping books. As he treated each patient he would make a notation of the amount due on the wallpaper above his desk. About once a year, usually in the spring, he would have the office repapered and a new set of books would be opened.

He once told a friend that the people who could pay him had already done so and the others probably never would anyway. When store bills were paid there was always a sack of candy thrown in for the kids and if the bill was large or the miner was a regular customer a jug of whiskey would be included also.

On holidays such as Christmas, all the regular customers would receive a bottle of whiskey or brandy, usually with a special label stating compliments of

"Suttons", "Newells Meat Market", "Welsh, Driscoll, & Buck", "Smith & Brim" , "Saulsbury & Stevens", or one of the other old-time stores. An antique Saulsbury & Stevens Christmas bottle sits on a shelf above the author's desk as these words are being written. All those old bottles are collector's items today.

In November, 1892, W.D. Shepard missed his neighbor, John A. Hughes, and went out to look for him. Hughes was an older man and will be remembered as being a partner with McHenry in the discovery of the McHenry Mine 18 months before the finding of the Ontario. Shepard and McHenry hiked into McHenry canyon where they found Hughes laying face up on the old McHenry Mine dump. He had been dead for several days and it was never determined whether he had died from exposure or some other cause. The death of Hughes was one of the first of the real old-time prospectors who discovered ore in the district.

Another death at about the same time was something less of a mystery. Louis Paradise and Hope Fuelling were "sweet" on each other but Paradise had a rival named Milton Trotman who was jealous of him and Hope. One April day in 1892 young Paradise and Hope took a spring walk down the railroad tracks past the 'Y', a railroad switch near the lower end of town, and continued down the main line for about a mile.

There Trotman caught up with the young couple and drawing a pistol he fired a shot at Paradise that missed. The young couple jumped to the side of the tracks as Trotman fired again, this time the shot hitting Hope and killing her instantly. When Trotman saw the terrible mistake he had made he placed the gun to his forehead and fired again. He suffered for several days before he died but Paradise suffered his loss and the bitter memories for years.

They were just 17 years old.

The old Park City Bank, on the corner where the present-day Post Office stands.

CHAPTER 10

THE SILVER KING

There were quite a number of 'go-getters' in early Park City who were in on the ground floor of just about every new enterprise, whether in mining or the town's business life.

R.C. Chambers, David Keith, D.C. McLaughlin, John Daly, John Judge, and the Ferry brothers were among those who let no grass grow under their feet. Sometimes, as in the case of E.P. Ferry's Woodside property, the immediate returns were something less than spectacular. It will be remembered that the Woodside claims were located in 1873 in Woodside Gulch by John Nelson and sold to E. P. Ferry shortly afterwards, to be worked haphazardly at best by various lessees for the next dozen or so years. Although several small shipments were made from the claims the Woodside was not at that time considered to be an outstanding property and even the lessors themselves were less than enthusiastic about it.

In 1888 the Woodside claims were under lease to James Drake, John Farrish, and Frank and James Wellman. On Sept. 5th, Drake and James Wellman decided to take a day off from their work to go fishing at nearby Morgan Lake. On their return to their diggings late that afternoon they crossed Walker and Webster Gulch and were following a ledge which would lead them back to their lease.

At a point about 100 feet off their wagon road and only 800 feet from their cabin they came upon an outcropping boulder which appeared to carry ore values. They lost no time getting some tools and soon had the outcropping uncovered.

It proved to be one of the few places in the Park City district where an ore vein was exposed on the surface. When the Record editor heard of the new discovery and learned that assay reports showed values of 45 per cent lead and up to 600 ounces of silver to the ton he personally visited the property. In the paper's next issue he reported that a vein five feet wide had been opened up and that six tons of high-grade ore were piled on the hillside ready for shipment. The 100 tons of ore shipped before winter set in returned over $8,000 to the lessees. From shipments made the following spring the lessor realized profits of $200,000 and when the lease was about to run out they sold the remaining time to Ferry for an additional $50,000.

On June 23, 1889, the Woodside Mining Company was incorporated for $1,000,000 with E.P. Ferry as president; D.C. McLaughlin as vice president, and John J. Daly as one of the directors. The newly formed company lost no time erecting a surface plant which included a boarding house where by midsummer 72 miners were living. The mine proved to be a real bonanza right from the start although there was near panic when the vein was lost for a few days. When it was found again at the shaft's 220-foot level it was twice as rich as before.

The Union Concentrator in Empire Canyon, built to mill ore from the Alliance Tunnel, started processing Woodside ore. The first month 6,000 tons, averaging $100 per ton, were shipped. The secret of Treasure Hill had at last been revealed, but the Woodside strike was only the key opening the treasure vault that would soon be known to the world as the Silver King.

During the time events leading up to the Woodside strike were taking place several things happened which changed not only Park City's course but also influenced the economic and political future of the state. The Woodside strike greatly increased mining activity on Treasure Hill, with every prospector who could get a grubstake searching its rocky, brush-covered flanks. Among the prospectors who came to search for the Leprechaun's treasure was Thomas

Kearns, a Nevada miner and former acquaintance of David Keith, who was then foreman for R.C. Chambers at the Ontario.

In the late 80s Kearns left the failing mines of the Comstock and headed for Utah to find David Keith, his miner friend of Virginia City days whom he had heard was doing well in the Park City district.

The story is told that Kearns walked into Park City with a pack on his back and only 10¢ in his pockets. If he walked he was "broke" for there was both a railroad and stage line serving the camp. It is also said that he stopped at Parley's Park where he pitched hay all day for a meal. At any rate when he arrived at Park City he looked up his friend Keith who gave him a job as a miner at the Ontario.

While working at the Ontario, Kearns studied the geology and mines of the district, hoping to locate a paying claim of his own or find a good job like Keith had done. He was advised by Keith that if he wanted to find a good claim he would do well to prospect on Treasure Hill and along Woodside Ridge where several promising claims had already been located, including Andy Lundin's Northland, Jennie Lind, and Northpole claims as well as Dodge & McGrath's Mayflower, and the Silver King group owned in partnership by them with John Farrish and Con McLaughlin.

On Jan. 12, 1889, Peter Boyce leased one of the Mayflower claims, the number seven, from W.H. Dodge and in March was joined in the lease by Con Hunt and William Bennett. By April they had sunk a shaft 170 feet but were in need of more help as well as more equipment and financial backing.

It was then that Kearns, who had been prospecting in the area as Keith had advised him to do, tried them and believing they had a good property, agreed to join them. Keith was also taken in as a partner, not as a working partner but to furnish the needed equipment and financing.

It is interesting to speculate where Keith obtained the money necessary to finance the work at the Mayflower. Did R.C. Chambers provide that money perhaps obtained from Hearst or Haggin? In view of circumstances yet to be revealed, it appears that such was the case.

The Mayflower lessees decided to run a drift from the shaft's 170-foot level to try to cut the same ore vein the Woodside strike had been made in. Within a few days after Kearns and Keith joined the lessees, a body of ore that assayed 30% lead and 100 ounces of silver was found. The ore body became so rich and proved to be so extensive that more men were hired and the shaft sunk deeper. A horse-operated whim raised the heavy ore from the shaft until a 20-horsepower steam hoist could be installed.

The Silver King of Keith's & Kearns' day.

The first month of operation saw the beginning of an almost never-ending series of lawsuits that the Mayflower lessees and the claim's owner became involved in.

Both claim-owner Dodge and the lessees were sued by William Perego who claimed ownership of the property by an earlier location.

The suit was later settled in Dodge's favor but only after years of costly litigation. Meanwhile the Mayflower strike increased to bonanza proportions and steady shipments of high-grade silver ore were made by the lessees. The mammoth ore body attracted more prospectors to the area as well as a number of men who wanted to buy the lease. On Dec. 28, 1889, Boyce, Bennett, and Hunt sold their interests in the Mayflower lease to W.V. Rice, John Judge, and Albion

B. Emery, leaving Kearns and Keith partners with the new owners.

To say the new partnership at the Mayflower was a strange one would be an understatement. Keith was the high-paid foreman at the Ontario, while John Judge was making a fortune contracting the running of the Alliance tunnel. Neither actually worked at the Mayflower since they were both kept, plenty busy with their own positions. W.V. Rice was E.P. Ferry 5 secretary, a full-time job considering all of Ferry's interests, plus the fact that Ferry was frequently so ill he was confined in hospitals.

The "new" Silver King, visible from the Gondola Ski Lift.

Al Emery, who was a $3-a-day bookkeeper, was perhaps the strangest of the partners. Apparently he had no knowledge of mining and where he obtained the large amount of money needed to buy his interest in the lease was at first a mystery and later a scandal. Kearns, the poor boy of only a few months before, had become not only part-owner of one of the camp's richest claims but also its actual operator.

The Mayflower would make him a millionaire before his 28th birthday and make Al Emery's wife a silver queen. Mrs. Emery's wealth would soon rival that of Mrs. Thomas Walsh, owner of Colorado's famous Campbird Mine and then acknowledged as society's leading figure, and her story would be stranger even than that of "Baby Doe" Tabor and the Matchless Mine.

In 1890 the Mayflower lessees became embroiled in the first of numerous lawsuits alleging they had tunneled into adjoining properties and mined ore bodies belonging to other claims. The story is told that Kearns once said "If the ore goes into another claim, buy it if you can, but if you can't buy it, take the ore anyway!" The story is without proof and may not be true but later events do give it some credence.

For six months the lessees on the nearby Northland claim, Ezra Thompson, William O'Connell, Frank White, and Dan McDonald, had been following an ore chute and finally hit a fine body of ore on the claim's 100-foot level. They had worked on their new find for only a couple of days, however, when to their amazement they suddenly broke through into workings already mined-out by the Mayflower lessees!

On July 26, 1890, Ezra Thompson, representing the Northland, sued David Keith, as representative of the Mayflower, for mining Northland ore. Both men claimed the apex rights which would allow them to follow the ore but by a court order based on a pending underground survey Keith's miners were ordered to cease mining through the Mayflower workings. While an appeal was pending the Mayflower lessees continued working through the adjoining Northpole claim owned by Andy Lundin.

A legal decision handed down in 1892 finally allowed the Mayflower to follow the ore into the Northland ground. An interpretation of the mining laws at that time allowed a claim holder to follow a vein beyond his claim if it extended outside his claim's side lines but not if it crossed the end lines.

The Northland countered with another suit which was settled in 1898 with the Northland Company being paid $45,000 for the Northland, Northpole, Nevada, Jennie Lind, and Central Hill claims. The price was probably cheap since it was estimated that the value of the ore already taken from the Northland alone was many times that figure.

During the time the Mayflower and Northland were in litigation feeling in town ran high and tempers often flared in arguments over who was in the right.

On Sept. 18, 1890, while Kearns was in town with W.J. Moss, a friend of his and engineer at the Ontario, he was accosted by Alex Landon who accused him of being a thief for stealing the Northland's ore. An argument quickly erupted with Moss standing up for his friend Kearns.

In a sudden burst of temper Moss drew a pistol and shot Landon. Landon turned and ran for Dr. LeCompte's house which was nearby but fell before he could reach it. Dr. LeCompte, assisted by Dr. Wilson, tried to save Landon's life but he died within a few minutes. Moss was hurried to a Salt Lake City jail where he was kept in protective custody to save him from the same kind of justice a lynch mob had dispensed to "Black Jack" Murphy only a few years before. A coroner's jury later found him guilty of willfully killing the unarmed Landon and he was sent to prison.

By the fall of 1890 it became apparent to Kearns that the Mayflower's ore vein was dipping into the adjacent Silver King claims. The Silver King claims had no particularly impressive surface showings of ore so when the owners, Dodge, McGrath, Farrish, and McLaughlin were approached by Kearns with a good offer they readily agreed to lease the claims to the Mayflower lessees. Just as soon as the lease on the Silver King claims was obtained, Kearns lost no time following the ore body into that property. Kearns now had over 100 men working for the Mayflower and many of them were moved to the Silver King shaft where a new hoist was installed to allow it to be sunk deeper than its 210-foot depth.

Day by day the shaft was sunk deeper. To the owners of the property it must have looked like a useless expense for no ore was found but Kearns and his partners knew well what they were doing. When the shaft reached 800 feet a drift was started towards the Mayflower claims and just as expected, in January, 1892, the rich Mayflower vein was cut.

On April 23, 1892, the partners purchased the Silver King claims according to the bond and lease agreement that had been made with the owners. By spring the new property was shipping fabulously rich ore to the Mingo Smelter near Salt Lake City and had returned profits great enough to pay for the purchase of the adjoining Park City Mining Company. On Aug. 23, 1892, the Silver King Mining Company was incorporated for $3,000,000 with David Keith as president; Thomas Kearns as vice president; and John Judge, W.V. Rice, W.H. Dodge, & Albion Emery as directors.

Profits from the new company were so great that a fine new hoist which allowed the shaft to be sunk to the 1,300-foot level was purchased and a whole new surface plant consisting of shops, steam plant, and bunkhouses was built.

In September, 1892, John Judge died in a Salt Lake City hospital from miners' consumption, Keith had been appointed superintendent of the Anchor Mining Company in addition to numerous other responsibilities and Emery and his wife were on an unending tour of parties in California and Hawaii. Kearns was left to "mind the store" as the company's active manager, backed by Keith, always the shrewd and careful watchdog over the holdings.

The Silver King Company had been organized in a period of rapidly declining silver prices and tight money. Silver had been $1.13 an ounce when the company was incorporated but by mid-1893 the price had fallen to only 80¢. The Crescent, Anchor, and Daly properties had been forced to close down and in July, when silver dropped to 70¢, the Silver King followed them.

The decline of silver brought about a revision of wage scales being paid by the mines. Most of the men accepted a 50¢ to $1 cut in pay a day, compensated in part by a cut of 10¢ a day in the cost of board and room at the company boarding houses. The new wage scales combined with the Silver King's rich ore soon allowed the mine to be reopened and on Sept. 13, 1893. While most of the other mines were still closed, the Silver King was not only operating but paid its first dividend of $37,000. That amount might not have looked like much compared to the millions already paid by the Ontario but it wouldn't be long before the Silver King would be boasting dividends equal to the Ontario's.

No doubt about it, the Silver King was a great producer. Ore specimens were displayed in Park City business houses and at the Salt Lake City Stock Exchange. A decision was made to enlarge the shaft to three compartments. This was done in a somewhat unique manner since the shaft from the 700-foot level downward was made three compartments while above that level it was still a single compartment. The upper section was enlarged to three compartments from the 700-foot level upwards to the surface while the shaft was being sunk to the 1,100-foot level.

In January 1894 the shaft hit a new ore body on the 900-foot level even richer than the famous Mayflower fissure. By then W.V. Rice had moved to Canada but the remaining partners Keith, Kearns and Emery seemed to have really acquired the Midas touch everything they touched turning to gold, or as it was in their case to silver. And then on June 13, 1894, Al Emery died unexpected in a California hospital leaving Keith and Kearns the giants of Treasure Hill.

Emery left something else besides his interest in the Silver King, though, he also left the strange story of how a poor bookkeeper became part owner of a multi-million dollar mine. His story is also the story of how his widow, the woman always known as Mrs. Emery-Holmes, became Utah's famous Silver Queen.

CHAPTER 11

THE SILVER QUEEN

Albion B. Emery was an easterner who migrated to the Idaho gold fields in 1869. He made his way to Utah's Tooele district where he served from 1874 to 1875 as the first county clerk of Tooele County. He came to Park City in 1880 and became postmaster the following year, remaining in that position until 1886. During that time he met and married Susanna Bransford, a local girl who worked as a seamstress in a small shop. Miss Bransford was the daughter of M.B. Bransford, a bookkeeper for John J. Daly, and not long after his marriage Emery left the post office and became a bookkeeper for Daly. As already described the lessees Boyce, Bennett, and Hunt made a rich strike at the Mayflower in 1889 and later sold out to Rice, Judge, and Emery.

Emery's interest in the Mayflower lease cost him $8,000, a large sum for a poor $3-a-day bookkeeper to raise in 1889. The rich ore finds at the Mayflower soon allowed the partners to purchase most of the adjoining claims on Treasure Hill and install the best equipment at their newly acquired Silver King mine. The fabulous discoveries at the Silver King made the partners wealthy almost overnight. Not only did Emery make a fortune from his share of ore sales and dividends but also from the sky-rocketing price of the stock he held in the new bonanza. Keith and Kearns also realized great wealth but under Keith's shrewd business ways their wealth was invested in other profit-making ventures. No so with Emery, however, for he was not influenced by Keith's conservative ways. Instead he and his new with began a continual round of parties, enjoying to the full the lavish life their new wealth afforded them, traveling and entertaining at a whirlwind pace at the best hotels and clubs in America and abroad.

Mrs. Emery-Holmes, the Silver Queen.
- Utah State Historical Society -

In June, 1894, only two years after he helped organize the great Silver King Mining Company, Emery's riotous living caught up with him. While returning from a trip to Hawaii he was seized with heart and liver failure described as being due to chronic alcoholism, and on June 13 he died at San Francisco's Bella Vista Hotel.

At the time of his death he was Grand Master of Utah's Masonic Lodge and Speaker of the Utah House of Representatives, the first gentile to hold that position.

A large and impressive funeral was held in Salt Lake City with a special mourners train running from Park City. The press coverage at his pretentious funeral and earlier wild parties would be nothing however compared to that yet to come. A silver king had died but a silver queen was about to be born.

On July 28, 1894, Mrs. Emery applied through her lawyers to obtain her late husband's estate and filed a bond of $320,000 for the necessary papers of inheritance, which included 150,000 shares of Ontario stock, valued at more than $80 a share! Emery's death occurred at the same time the Northland's lawsuit was charging the Mayflower lessees with removing $500,000 worth of ore from their property. Mrs. Emery discovered that as the inheritor of her husband's mining stock she had become one of the defendants in the case. The trial had dragged on for three years with six lawyers on each side and it looked like it would be just another dull case of apex rights until September when once again the mystery man of Park City, R.C. Chambers, dropped a bombshell that shocked the entire camp.

On Sept. 22, 1984, Chambers sued Mrs. Emery for the amount of $174,712. In his suit he claimed that in 1889 he had given Emery $8,000 to buy a one-fifth interest in the Mayflower lease, to be held in trust for him. The large amount claimed by Chambers in his suit was for the value of one half of the 24,800 shares of Silver King stock the one-fifth interest had grown into as well as the dividends Emery had received. Chambers' claim was that there had been a verbal agreement in which Emery would turn half of the stock purchased over to him but that this was never done. Why he took such a devious way of obtaining the stock in the first place or why he had waited so long to press his claim wasn't explained. To the townspeople it was just another of the strange puzzles that was R.C. Chambers.

In October Mrs. Emery answered Chambers suit denying he had any right or interest in her husband's stock or estate. Her lawyers also pointed out that even if his claim was true the statute of limitations on the debt, if it had ever actually existed, had run out.

By then Chambers was quite embarrassed by the whole thing, appearing almost as a fool in the eyes of most Park City residents, and probably wished that he had never made the claim. Parley L. Williams was one of the lawyers for the Northland in their suit against the Mayflower and he thought that if he could prove Chambers was behind the lessees he might have the case settled in favor of Northland.

It was rumored that Chambers was leaving for California so attorney Williams lost no time calling him to the witness stand. Chambers took the witness stand, obviously embarrassed, and made a poor attempt to appear at ease. Finally, after several minutes of tense silence, attorney Williams began his questioning.

The Silver King Consolidated Mine. It made millions, but not for Solon Spiro.
- Courtesy United Park City Mining Company -

"Mr. Chambers, did you supply the money, some $8,000, with which A.B. Emery purchased a one-fifth interest in the Mayflower lease?" Chambers flushed visibly and after some hesitation finally answered, "Nope!"

"Did Mr. Emery ever borrow any money from you to buy an interest in the Mayflower lease?" After several minutes of strained silence Chambers answered, "I loaned him some money and he may have used it to buy an interest in the lease but the money has been paid back to me."

"You don't know then if Emery used the money to buy into the lease?" Williams then asked.

"Yes," Chambers slowly replied, "I think he said he bought an interest with the money."

"Did he promise you any part of the lease or do you claim any interest in the part of the lease he purchased with the money he got from you?" Williams asked.

"Nope. He borrowed some money from me and he

paid it back. I have no claim on the Mayflower lease or on his estate!"

The Northland's attorney was anything but satisfied for he had not gotten the answers he had hoped for but the hearing was declared to be over. Judge Merritt ruled that Chambers' money was a loan to Emery which had been repaid. Chambers suit against Mrs. Emery was dropped and he sulked dejectedly out of the court like a beaten man. Mrs. Emery was awarded her husband's estate making her fortune larger than that of any woman in Utah, with an income of over $1,000 a day in silver.

The Amelia Palace, home of the Silver Queen. Even the door knobs were silver!
- Utah State Historical Society -

At the time of her husband's death, Mrs. Emery was still a young and attractive woman who had learned the ways of high society and liked them. With her grand parties she soon became the toast of the '400' and the darling of the New York social whirl. On Oct. 14, 1899, she married Elvin S. Holmes, a millionaire mining and lumber tycoon from Chicago, who made his home in Salt Lake City. With their combined fortunes they added much to the social life of the Utah capital.

Mr. Holmes purchased Salt Lake City's famous Gardo House, built by Brigham Young for his wife, Amelia, and known as the Amelia Palace. It was fitted with the finest of furnishings and fixtures, many of pure silver.

The Silver Queen, as she was then known, invested heavily in Salt Lake real estate. Among the business ventures she owned was the Bransford Apartments and the Hotel Semloh, Holmes spelled backwards. Mrs. Emery-Holmes soon out-shone not only the leading social figures of Salt Lake City but New York, California and Washington also. In 1927 just when it seemed she had reached the very zenith of the social world Mr. Holmes suddenly died, leaving the Park City seamstress an even greater fortune.

The death of her second husband never slowed the Silver Queen's social life. Her favorite pastime was traveling and her journeys kept her on a continual tour of the world. While in Europe in July, 1930, she met and married Dr. Radovan Nedelkov Delitch, a Serbian physician. The Silver Queen's third marriage ended in divorce only two years later. After the divorce Delitch committed suicide by hanging, while aboard ship on an ocean voyage. Soon Park City was hearing rumors of her courtship with not just one, but two Russian princes! Prince Nickolas Engalitcheff from Russia's most prominent family, and Prince Dadiani, leader of Russia's Georgian aristocracy, both sought her hand. The question of which prince would win her kept tongues wagging for months.

The gossips soon heard that Prince Engalitcheff was the winner, for they were married not once but twice in two different ceremonies in New York City in 1933. At the time of their marriage the Prince was the official Russian Vice Counsel. Unfortunately the Silver Queen's fourth marriage was also a short one, for Prince Engalitcheff died only two years later. Years later when settling the Queen's estate, 10,020 shares of her Silver King stock was given to the Engalitcheff estate.

The Silver Queen later had a palatial home built in Pasadena, Calif., where she made her home but even then the stately, whitehaired millionairess was still the much sought-after society leader. On Aug. 4, 1942, while on her fourth trip around the world, the 83-year-old Silver Queen died at the Putnam Inn at Norwalk, Conn., still owner of the Silver King stock and its fortune in dividends that 50 years earlier R.C.

Chambers had claimed as his own.

She was buried in Salt Lake City's Mt. Olivet Cemetery by the side of her first husband, Albion B. Emery, as Mrs. Susanna Bransford Emery Holmes Delitch Engalitcheff. The one time Park City seamstress would always he remembered to Park City and her Utah friends as the Silver Queen.

While the Silver Queen was making the Silver King mine a household name around the world the mine was becoming famous in its own right. The three compartment shaft was completed to the surface and the huge ore bins were kept to over-flowing with silver ore. All of the Mayflower ore was being brought to the surface through the new shaft and the Mayflower had in effect become the Silver King. The entire property was fully equipped with the finest equipment and it was considered to be a model mine. The King, as it was known, was born in lawsuits and couldn't seem to escape them afterwards. Most of them alleged the theft of other companies' ore underground but one of the first suits was over water, not ore.

The Alliance Mine, showing the Massachusetts Mine at the upper left.

The King needed a dependable source of water for its mine boilers and boarding house so in 1894 the company purchased four claims at the head of Thaynes Canyon from Col. William Ferry. Shadow Lake was situated on the claims and a pipeline was laid from the lake to the mine. It was hardly in use however before the Crescent Company claimed trespass, claiming the King had crossed their ground with the pipeline and also that before the pipeline had been completed the King had tapped a Crescent pipeline and took water illegally for over a year before the Crescent Company became aware of it. After five years of costly litigation the King was allowed to use the pipeline by posting a bond.

A far more serious suit regarding water was filed by the King on Dec. 28, 1895, against the Alliance Company. It charged that the Alliance had tunneled 1,300 feet into King ground with a drain tunnel and what was even worse that if the tunnel should break into King workings the King mine might be flooded. The Alliance was being worked in ground heavy with underground flows while the King was comparatively dry.

By early 1897 Silver King dividends passed the $1,000,000 mark. Ground was broken for a new mill, the most modern in the camp, and an overhead tramway was started to eliminate the long wagon haul down Woodside Gulch. The new aerial tramway was completed and the first bucket of ore, decorated with flags and brightly colored streamers, was lowered along the high cableway on June 8, 1901. The tramway was nearly a mile-and-a-half long, had 80 ore buckets, and used 40 steel towers up to 85 feet in height.

Although the new tramway cost a small fortune it resulted in savings to the company. Hauling ore by wagon had cost $ 1.50 per ton but the cost of transportation on the tramway was only 22¢. It didn't take long to pay for it at that rate. Only one week after its start an amateur tightrope artist shocked watching housewives below with his daring antics. Nine-year-old Dick Smith, son of F.W. Smith, climbed one of the tallest towers and by walking on the 3/4" lower cable and holding on to the threadlike upper one he slowly inched his way to the next tower 180 feet away. He was returned unharmed to his mother, except for a "blistered bottom," just as soon as that poor lady could be revived.

In 1900 the King paid $1,000,000 in dividends, more profits paid out in one year than the entire total from the time the mine had started eight years before. M.J. Dailey, known as Mike Dailey, was foreman at the mine and was made assistant manager in 1901 Mike Dailey did more to make the King the great mine it became than almost any other man. He was well-versed in the district's geology and knew that if the pinched and narrow ore veins were followed often new and greater ore bodies would be uncovered. Many old drifts and stopes that had been abandoned by earlier foremen because of narrowing fissures were reopened by Dailey, resulting in the discovery of some of the King's greatest ore bodies. Under his direction it wasn't long before the King boasted $10,000,000 paid in dividends and had ever increasing ore reserves. On Nov. 15, 1902, Duncan Gillis, foreman at the King, was killed when he fell down a raise. He was replaced by Frank Dailey, brother of Mike Dailey. The brothers were fine mining men and had colorful careers at the King lasting well over 20 years.

Ontario Company Superintendent Robert Craig Chambers. - *Courtesy Utah Mining Assoc.* -

In June, 1905, the American Smelting & Refining company offered $9,000,000 for the Silver King Mine but the offer wasn't given serious consideration, not with King stock over $50 a share and $ 100,000 dividends a month being paid! So many rich discoveries were being made at the King that they hardly warranted news coverage. Even strikes of monumental proportions were reported in fine print on back pages of the Park Record.

In 1906 the King purchased E.P. Ferry's pioneer Woodside Company making its ownership of Treasure Hill nearly complete. Not quite complete though, for on March 31, 1906, the Silver King was sued for $900,000 by James McGregor's St. Louis-Magnolia Company for mining that company's ore underground. The lawsuit forced the King to cut its monthly dividends but in the long run it served to make the great mine even greater.

Early in 1907 Keith and Kearns called a special stockholders' meeting at which it was decided to form a new company. Instead of fighting the St. Louis-Magnolia suit in court the King purchased McGregor's company, consisting of 56 claims and 486 acres. Including the Pinion and Baltimore claims and all connected workings and surface plants it added greatly to the King's holdings. Also purchased was the old Keith and Kearns Mine in Walker and Webster Gulch and the Odin properties in Thayne's Canyon.

On May 25, 1907, the new company, named the Silver King Coalition, was incorporated with 1,250,000 shares of stock valued at $6,250,000. David Keith remained as president, and Thomas Kearns vice president, while other officials included W.S. McCornick, James Ivers, William Ferry, and Mike Dailey as superintendent.

The new coalition company had 550 employees at its start and was mining so much high-grade ore the mighty American Smelting and Refining Company smelter was forced to ask it to slow down since it couldn't handle the great volume of ore being shipped. The monthly dividend hit $187,000 and Mike Dailey was given a special bonus of $4,000 for his part in making the mine the El Dorado it was. Keith was devoting full time to the company, having resigned from his position at the Anchor several years earlier, and Kearns was a name known wherever mining men met.

It had been a long, hard, road from the days when Keith was a miner at the Comstock and Kearns walked into Park City with a pack on his back, but it was only the beginning. The new Silver King Coalition would soon become the best-known mine in the west. It wouldn't all be a path of roses though for there were more lawsuits and problems ahead, both for the Silver King and Park City, but both were destined to win the name of Silver King in their own right.

A close-up view of the Cornish Pump, showing the huge 35-ton, 70-foot diameter flywheel.

CHAPTER 12

JOHN DALY'S MINE

It was in 1881 that John J. Daly with only 24 unproven claims and the behind-the-scenes backing of R.C. Chambers built the Daly Mining Company. In less than ten years it became one of the camp's leading mines with 150 miners employed and its stock listed on the New York Exchange at $16.50 per share. It rivaled even the great Ontario and before the silver panic of 1897 struck the nation it paid nearly $3,000,000 in dividends. It was during the same period that Daly also organized the Daly-West Mining Company.

In September, 1891, Daly began sinking a new shaft using the hoist and machinery from the Ontario's No. 4 shaft, the old air shaft at mid-point in the 600-foot level drain tunnel. His new shaft was a three-compartment one that had workings connecting with the Daly shaft on the 800-foot level. The Daly-West Company was incorporated in 1898 with John Daly as president and R.C. Chambers as vice president.

The Daly-West had rich ore in all its workings and by summer of 1896 boasted the completion of a modern mill and the installation of a new hoisting plant. At that time the Daly-West had the reputation of being one of the best equipped mines in the west. Everything in the line of buildings and machinery was new and there was plenty of high-grade ore on every level. In May, 1897, just when everything looked rosy for the new company a tremendous underground water course was cut into on the mine's 1,300-foot level. Some of the most promising ore bodies had to be abandoned in the face of the advancing water until larger and more efficient pumps could be obtained.

Water troubles weren't Daly's only problem however, for R.C. Chambers, the company's vice president, disagreed with Daly's operation of the mine. Many of the company's miners had been temporarily laid off when the great 1,300-foot level water course was struck and because of the conflicting interests between Daly and the Hearst interests, represented by Chambers, the others were soon unemployed also and the mine closed.

The "temporary" layoff lasted for two years while the great mine lay idle. Miners weren't the only ones who lost out while the Daly-West was closed for the company's sawmill was also shut down as an advertisement in the Record on Nov. 20 proved: "A competent sawmill man needs a situation. Can run a sawmill and keep it in repair from engine to slab pile. P.S. If I cannot get a situation in a mill I would be perfectly willing to accept a situation with some widow, no matter how grassy, until the roses bloom again."

Finally an agreement was reached in which Jacob and Simon Bamberger, Salt Lake City businessmen, agreed to purchase the 47,000 shares of Daly-West stock owned by the Hearst interests. The mine, still one of the finest equipped and having immense bodies of valuable ore, was reopened in March 1899. The Bambergers taking over their interests the following January. No sooner had the mine opened than more rich finds were made. The ore was hauled from the mine through the Ontario's 600-foot level drain tunnel. By October the Daly-West was able to pay its first dividend of $30,000. The mine's ore was so rich, and there was so much of it, that soon the dividends were increased to $45,000, then to $60,000, and by 1902 to over $100,000 per month.

The Daly Mining Company and the Daly-West Company weren't Daly's only interests for he also obtained the contract for driving the Anchor drain tunnel and was a director in the Alliance Company. In 1900 Daly also had a crew of men working at the Jones-Bonanza Mine on Bonanza Flats but was having hard luck with large water flows in the shaft. John Judge, who was also prominent in Park City mining as foreman of the Daly Mine and contractor of the Alliance Tunnel and who had many irons in the fire before his death in 1892, had several promising claims adjoining Daly's Jones-Bonanza. Almost eclipsed alongside such bright stars as the Daly and the Daly-West a new mining company was born when John Daly combined his Bonanza Flat claims with the adjoining ones owned by John Judge. The new company, born almost unnoticed, was named the Daly-Judge. Another Park City mining giant was in the making.

For some time E.P. Ferry's Anchor Mine had been tottering on the brink of bankruptcy. A costly concentrator had been installed and that expense combined with the purchase of 11 claims owned by Silas Reed left the company's treasury nearly empty. While Ferry was confined to a hospital during the summer of 1901 his vice president, D.C. McLaughlin, organizer of the Park City townsite, died. David Keith had left the Anchor Company to devote full time to the Mayflower lease, leaving the Anchor Company in shaky hands at best.

To make matters worse for the Anchor Company, if that were possible, the Daly-West Company sued it for $200,000, alleging the Anchor Company had mined Daly-West ore while that company was shut down during the Daly and Chambers feud. The Anchor Company's problems came to an end on April 5, 1902, when the newly formed Daly-Judge Company acquired it. The Daly-Judge owners paid the Anchor Company $750,000 in cash for the mine and all its holdings, including the one-quarter interest still owned by Mrs. Mary Judge, John Judge's widow.

John Daly became manager of the newly acquired property while John McSorley was made superintendent. Among the directors of the Daly-Judge Company was George Lambourne, a name which would soon he almost as well known as Daly's in mining circles. Other prominent mining men who were closely associated with Daly in his mining ventures at Park City were Newton Dunyon, John Mason, and Fred W. Sherman. Sherman was an outstanding mill man who designed and operated some of the finest mills in the west. In June, 1902, the steam plant and hoist were moved from the Jones-Bonanza to the Anchor and were soon busy hoisting Anchor ore. New crews of men were hired to work the mine's 700-foot and 1,400-foot levels where Daly thought the best ore would be found, and before the month was out several new ore bodies that could only be called magnificent were discovered. The ore had high values in both gold and zinc, the first such ore found in the Park City district. A drift was driven for 2,000 feet with the ore increasing in quantity and value all the time. If ever anyone seemed to have the Midas touch it was John Daly. His new Daly-Judge Mine was proving to be one of the district's richest while the Daly-West and the Daly were beaten only by the Ontario. It was then, just when John Daly's star shone the brightest ever, that Park City's worst mine disaster and one of Utah's most heart-breaking tragedies occurred.

John Daly's original #1 Mine, Empire Canyon.

In Park City's early mining days, just as in other camps at that time, there were few safety devices or rules in effect. The fault was not that of the mine owners, the miners, or of government. Underground mining on such a large scale and at such great depths as was practiced at Park City was at best a trial and error system where safety hazards were discovered by mistakes made. One of the unsafe conditions that existed in all the large mines was the underground storage of large quantities of high explosives. Powder magazines where dynamite was stored were located in the depths of all the mines. Convenient to where it was needed.

At 11:20 p.m. on July 15, 1902, several unusual circumstances were noticed at different parts of the Daly-West Mine.

Shift Boss Hennessy was on the surface when he thought he heard the sound of a smothered report. He listened for several minutes but hearing nothing more he returned to his duties. At the same time hoisting room engineer Chet Barker felt a sudden tremor shake the hoisting room and he stopped the engine to see if anything was wrong. Unable to find anything unusual he brought the cage slowly to the surface and discovered several pieces of broken guide timber on it.

The Daly #2 Mine shafthouse in Empire Canyon. - *Courtesy of Ken Webb* -

Just then he received a signal to lower the cage to the 900-foot level where station tender Rooker got on and was brought to the surface. When he came into the engine room Rooker told Engineer Barker and Shift Boss Hennessy that a terrific explosion of some sort had shaken the mine somewhere below the 900-foot level.

Hennessy, Rooker, and a miner named Worthington were slowly lowered down the shaft to investigate. At the 900-foot level Rooker left the cage to give the alarm for men there to get to the surface. When the cage reached the 1,400-foot level Hennessy and Worthington found the body of Elias Nelson at the station. Nelson's body was raised to the 900-foot level where Hennessy called for volunteers to return to the 1,400-foot level with him.

With three volunteers, Richard Dillon, R.P. Statz, and W. Harlin, they returned to the 1,400-foot level and soon found both John Devlin and J. Featherstone dead.

Meanwhile in a stope on the 1,200-foot level the body of W.A. Weggland was found. Hennessy became sick from gas and was taken back to the 900-foot level.

When he regained his senses he was told by Statz and Harlin that they had found three more bodies and also that Dillon had fallen unconscious and after dragging him 200 feet they had become so sick they had to leave him. Statz and Harlin crawled back to the station after leaving Dillon, passing Mike Conlon on the way. Rescuers later found Conlon dead at the same place they had passed him earlier.

The cages were raised and lowered as fast as Barker could operate them, each time bringing up more of the dead and rescuers overcome by the gas. Foreman Nimmo went down to the 1,400-foot level, where most of the dead had been found, and directed the search until 19 bodies had been recovered. Several of the rescuers had already been overpowered by the terrible fumes or were missing so when morning finally came Foreman Nimmo refused to let the cage go down again.

Friends of the lost rescuers begged and pleaded with Nimmo to let them search for the missing miners and finally yielding to their pleas he joined them on the cage and they were lowered down into the black pit of death once more.

An eternity passed for the waiting miners on the surface before the cage came up again, this time bearing the bodies of Richard Dillon and John McLaughlin. Some of the men thought George Richardson had gone down the shaft with one of the rescue crews but no one was certain for he hadn't been seen for several hours. His fate was discovered late that afternoon when his body was found 70 feet down an incline, still standing erect, suspended by an arm which was wrapped around an air pipe. He was only 17 years old.

All through the long black night and the dismal

day to follow the cage brought more bodies to the surface where anxious wives, mothers, and friends kept a lonely vigil. When the search ended, 25 bodies had been located and taken to Park City's two mortuaries, S.I. Richardson's and Barton & Phillips. By then the cause of the terrible tragedy had become known. John Burgee was the "powder monkey" on the night shift. His job was to count out the sticks of dynamite each miner used and then distribute them to their working places. He would separate the amount of powder each miner needed plus the necessary blasting caps and fuse at the mine's well stocked powder magazine on the 1.200-foot level.

Exactly what happened would never be known for sure but it was later surmised that either Burgee's candle dropped into the charges he was preparing or that he was smoking and live ashes fell into the powder or blasting caps. Burgee apparently had time to try to escape but he never made it for later when the powder magazine level could be entered again bits and pieces of cloth and leather were found clinging to the smashed timber and near a side drift that he had probably tried to reach one shoe with a foot still in it was found. But the horror wasn't over yet for while the grisly search at the Daly-West was continuing a gruesome discovery was made at the adjoining Ontario.

At 12:30 a.m., just about an hour after the awful blast at the Daly-West, Ken Crawford, an Ontario miner, was lowered down the Ontario shaft to count some cars loaded with coal. As he made his way from car to car he stumbled and fell over the body of his friend, George Garvin. An almost fatal dizzy spell hit Crawford but he managed to crawl back to the fresh air at the shaft and ring for the cage. When he was brought to the surface he told Shift Boss William Campbell of his discovery. With Crawford to guide them Shift Boss Campbell, his brother, Sandy Campbell, and Mac Norton were lowered to the 1,200-foot level. When they reached Garvin's body Crawford again collapsed from the fumes. Shift Boss Campbell dragged him back to the shaft where he sounded the alarm for men at every level to get out of the mine. Foreman Matt Conley arrived at the mine and lost no time organizing a search party.

The body of William Zweifel was found in the connecting tunnel between the Ontario and the Daly-West. Chris Sandrup was found alive nearby but died before he could be moved. Steve Baratta and Wade Gladski were found dead in a raise they were running just off the 1,200-foot level and Foreman Conley discovered Charles Niemi's body near the station. J.B. Tindall and J. Malony were found dead where they had been working. The natural flow of underground air currents had carried the deadly fumes from the Daly-West into the Ontario without warning and out the 600-foot drain tunnel into Ontario Canyon.

An ore train before the days of locomotives. Note the ore wagon in the canyon below.

The deadliness of the poison gases created by the giant blast was even felt at the mouth of the drain tunnel for a horse kept just outside the tunnel's entrance suddenly dropped dead when the fumes reached it.

When the final count of dead was made at both mines it was learned that 25 men had died at the Daly-West and nine at the Ontario. Besides those already named the following were also killed by the terrible blast and the toxic fumes: James Murnin, Peter Haron, Henry Devlin, Chris McAlinder, Thomas Kelly, Roy Johnson, John Gill, William Lance, William Simms, M. Cowley, J. McAullife, J. Lively, Chris Cullen, Thomas McKowen, John Carney, J. Eckstrom, and Pat O'Neil.

The tragic death of the 34 men killed at the Daly-West and Ontario mines was the worst mine disaster ever to strike Park City. It did bring about safety reforms however, for the blast was directly responsible for the speedy passage of state laws prohibiting the underground storage of explosives in quantities greater than actually needed for daily operation. The Daly-West Company did everything possible to help alleviate the suffering and loss caused by the explosion. Only a few days after the tragedy the Daly-West announced that a settlement would be made with families of the victims. Every family that lost a husband, father, or son, was given $2,000 plus $500 for each child in the family. Families of single miners were given $1,000 each. All claims were paid by the following spring and monuments were placed on each of the graves. The loss was not made up but the burden was eased.

Daly-Judge Mill & shops, Empire Canyon. George Kruger's home at upper left.

The explosion was only one of the problems to be solved that year for the Daly-West was starting to have troubles with its neighbors. In March, 1902, the Daly-West sued the Quincy, a company whose property was located just up the canyon. The lawsuit alleged that the Quincy was mining ore in ground owned by the Daly-West. The Quincy Company quickly countered that the ore was theirs by the right of the apex law. The prize was estimated to be worth at least $1,000,000 to the winner.

The Quincy had originally been located as the Putnam and had been known as the Putnam group of claims until 1899 when it was incorporated as the Quincy Mining Company with D.C. McLaughlin as its president. By then an incline shaft had been sunk following a vein which apexed on the Quincy claim of the Putnam group. The ore was some of the best ever found in the district up to that time. One rich stope was worked for seven weeks without a pound of waste rock being mined or the end of the ore body reached. Col. William Ferry, a company director, had the hoisting works moved from the Woodside Mine to the Quincy where a new shaft-house had been built for it.

When the Daly-West sued the Quincy that company initiated a lawsuit of its own claiming it had the apex of the ore and also that the Daly-West had secretly been taking at least $5,000 worth of ore a day from Quincy ground. Also included in the Quincy's suit was an injunction to stop the Little Bell Mining Company, organized in 1900 and consisting of 25 claims just south of the Quincy and adjoining the Daly-West, from removing any more ore from the ground in question. In 1901 Solon Spiro purchased the Little Bell Mine for $110,000 and started a shaft which was drilled by hand with three shifts of five men each. A hoist was installed when the shaft reached 50 feet in depth.

On Feb. 22, 1902, the Daly-West Company acquired the Little Bell Mine from Spiro but allowed it to continue working as a separate company. By the time its shaft reached 300 feet several rich ore veins had been cut and cross drifts were started into them. It was these drifts that the Quincy Company claimed were being driven into their ground.

The lawsuits and counter suits were finally resolved on April 5, 1902, when the Daly-West and Quincy companies consolidated. The Daly-West Company turned over 30,000 shares of its stock, then valued at $29 a share, to the Quincy for which it received full title to all the Quincy holdings and equipment. All three properties, the Daly-West, Quincy, and Little Bell, were soon pouring forth their streams of silver wealth and although each company continued to operate independently it mattered little from which shaft the ore came, for John J. Daly was the guiding hand behind all three. The stocks of each soared on the exchange and the fame of Park City soared with them.

Both the Daly-West and the Daly-Judge were among the most modern and up-to-date properties in the West. In 1903 the Daly-Judge ordered a new electric locomotive to replace horse-drawn ore trains in the mine and in 1904 the Daly-West began installing air-driven rock drills. It was claimed that one of the new air-powered drills could do the work of four men drilling double handed. Perhaps some of the innovations being implemented at Daly's mines were just a little too modern for the camp's old-timers. When the company tried to introduce oil lamps the miners walked off the job, claiming the new lamps were unhealthy, dirty, and inconvenient. The walkout was settled nine days later with the men returning to work with their old candlesticks.

In May, 1903, a new wage scale put into effect announced pay for miners at $3 per day and muckers at $2.75. In 1903 Daly's health began to fail, caused in part by the demands of his many interests, and also because of his years of underground work. He retired from active duties although he continued the management of his companies. In March, 1904, Jacob Bamberger succeeded him as president of the Daly-West Company while his son, Ernest Bamberger, became general manager.

Although the Daly-West was paying a monthly dividend of $108,000 reports were being circulated that the company was actually in financial trouble and almost out of ore. The false reports were circulated by stockholders in the east, both to manipulate the price of company stock and also to embarrass the Bambergers whom they did not want in control of the company. To disprove the false reports the Daly-West published a frill report of all its resources and holdings and a tour of the mine was arranged for the stockholders to satisfy them once and for all of the great quantity and richness of the mine's ore reserves. Rumors of trouble in the company were thus squelched, at least for the time being, for the dissident stockholders opposed to the Bambergers were yet to be heard from once more.

An interesting feature of the ore being mined at the Daly-Judge was the fact that it contained a considerable amount of zinc, a metal then thought of as being practically worthless.

John Daly had foreseen, however, that zinc would not always be without value and had it stockpiled as it was separated by the milling process at the Judge mill. His foresight was vindicated for in September, 1905, the zinc stockpile was shipped and paid off a $300,000 debt the company owed. Not only was Park City a silver, lead, and gold camp but also one of the first producers of zinc. By 1906 the Daly-Judge Company's earnings were exceeding $50,000 per month with over $30,000 of that amount being paid in dividends. John Daly had come a long way from his group of 24 claims that R.C. Chambers had passed by as worthless, and he was ready for a rest.

On May 21st, 1907, John Daly announced he was retiring from active participation in Park City mining. He had come to Park City in 1880 and had progressed from a miner at the Ontario to the contractor of the Anchor drain tunnel and partner in several pioneer leases and companies. He organized the Daly Mining Company, the Daly-West Company, and later the Daly-Judge. All three were among the best mines in the camp and the most progressive of their time. A Park Record editorial described the many services he had given the town and voiced its regret that he was leaving. He was always fair with his men and well liked by all the townspeople.

John J. Daly. From miner to millionaire he had Park City's interests at heart.

CHAPTER 13

LITTLE BONANZAS

While Keith and Kearns were building the Mayflower lease into the great Silver King, and Daly was organizing his Daly, Daly-West, and Daly-Judge, other mines, perhaps not so famous but just as important to Park City, were getting their start. The Thunderer group of claims, located in Empire Canyon in 1898, was purchased by William Curtis and John Rhodin in 1901 and consolidated as the American Flag Company. The Flag, as it was known to Park City, had high gold values right from the start. Ore carrying 700 ounces of silver per ton in addition to $100 and more in gold was found as the shaft was being sunk.

Samples of ore aroused great interest wherever they were shown. A double drum hoist, powered by two 60-horsepower boilers, and reported to be the finest hoisting plant in the camp, was installed in 1905. The Flag workings were in an area with a great amount of underground water but most of it drained through natural channels into the deeper workings of the Ontario.

The gold content of the Flag's ore was giving ever greater promise that the mine would be another great one, when the unexpected happened. A cave-in which occurred deep inside the Ontario drain tunnel in 1905 backed an underground lake of water behind it, flooding the Flag's best ore-producing areas below the 600 foot level. While its richest workings were deep under water the long, slow job of reopening the caved tunnel went on with most of the Flag's miners working the mine's lower grade ores on its upper levels.

In 1909 the American Flag Company acquired the Constellation Company and all of its properties giving the company a total of 360 acres of surface land owned. The Constellation mine, located at the top of a wooded gulch just above the Ontario mill, had been started in 1889. A whim hoist was installed at the time and officials reported the shaft would be sunk 150 feet. Eight years later the owners reported the shaft was only down 23 feet but even at that shallow depth the ore was showing values of $41 in gold and 10 ounces in silver. The American Flag Mine was finally drained when the caved Ontario drain tunnel was reopened, allowing the Flag to mine to its 1,100 foot level again. The rich ore that was being shipped when the mine flooded was worked again and in the words of George Rathmore, the company's president, "everything at the Flag is lovely."

Another early company was the Comstock, organized in England in August, 1888, with 250,000 shares of stock priced at one pound sterling each. The Comstock's property was located near the head of Thaynes Canyon, not far from the Crescent Mine. Work went slowly at first for by 1900 its shaft was down only 100 feet but like the sturdy Englishmen who owned it, it was well built. It had a three-compartment shaft timbered with 12" x 12" timbers, far heavier than most of the larger mines with deeper shafts had.

The California Company was incorporated in 1900 with nine claims on ground adjoining that owned by the Comstock. In September, 1903, the Comstock and the California companies merged their holdings to form the California-Comstock Company. The California-Comstock soon made a real name for itself when it started making steady shipments of high grade ore. The mine boasted a new mill, rated as one of the best in the camp, as well as other substantial buildings and equipment.

Since the early 1880's John Morey had worked his Naildriver claim just above Lake Flat, knowing the mine had good ore at depth but never able to get adequate financing to reach it. The tunnel Morey had started and worked in for so long was eventually taken over by Jack Creen who continued it and in time proved that Morey had known what he was doing. In 1899 a face of ore 12 feet wide that assayed 400 ounces of silver and 30 per cent lead was found after the day's round was blasted. The tunnel was pushed deeper into the rich ore and when it reached 1,000 feet from the portal an incline was started, run in fine ore all the way, and by first snow a stockpile of galena and silver ore was piled near the tunnel's mouth.

The ore averaged 200 ounces of silver and up to 75 per cent lead and contained enough gold to offset most of the cost of mining. In October, 1902, Jack Creen incorporated the Naildriver Mining Company with 300,000 shares of stock selling for $2.00 each.

In January, 1903, a shaft was started higher on the mountain to connect with the tunnel and other workings below. A gallows frame 44 feet high and built of 16" x 16" timbers stood guard over it. A boiler and engine for a newly ordered hoist was installed while shops and bunkhouses were built nearby. In June, 1904, the shaft and tunnel were connected. Before the snow was gone from under the high pines, wagon loads of rich silver ore were rumbling down Ontario Canyon. Close by the Naildriver were several other good claims, some of which would make a name for themselves before long. Among them were Col. Trewicks Wabash, Jimmie Burn's Star group, and the New York Mine.

The Creole on Treasure Hill was started in 1884 by D.F. Condon who told the Record editor he was the owner, shift boss, and crew! Condon leased the Creole to E.N. Jenkins, Dan Dorey, and Pat Blaney and in 1889 they uncovered a valuable vein of ore. For several years they made steady shipments from the Creole and stockpiled a large amount of mill rock. In 1893 they discovered a 2 foot vein of some of the highest grade chloride ore ever seen in the camp. In short order the Creole became another of Park City's leading producers and continued as such for many years. The Creole was located in an area where many rich claims had been staked, including the Uintah Treasure Hill owned by Eureka's "Uncle Jesse" Knight. In 1907 the Creole was consolidated with Knight's Uintah Treasure Hill and became part of that company's lawsuit against the Silver King owners.

The list of mines which flourished in those early days is a lengthy one and includes among others the Lucky Bill in upper Empire Canyon, the Odin and

Solon Spiro & Mrs. Spiro, second from right, standing and sitting. - *Utah Mining Assoc.iation-*

Scott Hill Consolidated in Thayne's Canyon, and the Midnight Sun and Scottish Chief at the district's west end. There were literally hundreds of small mines located in the hills around town, some just prospect holes while others were stock companies listed on the Salt Lake City stock exchange.

Often they were only one-or-two-man diggings where time went slowly on long winter nights. Many of those lonely cabins had walls decorated with fancy calendars and with poems and verse composed by its occupants to pass the long hours. One of the most common poems found written in isolated cabins and on bunkhouse walls was the Miner's Ten Commandments. Although it appeared in many forms the following is typical.

"THE MINER'S TEN COMMANDMENTS"

"The ragged old man spoke these words and said unto me, I am a miner who wandereth from the East to sojourn in a strange land and see the elephant. And behold! I saw him, and bear witness that his whole body passed before me, and I followed him until he stopped before a rough cabin, and with his trunk extended he pointed to a printed shingle tacked to the cabin, as though to say, read the Miners Ten Commandments!"

1.Thou shalt have no other claim but one.
2.Thou shalt not take unto thyself any false claims, nor shalt thou jump one.
3.Thou shalt not go prospecting again before thy claim gives out nor shalt thou take thy hard-earned dust to the gaming tables in vain for the more thou shalt put down the less thou will take up.

Underground station at the Ontario. Note the overhead kerosene lamp.

4.Thou shalt dig or pick only six days for on the seventh thou shalt washeth thy dirty clothes and darneth thy socks and choppeth the whole week's wood.
5.Thou shalt not think more of thy gold than thy father's blessings or thy mother's love.
6.Thou shalt not kill thy body by working in the rain nor by getting stewed or three sheets to the wind from drinking down whiskey punches, rum toddies, or brandy slings.
7.Thou shalt not grow discouraged nor go home before thou strikes it rich lest in going home thou will work for fifty cents a day while thou might strike a lead and make fifty dollars a day by staying.
8.Thou shalt not steal a pick or shovel nor take thy neighbor's tools nor borrow those he cannot spare and return them broken nor remove his stakes to enlarge thy own claim.
9.Thou shalt not tell false tales about thy diggings in the hills nor salt thy claim to deceive thy neighbor.
10.Thou shalt not covet thy neighbor's wife nor trifle with the affections of his daughter but if thou truly love and covet each other thou shalt pop the question like a man.

On the eastern slope, Col. Shaughnessy, who had beaten R.C. Chambers at his own game during the Ontario and Union claim feud, was working the pioneer Glen Allen property. Ore values weren't spectacular at the mine, now renamed the Glencoe, but they were encouraging enough that a concentrator was being planned. The Valeo, located in a gulch about a mile from the Glencoe, was organized in 1896 and within a year was shipping $200 a ton ore. It was incorporated in 1898 with Thomas Kearns as president and Mrs. Emery-Holmes, the Silver Queen, as vice president. A smelter was built and the Valeo was added to Park City's growing list of producers.

In 1901 the pioneer McHenry and Hawkeye mines in McHenry Canyon were combined as the Hawkeye-McHenry Company. They had been idle for 17 years while under control of a German company which made no effort to work them. The first miner lowered down the old McHenry shaft found the water level was just 323 feet below the surface, not far from where it had been 30 years earlier When George Hearst passed it up to buy an unknown claim named the Ontario.

Although the Ontario hadn't been making as much noise as new competitors work there was still going right along. The drain tunnel had been extended from the No. 2 shaft to the No. 3, allowing still newer ore bodies to be developed. The Ontario's workings were now over 1,500 feet deep and totally dependent upon the long 3 1/2 mile drain tunnel. On Feb. 29, 1896, a flow of water so great that the men had to abandon their tools and flee before its force was struck in a 1,500 foot level working but the drain tunnel easily handled the added water in addition to the 10,000 gallons per minute it was already carrying. As soon as the water subsided, the men went back to work for the vein was 20 feet wide and assayed 150 ounces in silver as well as being 25 per cent lead.

The following year such a tremendous flow of water was struck in an extension of the drain tunnel being driven into the Daly that the water filled the flume and rose a foot above the ore car tracks.

Apparently the Ontario Company was beginning to become more involved in the life of the community than it had in the past for in 1898 the company obtained a franchise to operate a power company competing with the city's power plant and also to build two wash houses in Chinatown. In 1899 the new Aschiem store was started with R.C. Chambers as principal stockholder. Only a year later the new Ontario Power Company absorbed the Park City Heat, Light, and Power Company.

In July, 1899, R.C. Chambers and J.J. Daly joined with officials of the Union Pacific Railroad to survey a spur track known as the "high line" to the Ontario Mill and Loading Station in Ontario Canyon. It was completed in 1900 and soon Union Pacific engines were moving 16 cars of ore a day over the new track. That same year the Ontario's dividends passed the $14,000,000 mark, the company having shipped some 36,136 bars of silver bullion.

During 1902 the Ontario shaft was sunk to the 2,000 foot level, a depth not thought possible only a few years earlier. In October, 1903, while leveling ground under the mill to put in some needed supports it was discovered that quicksilver which was used in the mill's amalgamation process had been seeping from the storage vats on the floor above. A flume was set up and from the topsoil that was washed through it 575 flasks of the silvery metal was recovered.

The following August a small fortune in silver was recovered from the retort room at the mill. The recovery of the silver and the quicksilver represented the last income the Ontario would have for a while for on June 25, 1904, the fine hoisting works and the engine house erected in 1881 were destroyed by fire. The financial loss was placed at $500,000 in addition to the loss represented by the men who were put out of a job. The hoist and gallows frame from the Daly Companies No. 2 shaft were moved to the Ontario but their use was destined to be a short one.

Early in 1905 the heavy ground in the drain tunnel began crowding in ever harder, resulting in a number of small cave-ins and on June 10 a serious cave-in blocked the tunnel. Water rapidly backed up behind the caved ground and by July 1 the tunnel was completely flooded and water had raisen to the shaft's 1,200-foot level, 300 feet above the drain tunnel. With its miners laid off and the mine flooded what seemed like a final indignity was imposed.

On Sept. 16, 1905, an assessment was levied against Ontario stock! Unthinkable! The mighty multi-million dollar Ontario calling for an "Irish Dividend"! The fire which had destroyed the hoisting works followed by the caved drain tunnel and the huge cost of trying to reopen it were given as the reason for the assessment.

On Nov. 11, 1905, the final cave-in between Camp Florence and the Ontario shaft was removed and the great underground ocean of water released. Water in the shaft fell 300 feet in only a few hours, its force literally making a shambles of the tunnel. Andrew Nystrom, one of the miners in the tunnel, was washed into the flume and drowned by the great flood of icy water. It was a wonder he was the only casualty. Work was started immediately to re-timber the weakened tunnel as far as the No. 2 shaft. The tunnel was still closed tight between the No. 2 and No. 3 shafts by another cave-in and also between the Ontario and the Daly and American Flag properties to the west.

During 1906 water slowly lowered in the Ontario's workings and some of the miners were rehired.

In June, C.L. Rood, who had taken Chamber's place upon his death, resigned and the Bamberger interests which were running the Daly properties gained control of the company. Matt Connelly, long time foreman at the Ontario, didn't like the new management and resigned, moving to Oregon where he purchased a ranch. Matt Connelly had always been a favorite with the miners and although most of them were near "broke" because of the long shutdown they all chipped in and bought a fine new carriage which they had delivered to his ranch as a token of the esteem they felt for him.

Finally, on May 22, 1908, three years after the tunnel had caved in, it was reopened all the way to the Daly and Daly-West mines. Those properties as well as the flooded sections of the Ontario No. 3 and several smaller interconnected mines all began draining in fine shape. When the final cave-in was dug through an awful flood of icy water swept through the tunnel. The swirling waters quickly rose waist high on the miners and in the next five minutes raised yet another foot to chest height and many of the shorter men must have thought their time had come. But then, just when it appeared that many would be drowned, the angry waters slowly receded, allowing the difficult job to be completed without loss of life.

A great celebration was held at Park City and attended by all for the reopened mines meant much to everyone. The miners would have jobs again and the stores would have customers. A grand parade was held and there were sports and contests with free shows at the theatres and a barbecue for all. A dance was held that didn't break break up until morning. Park City had only been down, not out. With its mines being drained and men being hired the camp was to remain the great mining camp it had been.

CHAPTER 14

THE GAY 90s

The coming of the "gay 90s"found Park City no longer a rough camp of clapboard shacks and tents but a regular town. It had outlived most of its wild days and had survived a dozen or more bad fires, all of which luckily had been contained by the 'fire laddies'. Some of the pioneers from its turbulent days were no longer on the scene, John Judge and John Hughes notable among them. Fine schools had been built, there were electric lights and telephones, and brick and stone buildings were replacing the false front business houses along Main Street. The mining camp had become a city. True, there were still a few rough edges and a few rough characters; but it was a city.

In July, 1892, Thomas Kearns paid $9,000 to have a fine new two-story brick and stone building built on Main Street's upper west side. It housed several new firms on its ground floor. Foremost among them was Conlon, Welsh and Company, later to become Driscoll, Welsh, and Company and finally Welsh, Driscoll, and Buck but known to Park City for over 60 years as "Welsh's"

J.C. Weeters lumber yard advertised all kinds of building lumber and their huge stock attested to the prosperity of the town. The New York Theatre Company presented "A Celebrated Case" at the Opera House and on April 19, 1893, "Gentleman Jim" Corbett, champion prize fighter, appeared on its stage.

The Record of May 27 notified all 'celestials' that they must register or face deportation. R.C. Chambers brought all the Chinese cooks and other 'celestials' who worked at the Ontario into town to comply with the new law. The Record also reported that Marshal Bennett broke his right arm but there was no problem since all he had to do was take it off and send it into Salt Lake City for repair!

Apparently early Park City had no truant officers for the Record gave the following breakdown of school-age children. With a total number of 791 there were 508 in the public schools and 181 in private schools. The remaining 102 were probably hiding in the hills. There were 422 boys and 369 girls and their numbers were further broken down as being 64 Mormons and 727 non-Mormons. But even with that many school children in town Park City hadn't claimed all of the population from the surrounding canyons, for in the mid-90s the Record reported that the residents of Lake Flat had held a surprise party for John Dunsmore and his family.

Among his neighbors who attended the party at Lake Flat were James Dagliesh, George Haylot, William, Thomas, and John Taylor, Sam Mitchell, Peter Martin, and Patsy McCarty. Although the Record didn't say so their families probably attended the party also. And that same year the Record was still trying to get the county seat moved from Coalville. The people must have been pretty sure Park City would get the prize for a site was chosen for the new courthouse and $5,000 was raised to help build it. Finally a petition was started and when everyone had signed it, it was presented to the county commissioners. The Petition claimed that Park City had half of the county's population, seven-tenths of its business, and almost all of its money! All of which was no doubt true but in the November election that year Coalville aided by Kamas, Henefer, Echo, and the other small farm towns in the lower valleys, carried the vote by a narrow margin and retained the county seat. And that was that.

As strange a tale as was ever reported in the Record appeared in 1893. It had been known for years that gold ore of great richness had been found at several widely separated spots in the Park City district, particularly in the workings of some of the smaller mines like the Constellation and the American Flag. On a property about a mile from the head of Snake Creek that was owned by Col. Trewick, wire gold, that assayed $23,000 per ton, was found in float galena but its source could never be found. The Record's strange story was about just such a discovery.

It seems that while two old-timers were exploring a side drift in an abandoned shaft they came upon the skeleton of a man. His clothing had long since rotted away and his bones had been picked clean by rats. His heavy shoes were still in fair condition and nearby lay a rusty lunchpail with the initials R. S. punched in the lid. In that rusty lunchpail the two old miners found samples of fabulouslly rich gold ore, the like of which had never been seen in Park City.

Also found near the skeleton was a scrap of yellowed paper, so fragile it crumbled at a touch. Writing on the paper could be made out as follows: "Good God, I am dying! I have found wealth at the cost of my life. The samples in my bucket are from a ledge one . . . my hand trembles, my eyes are dim, I am . . ." It was supposed that the man had been returning to his camp at night and fell into the open mine shaft. He was unable to get out and crawled into the side drift, fatally injured, but managed to write out his last message before he died. The Record editor claimed to have seen the ore samples and the pieces of rotted paper. Many old-timers still talk about a lost gold ledge hidden somewhere in the deep rocky canyons above Park City. Who knows?

Three quarters of a century after the Record reported the story of the lost gold ledge an easterner arrived at Park City and began making inquiries about a long-lost relative who had been a prospector during the camp's boom days. According to the story the easterner told, his relative was a footloose prospector who roamed the west for years. Finally, after a lapse of some years, he wrote to his brothers in the east that he had made a rich strike, a fabulously rich gold strike in Henry's Fork, just out of Park City, Utah. For some unknown reason the old prospector had been unable to return to his find until the following year but by then a forest fire had burned through Henry's Fork, changing the country-side so that landmarks once known to him were unrecognizable. Though he searched in vain for years he could never relocate his golden prize and in time his brothers lost all trace of him again, their letters coming back unanswered.

The easterner's story was received with skepticism in Park City for the district had no Henry's Fork, although the prospector may have meant McHenry Canyon, nor could anyone remember a major forest fire in the area. But it was probably the prospector's name that made Park City people most skeptical for the easterner said his relative's name was Truelove Manhart! Park City had its "Hard Water" Bill, and "High Grade" Bob, even "Black Jack" Murphy, and "Hardrock" Harry, but never a Truelove Manhart! With its usual dry humor the Record stated it was little wonder his relatives lost touch with him for with a name like Truelove Manhart somebody probably shot him.

Ruins of Lake Flat ghost town, site of the first settlement of Park City.

Over the years new evidence has come to light which indicates there may be more to Manhart's Lost Ledge than was once thought. There really was a Truelove Manhart, and he did prospect in the Park City area. He came from the Arizona country in the 1880s, leading a burro, something people noticed and remembered for burros were seldom seen around Park City. He found rich ore somewhere near town, not up near the Wyoming border, which assayed a reported $50,000 to the ton. Park City was a silver camp not noted for gold discoveries, but rich gold ore was found in many early day claims, like that found near the

American Flag property, at Snake Creek, and later at the New Park Mine. Manhart loaded his burro with supplies and left to return to his prospect somewhere in the mountains south of town. He was never seen or heard from again.

Was the body found in the shaft Manhart's? There was such a person, for court records at Salt Lake City reveal that a Charles Manhart and two sons, Truelove and Freelove, had been arrested for horse stealing. The records state in part that they were "reckless and theavish" and were "put in confinement to await trial, and on Wensday one ware centenced to the penetentary for one year and one ware centenced for one year and eighteen months, but one of the Manhart boys ware not convicted." They were not long in prison though, for the record adds that Judge Eckels later discharged them "without ceremony of investigation."

The Marsac Mill. Note the 1885 date on smokestack. - *United Park City Mining Co.* -

Is there a gold ledge, the Lost Manhart Lode, just waiting somewhere out there? Stranger things have happened!

Early mills and smelters were often at best only crude affairs, not far removed from the ancient Spanish arrastra. Great clouds of noxious yellow smoke drifted over the town and their tailings poisoned the streams. In January, 1894, the Record editor asked that something be done about the terrible fumes coming from the Marsac mill. The Marsac was located only a stone's throw from Main Street and was therefore the one easiest to condemn although others were equally as offensive. When canyon winds laid the smoke low over the hills a heavy pall of acid-laden fumes choked both man and beast. Women in Ontario Canyon complained that when they hung their washing out the smoke would eat holes in the cloth! Even the glass windows in many homes were etched by the corrosive fumes. Annie Gibson, one of the towns early settlers, used to recall when she could catch a fine mess of trout from the sparkling little stream behind Main Street called Silver Creek. After the mills were built the creek was fouled and there were no more fish. Today that little creek where Annie Gibson caught fish is called Poison Creek!

The poisoned creek waters and deadly smelter smoke were a constant annoyance to farmers living as far away as Snyderville, Coalville and Heber City. They claimed the fouled water affected their lifestock, and lawsuits were sometimes lodged against the mining companies. Of course not all of their claims were legitimate, and as one editor suggested in the following poem, farmers would blame all of their trouble on the mines, from drought to early frosts, if they thought they could get a cash settlement.

SMELTER SMOKE

If his horses have the glanders, If his turkeys have the roup, If the deadly chicken hawk is flying Into his chicken coop.

The farmer has his innings, The matter is no joke,
For he traces up his losses Direct to smelter smoke!

The frost may blight his melons, The crows may get his corn, The pigs may have the cholera Or his cow a crumpled horn.

The farmer just grabs his pencil, He charges all to smoke,
He swiftly sends his little bill But doesn't think it's a joke.

The water in his streams dry up, The south wind blasts his field,
His daughter has the whooping cough
And his wheat it fails to yield.
But the farmer's never troubled, He banks his gold in town, And never feels the want of cash Until the smelter closes down!

Even after arrival of the railroads heavy snow storms often kept the community isolated, sometimes for weeks at a time. In March, 1894, the Record reported that the Utah Central had taken a crew of men to the summit to shovel out the pass into Parley's Canyon. The men faced the howling storm all day without heat or food and then at nightfall were told the engine that had brought them from town was helplessly stuck and they would have to get back to their homes however they could. It was a thoroughly chilled and mad crew that finally waded through to the rock quarry at Snyderville where they were fed and spent the night.

It wasn't until St. Patrick's day that the first train to reach Park City in two weeks arrived. On the 9th of December that year Tom McLean, an old-time prospector, was found frozen to death where he had fallen in exhaustion while trying to cross the divide south of the Lucky Bill Mine. It was the last divide for Old Tom.

Park City had its share of hard times so the townspeople were always quick to help whenever other camps were in trouble. In May, 1895, a terrible explosion tore through the coal mines at Alma, Wyo., killing 60 miners. Within days nearly $1,000 was raised in Park City and sent to the victim's families. A few years later when another explosion rocked the coal mines at Scofield, Utah, Park City's miners raised $2,000 to help the stricken town. When the great California earthquake ruined San Francisco Park City was one of the first to help with a check for $4,000 and a railroad car full of provisions, supplies, and clothes. People of Park City didn't know it then but their town would have its disasters in the coming years and would receive just as it had given.

The 90s saw many new business houses and fraternal lodges come to Park City. The McLaughlin Mercantile succeeded C.P. Davis and Company while the Woodruff Brothers purchased the stationary and newspaper shop owned by J.E. Smith. George Pace purchased the old Park Hotel from L. Simmons for $12,000. Welsh, Driscoll, and Buck carried a full line of dry goods and clothing, as well as many heavy mine supplies and a variety of liquors. At one time its furniture and hardware departments spilled over into a separate building across the street from the main store. Welsh's bought their goods by the railroad car load and it wasn't uncommon to see a whole car with nothing in it but potatoes, apples, nails, or dynamite. When the store didn't have display space for the car loads of furniture it received some would be stored in the basement of the Dewey Theatre and often would be used as stage props for the road show playing there.

The Park Record did have some competition, even if it was short lived. Only a year after "The Call" failed in 1889 "The Miner" made its appearance on the city streets and though it struggled valiantly it finally had to throw in the sponge in 1892 The "Utah Patriot" began publication in 1895 but, like "The Miner" lasted only two years, failing in 1897. It was more than five years before the "Park Miner", the Record's last serious competition, made its appearance in 1902. Its life was even shorter than its predecessors however for it took its final bow less than a year later. The Record's editorials were often vitriolic and its humor often dry but it reported the news faithfully and honestly and the miners liked it. And they still do.

The clothing department of Welsh, Driscoll & Buck.

Tim O'Keefe opened a cigar store in 1894 and W.A. Adams, the pioneer photographer, opened his photo shop the following year. In June, 1895, Pat and Larry McPolin were operating the Park City Bottling Works and the Kimball Brothers began stage service to Brighton. More fraternal lodges were being organized also for in May, 1894, two newcomers made their appearance. The Ancient Order of Hibernians opened their lodge in the Feeney Building on Upper Main Street and The Sons of St. George was organized by R. Tretheway and J. Nancarrow.

Not all of the Record's news in the 90s was so tame for on Dec. 15, 1894, it reported that A. B. Richardson, cashier at the Park City Bank, had "gone south" with $15,000 and in the same issue told how William Collier had been arrested for the murder of Gary Watson. A regular "wild west" shooting took place on Sept. 21, 1895, at Riley and Towey's gambling hall. Peter Clark had gambled at Henry Nugent's faro table from 11 p.m. until 7 a.m. the following morning and had lost steadily all that time. The longer Clark played the madder he became and when he finally lost all his money he left the game with a curse but came back within a few minutes, having obtained some more money somewhere. When he lost that also he got up and started towards the bar but turned about half way to it and covered Nugent with a .38 Colt revolver.

Andy Petersen's Corner Grocery.

Clark demanded $600, the amount he had lost, and Nugent quickly promised to return it to him. Without waiting Clark fired, hitting Nugent "dead center." While Nugent was still falling he drew a heavy .44 revolver from under his coat and shot Clark, hitting him in the arm. Clark ran out on the street, streaming blood, and frightening housewives who were doing their morning shopping. He ran up the street until he was stopped by John Shields, who tied a cord around his arm to stop the bleeding and probably saved his life. Dr. Wilson was called to treat Nugent, who did not think he was badly hit, and advised him his time was short for Clark's bullet had pierced both his lungs. Nugent scrawled out a last will on a scrap of paper, fell back on the floor, and died at 11:30 a.m. Which just goes to prove that gamblers didn't always make their money easily.

An especially heart-rending murder-suicide of a prominent family was reported on September 9th, 1897 in one of the few "extras" ever printed by the Record. James Quinn, well-to-do partner in the Quinn & Hyde Livery and owner of valuable Ontario and Valeo mining stock, killed his wife and then committed suicide, all in the presence of their small children. Quinn had planned the murder-suicide well, though his wife and children had no thought of what was to come. Earlier in the day, while discussing the poor state of business with several acquaintances, Quinn had said, "Well, it makes no difference, I'll finish my business for good today." The remark meant nothing to them at the time, but his friends reflected heavily on it after the foul deed was done.

On his way home at day's end, Quinn stopped at a barber shop where he was given a fresh trim and a shave, which later saved the mortician that task. On arriving home he told a daughter, age 7, to always remember to say her prayers, and then turned to ask his wife if she had any last remarks to give to her family. Mrs. Quinn, suspecting nothing wrong, asked, "Why Jim, what do you mean?" Then according to the children, Quinn pulled a pistol from his pocket and answered, "I mean this!", and shot his wife through the head. He then turned the pistol to his own brow and committed suicide.

They had a happy marriage and a respected home. The only guess ever made was that for some reason Quinn became insane, perhaps over an imagined love affair. All Parkites were saddened by the senseless tragedy.

Early Park City escaped the labor troubles and strikes that crippled many other mining camps. When the price of silver fluctuated, as it often did, a committee of miners would meet with the mine owners and together work out a settlement. The companies had always been fair in paying good wages when metal prices were high and the men were philosophical about taking wage cuts when prices were low. One old miner put it this way when a 50¢ per day wage cut was announced: "During the Cleveland, panic of '93 they took 50¢ off our wages and now the McKinley boom takes another 50¢!" Direct bargaining between the miners and management was about over though for in November, 1895, James Martin, a union organizer from Butte Mont., rented Dudler's Hall and called a mass meeting of miners. His promises of higher pay and better conditions resulted in the organization of The Western Federation Of Miners. O.E. Lawrence was chosen as union president and Dan Hurley, Louis Lundin, and Gus Lindstrom were put in other official capacities. The Western Federation's birth in Park City had been a quiet one but its growing years would be anything but quiet. The close feeling between the miners and management and the pride that a man had in working for a particular company would soon be gone forever.

Park City experienced a population explosion as well as a building boom during the 90s. When Utah attained statehood on Jan. 4, 1896, Park City was boasting a population of over 7,000. It could also boast having a representative at the constitutional convention for Thomas Kearns had been chosen as one of the delegates. Kearns was also nominated for the U.S. Senate but was defeated by Frank J. Cannon, a Salt Lake and Ogden newspaperman. Kearns was nominated again in 1900 however and was elected easily, defeating his opponent hands down. Kearns was defeated in a second term attempt and to regain the public's favor he started a third party known as the Utah Americans. The new party wasn't popular and he never gained public office again. Still, Park City had sent a senator to Washington, and that's more than most towns can boast.

Many are the tales told of Tom Kearns, some true and some colored by time. Kearns was an Irishman born in Canada, and some said he was an ignorant Irishman. If he was, he didn't stay ignorant very long, for by his own admission he walked into Park City with only ten cents in his pockets, but was a millionaire by the time he was twenty-eight years old. Still, he was controversial.

While at a local saloon one night, Kearns got in a fight with a man who, it was later learned, was a professional fighter. After punches were traded back and forth, Kearns finally knocked his opponent down, striking his head against the brass rail. The following day the professional came to the mine where Kearns was working, accompanied by four ruffians, where he challenged Kearns to another fight. Kearns jumped up and hollered. "Sure, and you bet I will, and I'll lick the whole damn bunch of you!" The ruffians backed away, the fighter had second thoughts, and Kearns went back to work.

The Paymaster, his saddlebags full of gold coin for payday. - *Utah State Historical Society* -

On another occasion Kearns and several friends were watching a boxing match at Salt Lake City, when the "Terrible Turk" offered $1,000 to anyone who would get in the ring with him. There were no takers, so Kearns pulled off his coat and tie with its diamond stickpin and jumped into the ring. In less than a minute Kearns threw the "Turk" clear out of the ring. His friends said that Kearns sent the $1,000 home to his mother, expecting a letter of thanks, but instead received an "Irish blessing" admonishing him for fighting! Kearns kept the envelope his mother's letter came in, hiding it away deep down in a trunk. Years later it was found, and on the envelope Kearns had written, "But she kept the money!"

A humorous tale has it that when Kearns built

the Alta Club for his millionaire friends and it was almost completed, the architect was showing him through the fancy rooms. When they came to the main lobby, the architect supposedly said, "What we really need in here is a beautiful chandelier." "No, by hell!" Kearns is supposed to have roared, "There will be no damn chandelier!" "But why not?" asked the astonished architect, and Kearns shot back, "Why, there's not a man in town knows how to play one of the damn things!"

Houses below Ontario School were those of the Murray's, Mulcahy's, Mitchell's & Kervan's.

Many fine shows were playing at the Opera House even while a finer and more impressive theatre was being built. Some of the last plays shown at the old opera house were 'The American Girl" and "A Yenuine Yentleman". When the new opera house opened in 1898 its first show, "The Dazzler" played to a standing-room only crowd. There was other musical entertainment in Park City also for on Christmas and other holidays all of the town's bands would parade. There was the Park City Band, the Independent Band, and the always popular Brass Band, as well as others from time to time. On New Year's the bands accompanied by members of the various lodges dressed in gay costumes would parade through the streets, and from house to house all day long. A few of the parades didn't last quite all day though, thanks to the many free drinks handed out along the way.

An interesting note regarding New Years appears in the Record of Jan. 2, 1897. It states that considerable claim-jumping had occurred at midnight on New Year's eve and that one particularly good claim near the Daly West had been jumped. At that time mining claims reverted to public land at the end of each year unless a certain amount of development or assessment work was completed. If the work wasn't done and the owners rights expired the claim belonged to anyone who relocated it. As an example of what could happen when a claim was jumped the Record printed the following poem, composed no doubt by some local wit.

"JUMPIN' CLAIMS"

Behold the prospector
who wandereth over
the face of the earth,
He traverseth the hills
and picketh the mountain
with his pick,
The pangs of hunger grip
his bowels in the morning,
And at night he lieth down with
only a blanket to cover him,
And the Greybacks come forth
and rend him.

And he lifteth up the voice of
lamentations in the wilderness.
And crieth aloud to heaven,
Why is this affliction come upon me,
And why do the terrors of Hell compass around me,
And while he sleeps the wolves devour his substance.

And he findeth the outcroppings and he diggeth in the ground,
And sticketh up a location notice on a board,
He then hieth to the valley and sayeth to the capitalist,
"Hearken unto me, for I have struck it big,
Here are the samples from the ground."

And behold, the gold maketh the rock lousy with its richness,
And the twain returneth to find others working the claim,
And the prospector grabbeth his gun saying,
"Get thee from here, for this is holy ground!'

And a fire cometh from out of a bush and smiteth him on the hip,
And he calleth in a loud voice, "I'm done for, taketh off my boots!"
And he giveth up the ghost and is gathered to his fathers
And behold! Others worketh the mine!

In June, 1897, the Rio Grande Western Railroad purchased the Utah Central and soon after began converting the narrow gauge line into a standard gauge. The wide track rails crossed Parley's Summit in February, 1900, and on Aug. 4, the Rio Grande's first standard gauge engine puffed into Park City. It was something of a first all the way around for at the throttle was Engineer Billie Chatterton, the engineer on the first Utah Eastern locomotive to reach Park City in 1881, and also the engineer on the first Utah Central in 1891. Park City was now served by the Union Pacific which had succeeded the Utah Eastern and by the Rio Grande Western which in later years became the Denver and Rio Grande Western.

The year 1897 also brought some bad times for in February a diphtheria epidemic struck the town. A new type anti-toxin was administered by Dr. Avid and it proved to be a lifesaver for most of the people taking the new serum survived the disease.

Also in 1897 silver prices took a sharp decline and by midsummer many of the smaller mines were being forced to close. Men at the larger mines accepted a wage cut rather than lose their jobs altogether although a few left for other camps hoping things would be better there. Many blamed the price decline on the nation's change to the gold standard, making the demand for silver almost non-existent.

Three times, in 1896,1900, and in 1908, William Jennings Bryan ran for president on the platform of "16 to 1", the ratio he advocated for the value of silver compared to gold, a ratio he claimed would keep all of the silver mines of the west operating steadily. The "Silver-Tongued Orator Of The Platte" campaigned in Park City standing on the top rung of a ladder leaned against the side of the Union Pacific depot where he pleaded "that mankind not be crucified upon a cross of gold." Although he drew the miner's cheers and support it was not enough for he lost all three campaigns.

A few of Park City's unemployed miners found an unexpected job waiting for them when the mines closed. On April 23, 1898, Congress declared war on Spain and the Spanish-American war began. The Record reported 12 Park City volunteers were inducted into the army on April 30 and five more left the following week. Park City probably furnished the army's youngest recruit for when the volunteers left for the induction camp at Salt Lake City young Bobby Donohue, age 14, was on the train. When his age was discovered he was sent home but when the troops arrived in San Francisco he was among them again. The young would-be soldier was sent home again but when the ship carrying the soldiers to Manila reached mid-Pacific a stowaway was found and it was none other than young Bobby Donohue. From that time on he stayed with the Park City volunteers as a mascot and was even furnished with a flashy uniform tailored to size.

The Record dedicated columns to "the splendid little war", especially to the hometown boys who were among the first to volunteer, and when in August, 1899, they returned, a huge parade and celebration was held, with Bobby Donohue, Park City's 14-year-old soldier, leading them all. The war had forced the price of silver upwards and the close of the 90s found things looking better. Many interesting, exciting, and strange stories had been reported by the Record during those years but the strangest and most exciting was told in 1893 about a box of strawberries.

Col. Patrick E. Connor. His California Volunteers made the ore discoveries that gave birth to Park City.
- Utah State Historical Society -

CHAPTER 15

A BOX OF BERRIES

A story far stranger than that of the lost gold ledge and more exciting than the shooting of gambler Nugent had its start in the Park City of 1893. A small two-line item in the Record of April 29 almost casually reported that Patsy Coughlin, age 21, was in the penitentiary for shooting Patsy Haddigan. "Patsy" was a popular nickname then for the name Patrick. The following September an equally small item added that Coughlin had been acquitted of the shooting charge and released, a court having decided the shooting had been in self defense. In October, 1894, still another article reported that Coughlin had been arrested on an old charge when he returned to town. No reference was made to the charge but for months past miners had been complaining that their cabins were being rifled. Dan McPolin also reported that his home had been broken into and some valuable jewelry taken. The morning after the burglary everything taken was found piled on his lawn except for a $10 gold piece and a diamond earring. Perhaps the unexplained burglaries constituted the "old charge" that Coughlin was arrested for.

Coughlin and his closest friend, Fred George, had both been known as "tough nuts" around Park City for some time. George had served a term in the reform school for past escapades and while he sometimes drove a sprinkler wagon for Kimball's stables, his friend Coughlin was seldom known to work. Coughlin and George always seemed to have plenty of money to buy ammunition with and they practiced shooting constantly, both being able to hit a bulls-eye three out of four shots at 200 yards. On the 11th of July, 1895, a petty theft they thought of as only innocent fun triggered a chain of events that started them on a run for their lives and left a trail of dead and bewildered lawmen all across northern Utah.

As usual Coughlin and George were near "broke" and idle, with time hanging heavy on their hands, so when they saw a peddler leave his produce cart unattended for a few minutes they saw their chance to have some fun and maybe make a few dollars to boot. With another part-time acquaintance, Frank Kennedy, they quickly stole six cases of strawberries from the peddler's cart. Although each of them was carrying two cases of "hot fruit" they easily outran the mad and cursing peddler.

They sold the stolen fruit to a "madam" on "the line" and then parted company. Coughlin and George making themselves scarce for they knew that Sheriff Harrington took a dim view of their antics. Kennedy returned to his home where he was met by Deputy Williams who arrested him for his part in the "fun". When Coughlin and George heard about Kennedy's misfortune at being caught and of the $20 the judge had fined him they decided to skip town for awhile. Coughlin "borrowed" a couple of horses and they "shook the dust" of town, heading for an abandoned sheep camp in Crandall's Canyon where they sometimes "holed up" while "on the dodge."

A few days later, after things had quieted down, they returned to town and visited "the line" where they met another part-time friend named Earl Williamson. Williamson told them that Sheriff Harrington was still watching for them so they left town again, riding to the top of Emigration Canyon and then back-tracking to Roach's Half-Way House in Parley's Canyon. Williamson rode as far as the divide with them and then started back to town. He hadn't gone far before he met Sheriff Harrington and and Deputy Williams. Williamson made the mistake of teasing the Sheriff about not being able to find Coughlin and George and was convinced right then and there that he should be a good citizen and help the sheriff find his friends. After Williamson was "convinced" he should help the sheriff he led them to the sheep camp in Crandall's Canyon where he believed Coughlin and George would be hiding. As the trio came upon the sheep camp in the early morning they saw the missing horses that Coughlin had taken hobbled nearby.

Knowing the shooting skill of Coughlin and George the lawmen dismounted a safe distance from the camp and called out for them to surrender. Someone, no one was later sure who, began shooting and in the next few minutes a large number of shots were exchanged. The Sheriff was standing behind his horse when a bullet glanced off the saddle horn, part of it lodging just below his left eye. Williamson was recognized by the two men in the sheep wagon and since he was considered to be a turncoat he was fired on also, one bullet knocking the grip from his revolver and another breaking a whiskey flask he was carrying under his jacket. When a cartridge jammed in Sheriff Harrington's gun, he and Deputy Williams, with the frightened Williamson, made a hasty retreat out of rifle range. As soon as they were gone Coughlin and George, both probably wishing they had never heard of strawberries, quickly mounted up and rode off in the opposite direction.

The two young outlaws, for that is what they were by then, rode down into the little town of Wanship where they stocked up on ammunition and supplies. They continued down the Weber River past Coalville to Chalk Creek which they followed to the head of the Wasatch Divide. Just at dusk they met a rancher driving a band of horses and stopped to make a horse trade with him. The rancher wouldn't trade and although they could easily have taken his horses they didn't do so. They rode until long past dark when finally they came upon an abandoned cabin near the head of Duck Creek where they wearily unsaddled their tired horses and quickly fell asleep.

Meanwhile Sheriff Harrington was tired of the whole business and had telegraphed law officers throughout the surrounding counties to watch for the two men. Near Evanston, Wyo., the rancher who had declined to make a horse trade with Coughlin and George met a four-man posse who were out searching for the young outlaws. The posse, headed by Echo City Constable Perry Stagg, quickly returned to Evanston where they loaded a wagon with supplies and ammunition and started on the trail the rancher had described to them. A couple of hours past midnight the posse spotted the outlaws' horses grazing near the abandoned shack on Duck Creek. During the remaining hours of darkness they crept close to the cabin, Constable Stagg and Deputy Sheriff N.E. Dawes taking cover only a hundred yards in front of the cabin door while Deputy Sheriff Kim Calverly and Evanston City Marshal William Taylor watched from the higher ground of a ridge nearby.

The old steam hoist at the Silver King Mine. - *United Park City Mining Company* -

Just as the eastern rim of the Wasatch grew light with the approach of morning Marshal Taylor crawled to a spring close by the cabin to quench his thirst. While Taylor was drinking from the spring Deputy Dawes was startled to see the cabin door open just a crack and panicked lest the lawman at the spring be killed unawares he fired a fast shot through the narrow opening. Immediately a barrage of shots were exchanged, with the lawmen trying to protect Taylor who was cowering behind a low mound of dirt near the spring, and Coughlin returning their fire as fast as George could re-load and hand their rifles to him. One of Coughlin's first shots hit Deputy Dawes in the left arm, making a terrible wound. A few seconds later another bullet hit Constable Stagg in the head, killing him instantly. Marshal Taylor, who had been caught with only the ammunition he had in his gun, and Deputy Calverly both jumped up and ran from Coughlin's withering fire. Neither were shot at although Coughlin could easily have hit either of them and they reached their wagon safely and escaped. The first blood had been drawn and one of Utah's biggest manhunts was under way.

Coughlin cautiously left the cabin after Taylor and Calverly were gone to take care of the dying Dawes. He tried to make the lawman comfortable and brought him a drink from the spring. To Coughlin and George it appeared that Constable Stagg had been killed by cross fire from his own men but they knew it would be useless to try to convince a jury of that. Their own losses were slight. Coughlin's rifle had been damaged when it was shot from his hands and George had received a minor flesh wound. They took Constable Stagg's rifle, leaving his watch and money untouched, and as soon as they could round up their spooked horses they bid the dying Dawes goodby, being unable to stop the flow of blood from his shattered arm and knowing an even larger posse would soon be on their trail.

Within days posses were organized in all the surrounding counties. Marshal Taylor and Deputy Calverly led a large band of angry men from Evanston and Sheriff Harvey Hardy of Salt Lake County brought a well-equipped posse from Salt Lake City on a special Union Pacific train. Still another posse formed at Morgan searched the Lost Creek area. And while all the possemen were searching the brushy foothills Coughlin and George were having a leisurely dinner with a sheepherder atop Monte Cristo Mountain above Ogden. After their dinner they rode down past Huntsville, stopped at an Ogden store where they bought some bread and cheese, and then headed south. They crossed the sandridge, now Clearfield, at the mouth of Weber Canyon and just before dark passed through Kaysville where they were seen by several people. Word of their presence was flashed ahead to Salt Lake City where Police Capt. Donovan gathered together a group of city policemen and headed north in a patrol wagon to meet them.

Nordberg electric hoist, the old Silver King hoist electrified, the flat hoist cable retained.

It was dark when Capt. Donovan and his men, all inside the horse-drawn patrol wagon, met a train of produce wagons heading for the capitol city's markets. About half way past the produce wagons the driver of the patrol wagon suddenly came face to face with two heavily armed men riding along side the wagons. With a wild yell to his fellow officers inside the patrol wagon he quickly turned his horses in a wide bouncing turn off the roadway.

The half-asleep lawmen were pitched head over heels and while they were trying to find their weapons Coughlin and George rode off laughing into the darkness. The Salt Lake policemen finally got two horses saddled and Capt. Donovan and Officer Janney followed the outlaws' trail up the mountainside. About daylight they met two other officers who had ridden north from Salt Lake City.

After the four Salt Lake City policemen exchanged notes they continued up to the mountain's crest above City Creek where at about mid-morning they spotted two riderless horses and Coughlin and George resting on the ground nearby. Officer Pratt quickly drew his rifle and taking a fast aim fired at the unsuspecting men. He missed his target widely and while the shot was still echoing Coughlin and George sprang up and started to mount their horses. The next shot struck Coughlin's horse, knocking it from under him. George abandoned his horse, which was too lame to go much farther anyway, and on foot, with bullets raining down all about them, they climbed a steep, rocky ridge and disappeared over its crest. When the police officers cautiously topped the ridge all that lay before them was a jungle of oak brush. The outlaws had escaped again!

The officers started to give pursuit into the dense underbrush but soon it became a question of who was hunting whom. Discretion being the better part of valor, they decided to retreat and wait for reinforcements. At daylight the next morning posses from Salt Lake and Park City started cautiously up City Creek Canyon to trap the young outlaws between them and the waiting lawmen on the ridge above. All day long they searched the thick brush and when nightfall came no sign of the killers had been found. Sheriffs from eight counties and two states as well as countless possemen were baffled. The newspapers were having a field day over the comic opera antics of the "Keystone Cops". While the tired possemen were riding themselves ragged in the thick oak brush Coughlin and George were soundly sleeping among the tombstones in Salt Lake City's Mt. Olivet Cemetery.

The next day Coughlin and George slowly made their way around Salt Lake City, past the mouth of Parley's Canyon, and into the foothills near Mill Creek. Rumors that they had been seen brought fresh posses into the area and soon all escape routes were sealed off, guards being posted as far south as Provo City and the Jordan River. But while the possemen were watching the foothills Coughlin and George walked into town and stole two horses from a hitch rack in front of the Union Pacific Saloon in Murray. Late that night they crossed the point of land at Black Rock Beach on the Great Salt Lake and passed into Tooele Valley. Late the afternoon of the next day the weary long-riders rode up to the bunkhouse of the Third Term Mine near Grantsville and asked miner Ruel Barres for something to eat. After eating everything the suspicious Barres set before them they thanked him and continued riding west toward the Nevada line.

Barres had become suspicious as soon as he saw the roughlooking youths, their clothes ragged and torn, and their horses loaded down with six-guns and rifles. As soon as they were out of sight he rode into Grantsville where he learned of the great chase. New posses were quickly formed at Grantsville and Tooele and the word telegraphed ahead to Nevada that the outlaws were headed that way.

Just after daylight the following morning while the Grantsville posse was making its way up Willow Creek John Rydalch and J.P. Mecham spotted the outlaws' horses staked near a large cottonwood tree. Waving the other possemen to fan out on either side Rydalch and Mecham rode quietly on and came upon Coughlin and George, both stretched out on the ground and apparently just awakening from a much-needed sleep. Rydalch called for them to throw their hands up and Coughlin quickly complied but George rolled into a thick stand of willows and disappeared. Coughlin yelled for the posse not to shoot and he was assured they wouldn't be harmed. Coughlin told Rydalch as he walked up to him, "This is the first chance I've had to surrender without being shot, up to now its been shoot or die."

While Coughlin was being tied up Sheriff McKeller and the Tooele posse arrived and all the lawmen began searching for George. Coughlin asked to be allowed to call to George and with the sheriff's permission he walked to the edge of the brush and yelled to George that this was not the Salt Lake City posse and for him to come out. A few minutes later George, white-faced and shaking, came from the brush with his hands raised. The two outlaws were returned to Grantsville and then taken to Ogden where they were charged with murder and horse stealing. A few days later their trial was moved to Randolph in Rich County where the killings of Constable Stagg and Deputy Dawes had taken place. They were both found guilty but the jury recommended mercy for George and he was sentenced to life in prison while Coughlin was sentenced to be shot, the date of the execution being set for Dec. 15, 1896.

On Dec. 14 Coughlin was visited at the Randolph jail by his mother and Father Galligan of Park City's Catholic Church. He ate a hearty meal and his last words to his mother were "As I'll never see you again you know I'm telling the truth. The first shot was fired at me by Sheriff Harrington!" Early the following morning Sheriff Dickson of Rich County took Coughlin to Sage Hollow, about a mile from Randolph, and tied him to a chair which had previously been placed. About 30 feet away was a white wall tent with five holes cut in its side and five men waiting inside. Each had a loaded rifle, however, one of the weapons contained a blank cartridge.

Sheriff Dickson asked Coughlin if he had anything to say and he requested that "They don't take my picture." Father Galligan stepped up and assured him they would not and told him to keep his courage up. "You bet I will!" Coughlin answered. A few moments later five rifles echoed as one in the near zero temperature above the icy Bear River and Patrick Coughlin died. It was a terrible price to pay for a few strawberries.

CHAPTER 16

TRIAL BY FIRE

As the 90s came to a close Coughlin and George were nearly forgotten and the Spanish-American War was making all the headlines. But soon even the war news would take a back page for in mid-June, 1898, one of the worst disasters ever to strike Utah came unexpectedly. On the 19th of June, 1898, Park City burned to the ground. At 4 a.m. a Chinese cook spotted flames shooting from Harry Freeman's American Hotel and alerted night policeman Waldon who fired the traditional three pistol shots to waken the sleeping town.

A few minutes later the Marsac Mill whistle added its shrieking voice to warn the half awake townspeople. Residents knew the warning sounds well enough for they had heard them often before, twice for other fires at the same American Hotel. But they were not prepared for the awful sight that confronted them on that warm June night. In the few minutes since the alarm had been given the tinder dry building had become a blazing torch, sending flames high into the night sky and illuminating the terrified spectators below with a ruddy glare. The strong south winds that blow every morning from the mountain canyons fanned the dancing flames to white heat, sending licking tongues of fire over the closely packed buildings.

Col. Nickolas Trewick, mining promoter.
- Utah State Historical Society -

Frightened home owners and worried merchants carried treasured goods and furniture from buildings in the fire's path and piled them in the narrow street but the goods only served as fuel to carry the hungry flames across the street to equally old and dry buildings. Soon both sides of the street were ablaze, sending an angry red glow over the entire town. With the fire jumping from building to building the helpless people knew their town of false front wooden buildings was doomed.

Although Park City had as stout-hearted and willing a volunteer fire department as could be found anywhere it was no match for such an awful conflagration. By 4:30 a.m. both sides of Main Street were engulfed in flames too hot to approach and by 5 a.m. the fire had roared through several homes to the Episcopal Church and on to Park Avenue. Fire hoses burst into flame in the terrible heat into which no fireman dared venture. As the morning winds shifted, burning firebrands were carried onto the matchbox-like shacks of Chinatown. Almost in a twinkling they exploded in a sudden angry burst of flame and carried the inferno to the foot of Rossie Hill. The fire roared from house to house up Rossie Hill like a forest fire sweeping through a thick stand of pines. Housewives carrying children escaped only moments ahead of the fiery onslaught, saving only the clothes on their backs, and often they were scorched and smoking.

As soon as it was seen that the fire was out of hand and beyond the ability of the fire department to control an appeal for help was sent out to surrounding towns. As quickly as men and equipment could be assembled special trains were dispatched from Coalville, Ogden, and Salt Lake City. The distance to come was so great however that the miners despaired of help arriving in time and took drastic action to save as much of their town as they could. They knew the tiny streams of water being thrown into the holocaust were useless and being experts in the use of dynamite they resorted to blowing up buildings in the path of the raging inferno to slow its advance.

It took strong men and brave women to watch as their homes were blown up and a lifetime of work and property destroyed in minutes but it seemed the only way to slow the flames' advance. The blasts did slow the fire's spread but by then most of the town was gone. When the train with the Coalville volunteers arrived at 8 a.m. only a blackened mass of smouldering ashes remained. The Salt Lake City and Ogden fire departments arrived by midmorning and although they were too late to fight the fire they unhesitatingly joined in the job of dowsing the last coals and starting the cleanup.

Park City as a city was gone, wiped from the face of the Wasatch as if by the wave of a magician's wand. Only the homes and buildings south of the American Hotel where the tragedy had its start and those in the side canyons and gulches remained. Nearly all of Main Street was gone, Chinatown had disappeared, nothing remained of the 75 homes on Rossie Hill, and most of the residences, churches, and schools on Park Avenue were lost. The total number of homes and businesses lost numbered in the hundreds and included 5 hotels, 2 dozen stores and markets, over 20 shops, a dozen saloons, more than 20 professional offices, half a dozen restaurants, 2 banks, 4 churches, and hundreds of cabins and homes.

Also lost in the flames was the Record Office, both Opera Houses, including the fine new one built less than a year before, and the city hall with all the legal records of the town and its residents, including deeds, mining records and birth and death certificates. More than 500 people were homeless and over $1,000,000 in property was lost, little of it covered by insurance since few insurance companies would write policies on Park City property.

Park City burns to the ground, June 19, 1898. - *Courtesy of Ken Webb* -

At first it was thought the loss was too great to replace, that Park City could never be rebuilt. Salt Lake City's Deseret News of June 30, 1898, reported that "Park City has been wiped out of existence, visited by the worst conflagration in Utah's history. It will be many years before it can be rebuilt, if recovery is at all possible." But the news writers grossly underestimated Park City's spirit for before the smouldering coals were cooled the task of rebuilding began and Park City, like the legendary Phoenix Bird, rose again from its ashes. Not a single life had been lost and although valuables were piled everywhere no looting or theft took place.

After a town meeting was held it was announced that no charity was wanted, that Park City would take care of its own. Although Park City was proud and asked no help those who had been helped so generously in the past by Park City when disaster struck their communities refused to watch idly from the sidelines. Both the Union Pacific and Rio Grande Railroads announced they would haul relief supplies and building material free of charge. Soon car loads of foodstuffs donated by valley farmers and city merchants began pouring in and clothing and other items gathered by Relief Societies all over the state were sent to the stricken people.

Welsh, Driscoll, and Buck announced their prices would be at the lowest possible rates and the Ontario Company sold lumber at cost. Cash donations were

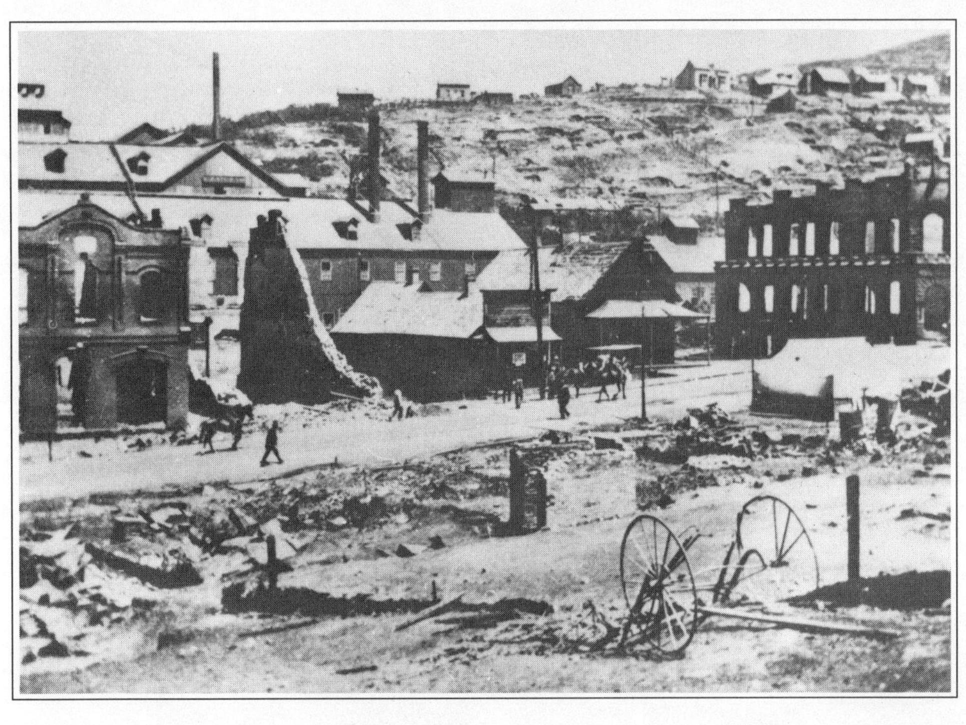

Ruins of City Hall after the fire. The building front is still in use. - *Courtesy of Ken Webb* -

received from far and wide. The Silver King Mine donated $2,000, and David Keith and Thomas Kearns gave $500 each. W.V. Rice donated $100; R.C. Chambers and D.C. McLaughlin gave $50 each, and Father Blake of St. Helena, Calif., sent $100. Many business houses contributed, including $75 from Welsh, Driscoll and Buck; $50 from the First National Bank, and $100 each from Auerbachs, Walkers Store, and the Walker Brothers Bank, all in Salt Lake City. The Salt Lake City Corp. sent $1,000; Evanston, Wyo., $220; Mount Pleasant $104; Eureka $70, and from Alma, Wyo., where Park City had sent relief only three years earlier, $175 was received. In reply to the newspapers that said Park City could never be rebuilt the Record answered. While housed in a tent pitched among the ruins the editor wrote: "This is the hand of charity the good book tells us is the greatest of Christian acts. It is the kind of thing that elevates mankind."

Though the first step on the way back had been taken the people knew there was no time to lose for winter's snows come early in the Wasatch. Buildings of rough pine boards appeared where once proud structures of brick and stone had been. Appropriately, perhaps, it was a saloon built by George Wanning that was the first new building to be built. Fire fighting and saloon building is dry work so it was fortunate that the brewery located in the basement of Joe Dudler's saloon was housed in the roughest of buildings but it was followed by other far more substantial structures. Among some of the well-built buildings that soon appeared was the Park City Hotel, Paul Bros. & Wilson's store, Adams Photo shop, Hurlbuts Drug, the First National Bank, several doctors and legal offices, and the Park Record office.

The Record had lost all of its printing presses and equipment in the great fire but still never missed an issue. It was printed by the Salt Lake Herald until July 30 when the first issue printed in Park City since the fire hit the streets. It reported that at least one new building a day was going up, including Charlie Street's new store, a temporary post office, Wiseman's Jewelry, George Smith's meat market, the Bell Telephone office, Riley & Towey's saloon and gambling hall, as well as a whole host of shops and office buildings.

A fine new building to house the First National Bank and Silver King Mine offices was built of brick and stone, all fireproof, and boasting a burglar-proof vault that weighed ten tons. Sutton's meat market, a completely modern butcher business having its own slaughter house and processing plant, opened for business. Like Henry Newell's early butcher shop the Suttons bought cattle in large number and kept them in their large pasture just north of town.

A great new opera house named the Dewey in honor of the hero of Manila Bay was started and had its opening on Christmas with a grand ball. The Dewey had a stage 25 feet deep and a tilting floor that could be raised for stage performances or lowered to level for dancing. It also had a bowling alley in the basement. At the arrival of the new year, when the new City Hall was completed, Park City could boast that it was still the west's leading silver camp and its newest as well.

On the trail old style, no fancy boots or ski fashions.

CHAPTER 17

MODERN TIMES

The turn of the century saw the building boom continuing with many fine brick and stone structures replacing the temporary wooden buildings that had been hastily erected after the great fire. In March, 1901, Julius Frankel purchased the old J.C. Weeter lot and erected a first-class clothing store. A high bell-tower was raised over city hall and a great 1,500-pound bell was hung, to be rung in the event of fire. A compressed air whistle had been used as a fire warning signal but it often froze during the winter so a more dependable signal had to be found. Finally, in 1905, an electric siren activated from the telephone company's switchboard was installed. Park City wasn't relying on three pistol shots for fire alarm anymore.

In the Fall of 1902 the new Jefferson School was completed, only a few months after the high school's first graduation was held. On the 24th of May Annie Deason, Claire Stevenson, Mae Williams, and Sam Raddon Jr. made up the entire graduating class of 1902. That same month M.S. Ascheim, the pioneer merchant, sold his store to the Blyth-Fargo Company of Evanston, Wyo. Sherman Fargo became the store's first manager. In July of that year a fine new dance and meeting hall named the Maple Hall was opened with a gala dance. C.V. Hodgson's Jewelry was located in the Maple Hall's north section. Later that year Madam Maude Davis, leading soloist for John Phillip Sousa's great band, sang at the new hall. The Dewey Theatre was featuring Bob Fitzsimmons, the world heavyweight champion, in "The Village Blacksmith", a play written especially for him.

In November, 1902, the Oak Saloon, destined to become Park City's best-liked and longest-lived tavern, was opened by Spriggs & Prior, with Henry Spriggs as manager. Later the business was owned by Spriggs and Crook and finally by Spriggs alone. Spriggs and the Oak were always among the first to contribute to the town's betterment projects. In 1903 the Oak stood the entire expense of building a bandstand next to Blyth-Fargo's "big store" where band concerts were to become a regular attraction. All of the new buildings and the return of prosperity made just about everybody happy, especially the saloon owners and gamblers.

With the mines going strong again and with plenty of miners with gold in their pockets the reforms of earlier city administrations were forgotten and the rattle of dice and whirring of roulette wheels could be heard far into the night.

The beginning of the new century also witnessed the loss of several of Park City's leading citizens. On April 13,1901, the man who had been Park City's pioneer mine developer, Robert Craig Chambers, died in a private San Francisco hospital. He often journeyed to California to report the Ontario's status to George Hearst and it was while on one of these trips that he suddenly became sick and was hospitalized.

Although he was often a figure of controversy and a mystery to many Park City residents it was he, more than anyone else, that made the Ontario Utah's greatest silver mine and blazed the trail for others to follow. Only a few months later, on June 22, 1901 David Chase McLaughlin, planner of the original Park City townsite and leader in many early day mining and civic ventures died in Salt Lake City's St. Marks Hospital. Both Chambers and McLaughlin played leading roles in the history of Park City and the mining industry of Utah. Park City and the nation was saddened again in 1901 when the crazed anarchist Leon Czalgozy shot and killed President William McKinley.

Store fronts were draped in black and memorial services were led by city and church leaders. At first many voters were distressed because "that damned cowboy" was in the White House but when in May, 1903, Theodore "Teddy" Roosevelt made a western tour 50 men rode on horseback to Salt Lake City to greet him and 500 more went by special trains to greet the new president.

The city wasn't alone in its new building spree for prosperity was also evidenced by the number of mining companies being organized and the appearance of new buildings and equipment at the older mines. New steam engines and hoisting plants were installed and a number of large new boarding houses built. The Record reported the following number of Thanksgiving turkey dinners served at the larger mines, indicating, at least in part, the number of miners still living at the mines instead of in town. At the Daly-West 205 dinners were served; at the Silver King 150; 100 each at the Ontario and Quincy; 70 at the California and Comstock properties, and 40 at the Little Bell.

The old Jefferson School. Note the bell tower that called children to class.

In addition there were many family men who lived at or near the mines as well as an unknown number of bachelors who had cabins all through the hills. It is easy to see why no exact population figure for Park City could ever be arrived at. In addition to those mines listed, two new companies were started in 1902. Jack Creen organized the Naildriver, which had been worked on and off since the early days, while Jimmie Burns headed the Star Mining Company, usually known as the 'Star Group', just south of the Naildriver.

After the disastrous explosion at the Daly-West in July, 1902, underground storage of explosives in large amounts was forbidden by a hastily passed state law. Still, blasting powder had to be taken underground, even if in smaller quantities, and some hazards still existed.

The Record of Sept. 27, 1902, reported what it termed "A Heroic Act". While working on the 900-foot level at the Silver King Mine, William Tretheway was momentarily frozen with fear when he came upon a case of burning dynamite near the station. Knowing the terrible consequences if something was not done quickly he lifted the burning explosives into a nearby mine car and pushed it onto the waiting cage. After getting into the cage with the potential bomb he quickly signaled the engineer to raise it to the surface where he breathlessly pushed the mine car away from the shaft and dumped the burning powder over the waste dump. Had the dynamite exploded inside the mine many lives would undoubtedly have been lost and it was that thought that motivated the heroic act.

In honor of Tretheway's courageous act Thomas Kearns called a special banquet at the Silver King boarding house with Tretheway as the guest of honor. He was toasted by all and paid the highest tribute by Kearns and other mine officials for his heroic act.

There were several newcomers who arrived at Park City just after the turn of the century who would be familiar to residents for the next half century. On May 23, 1903, Elija "Lije" Duke received a contract to carry the mail between Park City and Heber and for the next 50 years, from stagecoach to auto, he always brought the mail through. "Lije" could always find room for another passenger, including many through the years he knew couldn't pay a fare. Housewives would watch for his old Studebaker "white top" buggy and in later years for his Studebaker auto for whenever there was room he would always have a box of fresh eggs or some fruit or vegetables from the farms of Heber Valley.

Another figure long familiar on the Park City scene was Dr. Bardsley who started his practice in December, 1903. His shingle hung out for more than a half century. Since 1900 Dr. Monahan had maintained a small hospital for emergency cases at his home on Park Avenue but it was inadequate for the growing town. A real hospital had been needed for years but there never seemed to be enough people with money who were interested in building one. Finally in 1904 the Miners' Hospital, destined to be a landmark of long endurance, made its appearance.

The new Jefferson School. Its foundations and basement are today a modern home.

The miners banded together under the Western Federation of Miners to raise the necessary money, and Mrs. J.A. Nelson, whose husband had located the original Woodside and Tenderfoot claims, donated a building site on Nelson Hill. The miner's union sold shares in the new hospital at $25 each and just as soon as the building fund reached $5,000 work was started. Henry Spriggs donated $100 from the Oak Saloon. Not to be outdone other business houses chipped in and with funds raised at dances and other social affairs there was soon enough money on hand to finance and equip the much-needed facility. Col. & Mrs. Ferry furnished several of the rooms and the town's lodges furnished many of the others. On Oct. 1, 1904, the new hospital opened its doors for business.

Play Ball! That was the cry in 1904. The city council had purchased a lot to be used as a baseball grounds from the townsite company for $2,200. Interest in the new sport grew so fast that before long there was a team all decked out in fancy uniforms and ready to take on all comers. In June Park City beat Evanston 12 to 3 and Eureka 15 to 6. The famous Brass Band, all decked out in new green uniforms with gold trim, played at all the games. In 1905 the town's junior team won the state championship and the following year Park City and Eureka tied for the championship. Three games were to be played to decide the winner. Park City won the first game and Eureka the second. Park City had a most remarkable pitcher and everyone thought the game was in the bag for them. It didn't happen that way though, for Park City lost. To Park City fans there wasn't much doubt that the game "had been bought". There was talk for awhile of literally killing the umpire and the remarkable pitcher to boot. Apparently the pitcher thought the talk might lead to action for he pulled a hasty disappearing act that night, not even waiting to collects his bets or wages. It was later learned that he had pulled the same stunt in other towns just to get the odds up to where he could make a killing. At Park City the "killing" was nearly his.

Late in 1905 people were complaining that telephone service provided by the Bell Company was "simply terrible." A new company named the Independent Telephone Company was licensed and by the first of the new year was ready to start service. The new company had 45 customers signed up by February, 1906, with owners of businesses paying $36 per year while residential phones cost $24. A reporter for the Record claimed that talking to Salt Lake City over the new lines was just like talking to someone in the next room. A strike of telephone workers in 1907 hurt both companies with many subscribers having their telephones removed because of the poor service. The telephone companies weren't the only ones with trouble though for the Wells-Fargo Company reported their Park City agent had closed the office as usual on May 19, 1906, and "skipped town" with all the receipts.

A reward was offered and in August it was reported that he had been captured by Wells-Fargo agents in Kentucky, living high on company money. Just another proof of the warning that Wells-Fargo gave to robbers and highwaymen when they said "Wells-Fargo Never Forgets."

The Wells-Fargo office was located just south of Hodgson's Jewelry in the O'Hara Building's ground floor while the county sheriff's office was on the second floor just above it. A final proof that modern times had arrived was given in September, 1905. The Ontario Company reported that the world famous Cornish Pump was to be dismantled and sold for scrap!

After its installation in 1882 the 1,000-foot level drain tunnel had been dug, lessening its need, and later electrical pumps were installed to replace it. The great Cornish Pump, once the finest machine in the west, finally yielded to progress.

In the fall of 1905 snow started falling early and by the arrival of the new year old-timers were claiming it was the worst year in memory for storms. Numerous slides in the canyons tore out telephone lines and some resulted in the deaths of miners, especially those in unprotected cabins at isolated claims. Jerry Murphy, a Park City miner, was killed in a slide near Alta in January, 1906. The short summer of 1906 was hardly over before the blizzards began again and by January, 1907, old-timers were once more reporting the worst storms in memory. Telephone poles between Park City and Salt Lake were buried or blown down and men working at many of the mines were unable to get to work for days at a time. Perhaps the storms were an omen of things to come for 1907 turned out to be a year of panic with tight money and hard times all across the land,

The panic of 1907 sounded the death knell for many a western mining camp. Money became so scarce that company-issued script was used by some Park City mines. The use of script, which had no value other than the word of the issuer, contributed to the downfall of such prominent mining camps as Kimberly, then Utah's leading gold camp but now hardly remembered. The use of script was never very successful at Park City for most merchants refused it and before long the First National Bank announced it would deal in hard money only and was soon followed by the camp's other banks and business houses.

The "big store", Blyth Fargo, put their employees on a month on, month off, basis while the city laid off the dayshift policemen. Silver prices dropped from over $1 an ounce to 52c and it began to look like Park City might just follow the course of many other camps that were "folding up" that year.

The Miner's Hospital, built in 1904 by donations from the miners and business houses.

With money so scarce an evangelistic fervor grew, pushed by those who were appalled that the miners would spend what little money they had in saloons and gambling halls. A get-tough city administration was voted in, resulting in such old time gambling houses as Riley and Towey's going out of business and the "red light district" being confined to an edge of town location. The Record reported that respectable citizens were complaining about the "shirt-tail factory" in the residential section of town so orders were given to the "madam" to move within 30 days, "or else." A new location was found near the "green house" and the move was made. Before long a row of little "brown houses" grew up in a vacant lot near the "green house." Periodic fines of $40 for the "madam" and $20 for each "soiled dove" were levied instead of licenses being issued. The new arrangement kept the city's finances in the black and at the same time kept the "respectable citizens" happy.

Park City had many characters besides "madams" and "soiled doves". There were eccentrics like John The Baptist, a tall, skinny, wild-eyed stringbean of a man with long hair and a shrill voice. He would button-hole people along the camp's wooden sidewalks or preach to them from a corner soap box, calling down hell's-fire and brimstone on those who didn't repent. There's no record that many repented, but John The Baptist kept right on preaching.

The old 1923 Graham Brothers Dodge fire truck passing in front of the old Sutton Hotel.

And then there was Paddy The Pig, an old-country Irishman who lived at Sullivan's Boarding House. Paddy arrived at the dining room early one day, before the other miners arrived. Just as he sat down the cook placed a huge pork roast with all the trimmings in front of him. When the other miners came in, they found Paddy just finishing up the dinner which had been meant for all of them. The cook came running to see what all the commotion was about, and Paddy said, "Sure, Faith 'n be Jesus, I thought it wuz fer me!" He was Paddy The Pig ever after, but Parkites loved him just the same.

Besides inscrutable Chinamen wearing long queues and colorful silk pantaloons and "Cousin Jack" Cornishmen who called porridge "stir-about" or a pasty in their lunch pail "a letter from home", there were other characters, like Andy Gump, Slim Wheeler and Mike The Greek, who was really a Turk. And there was the poor single claim mine owner who needed help but who couldn't afford to hire more than one man. He tried all over town to hire someone, and when asked what kind of a man he wanted, would reply, "I want a man big enough to turn a winlass hoist alone, dumb enough not to mind, and so damn ugly no one will talk to him to keep him from working."

The cave-in of the Ontario drain tunnel had been responsible for much of Park City's depressed condition during the panic of 1907. Only the upper levels of the Ontario could be worked while the best ore at the Daly-West and Daly-Judge properties was under water. Smaller mines like the American Flag which depended upon the drain tunnel were also flooded and many had been forced to close. Then in May, 1908, the long tunnel was finally opened and the flooded mines began draining. About the same time silver prices began to creep up and by late summer notices stating "Miners Wanted" were being posted.

Merchants began buying new stock for their shelves and stores that had announced closing dates decided to stay open. On May 13 a gala parade was held to celebrate the reopening of the tunnel and speeches, sports, free shows, and barbeques were the order of the day. Dances were held until early morning and to a visitor it would have been hard to tell that times were bad. Such was the spirit of Park City.

The reopening of the drain tunnel seemed to be the turning point for Park City. By the end of 1908 things were looking pretty near normal again. Road shows were being booked at the theatres again and the welcome sound of machinery at the mines and mills could be heard above the tinkle of pianos along Main Street. Perhaps things weren't quite so exciting as when the Record reported "There is too much promiscuous shooting in the streets at night" but still Park City was a long way from ghost town status.

They had experienced hard times before but Parkites just weren't the kind to give up because times were a little tough. And probably they suspected that the Treasure House of the Wasatch had hardly been touched.

Robert C. Chambers, General Manager of the Ontario Mine,
confidant of millionaires, and enigma to Park City.

CHAPTER 18

LAWSUITS FOR HIGH STAKES

While new businesses were opening and times were getting better for the miners and their families, several new mining companies were getting their start also. One of these, the Uintah Treasure Hill located adjacent to the Silver King, was started in April, 1906, by the same William Perego who a few years earlier had claimed to be the original locator of the Mayflower claim which later became the Silver King. In August, 1906, "Uncle Jesse" Knight, a figure well known in Utah mining circles, came to Park City and purchased the Steamboat claim on Bonanza Flat,

"Uncle Jesse" had made his fortune in Utah's Eureka district with the Humbug Mine which he alone believed contained ore. The Humbug received its name while being located and driven into what looked like worthless country rock. "Uncle Jesse" offered a share of his prospect to a friend who is supposed to have replied that he wanted no part of such a "damned humbug" When he asked Knight what name he wanted put on the location notice Knight answered "You have named it, we'll call it the Humbug." Months later, after the tunnel had been driven deep into the mountain through worthless rock a fabulously rich body of ore was found, making Knight a wealthy man.

Late in 1906 stockholders agreed to merge the Uintah Treasure Hill Mine with the Creole Mine and in August, 1907, Knight gained control of both properties. Things went along quietly at the new Uintah Treasure Hill Mine until Nov. 13, 1909, when Knight filed a lawsuit against the Silver King Company demanding an accounting for ore mined from ground held jointly by both companies.

The suit alleged that the Silver King had mined the jointly owned ore through a lower tunnel level in the Silver King Mine and sold it as their own without the knowledge of Knight's company. The courts ordered the Silver King Company to stop mining in the disputed ground until an accounting was made. However in October 1910, miners in the Uintah Treasure Hill Mine reported they could hear the sound of Silver King drilling machines working only a few feet away. Just when it appeared that the decision would be awarded to Knight's company the Silver King Company settled out of court, paying $100,000 for all claims and property of the Uintah Treasure Hill Company. Keith and Kearns had learned that it was cheaper to buy their way out of litigation than it was to fight the costly lawsuits.

In June, 1907, another company owning ground jointly with the Silver King Company and also headed by a man famous in Utah mining got its start at Park City. The Silver King Consolidated was incorporated for $2,500,000 with Solon Spiro, formerly of the Little Bell Company, as president and Samuel Newhouse as vice president. Newhouse had made his fortune with the Cactus Mine located at Newhouse, Utah, the mining camp named for him, and later went on to build the well-known Boston and Newhouse buildings and the Newhouse Hotel in Salt Lake City. It wasn't long before the King Con, as the company was known in Park City, discovered, as had the Uintah Treasure Hill, that the Silver King had been mining ore from ground owned jointly by them without making any accounting of it. The King Con Company claimed that $250,000 worth of ore had been mined without their knowledge and sued for damages three times that amount as allowed by law. Both Keith and Kearns of the Silver King denied any knowledge of any such trespass into King Con ground,

The case was heard before the United States District Court. The Silver King claimed apex rights while the King Con charged that Keith and Kearns had ordered the Parson stope blasted to prevent a thorough investigation. In 1911 Judge Marshall announced a decision in favor of the King Con Company and awarded $750,000 damages. The Silver King Company immediately appealed to a higher court. In 1913, after five years of costly litigation, Judge Dickson concurred with the earlier decision, but increased the amount of damages to $900,000. The King Con lawsuit proved to be an expensive one for the Silver King in other ways also, for it encouraged other small companies to file suits of their own, several of which were not only very costly but also reached the United States Supreme Court where they established precedents in mining law.

The story of Solon Spiro is a saga of rags to riches and then back to rags. Sprio came to Park City from New York, a nephew of M.S. Aschiem, the pioneer merchant. He worked as a clerk in his uncle's store, saved his meager salary and bought mining stock. He made lots of money on Little Bell stock and became president of that company, and in time bought into a group of claims that he incorporated as the Silver King Consolidated. But although they bordered the famous Silver King, they produced little ore for Spiro, because the shaft and workings were flooded full of icy water. Spiro knew that the same deep ore bodies that were making fortunes for Keith & Kearns must also extend into his property, but he had no money to buy pumps to drain his shaft, and he was in a hurry, for he suspected that the Silver King owners were stealing his ore underground.

Spiro finally decided that the only hope of draining his deep water filled workings was a long drain tunnel from the base of the mountains, similar to the ones at the Ontario and the Daly-Judge. At the edge of today's golf course he started digging his tunnel. For 14,000 feet, nearly three miles, he dug it, so straight that daylight could be seen from the end.

While the tunnel was being dug, Spiro sued the Silver King Company for stealing his ore underground, and obtained a $900,000 judgment. With that small fortune, and with additional financing from Samuel Newhouse, he continued digging his tunnel nearly 25,000 feet deep, but finally, out of funds, he had to quit. He never found a pound of ore to help pay costs, and to add insult to injury, he was forced to sell to Keith & Kearns.

Then, in what has to be about the greatest indignity of all time, Keith & Kearns dug Spiro's great tunnel just 40 feet deeper and struck a huge body of silver ore Spiro had known was there all along. It was enough to make a strong man cry.

The Silver King Consolidated Mill, better known to Parkites as the King Con.

In April, 1908, Col. Nickolas Trewick, part-owner of the Conklin claim, brought suit against the Silver King for taking 10,000 tons of ore valued at $400,000 from its Elephant stope. As already explained the law of the apex allowed a claim holder to follow an ore body or vein beyond its sidelines but not past the claim's endlines. In his lawsuit Col. Trewick claimed that the Conklin claim's endlines were staked as its sidelines and therefore the Silver King could not follow their ore into the Elephant Stope to mine it. The case made its slow way through the courts until 1912 when a United States District Court dismissed it. The Conklin owners appealed the decision and the case continued with great expense to each side until 1916 when Judge Marshall reversed the lower courts' findings and ordered that a trial be held. In 1918 Judge Tillman Johnson ordered the Silver King to account for the ore taken in the amount of $540,000.

Both companies appealed the decision, the Conklin owners claiming the award was too small and the Silver King because it was so great. Both companies still claimed they could prove apex rights to the ore. The new appeal sent the case to the United States Supreme Court where arguments were heard in 1921 pending a decision which would be irrevocable. By then the original amount of damages claimed with interest added at 8 per cent totaled over $700,090. The Silver King Company was forced to suspend dividends pending the outcome of so great a settlement as well as paying the high costs of fighting the case.

Shoveling coal at one of the Ontario #3 boilers. Note date, March 14, 1901 on the boiler.

On March 1, 1921, Justice Holmes announced a decision in favor of the Silver King Company. His decision reversing that of the lower courts, was based on mining laws which required that all mining locations be distinctly marked with stakes or monuments on the ground to show without question the claims sidelines and endlines. The decision, coming after 13 years of appeals all the way to the nation's highest court, left the Silver King Company free of all litigation and undisputed Silver King of Treasure Hill.

Although the Conklin decision ended Keith's and Kearns problems over alleged trespasses and ore thefts from other properties another lawsuit not so prominent but one with equally high stakes was taking place at the same time.

Near the turn of the century a mine known as the Keystone began operating on the west slope of Pinyon Ridge not far from where the California and Comstock shafts were being sunk. Little work was done at the Keystone Mine however until 1908 when a crew of miners was hired and equipment installed. To their dismay the owners of the Keystone soon learned that the Silver King Company had already mined their property out underground. The Keystone Company owned the Red Fox, Wenner, and Bruser claims while the Silver King Company owned the adjoining Pinyon, Boss, Cumberland, and Monroe claims. The Keystone owners sued Keith and Kearns for $150,000, claiming they had knowingly allowed trespass through the Keith and Kearns Mine from 1901 to 1907 without the knowledge or approval of the Keystone Company.

Keith and Kearns countered that the apex of the ore was on their ground and also that their mine workings had always been open to inspection by the Keystone owners and that in fact the Keystone owners had made an inspection in 1906 and were aware that the Silver King Company was mining ore from their Red Fox claim. The case dragged on until 1916 when the amount of damages claimed was raised to $1,500,000 on the strength that investigation showed the value of ore taken was much greater than had at first been suspected. During the same time the Keystone lawsuit was in the courts Keith and Kearns were deeply involved in the lengthy and costly Conklin suit which had every indication of being decided against them so a settlement with the Keystone Company was agreed upon.

In January, 1920, the Silver King Company paid the Keystone owners $100,000 in cash and agreed to allow the rival company use of the Silver King's Hanauer Tunnel to haul their ore through and the use of the Keith and Kearns Mine mill to process it. Andrew J. Hurley, formerly superintendent of the Cardiff Mine at Alta and long-time and well-liked mining man of Park City, was put in charge of the Keystone Mine and within a year the mine was shipping 250 tons of high grade ore valued at $30,00 to $40,000 each month.

The settlement with the Keystone in 1920 and the decision of the Conklin case the following year ended the long series of lawsuits and almost ruinous litigation for the silver King. Its entire history from the time of its stormy birth at the old Mayflower No. 7 to the time of its reorganization as the Silver King Coalition had been a turbulent one. No doubt some of the methods Keith and Kearns used to get and mine ore bodies was to blame for their troubles but the temptation for smaller companies and claim owners to sue the "giant" for real or imagined grievances was equally responsible. Many times it was all too easy for a small claim owner to claim a trespass or theft of ore in the hope of getting a handsome settlement. At any rate, the Silver King's legal battles were mostly over and the company's resources could at last be directed to exposing to the world the vast treasure still concealed beneath the rugged face of Treasure Hill.

By 1912 the Silver King Mine equalled the world-famous Ontario with dividends paid, $14,000,000 for each. Also in 1912, Con O'Neil, a man who would one day be known throughout the west as 'Mr. Silver King', became foreman at the mine. In 1913 the Silver King began work on the world's largest underground station, to be known as Silver Hill. The huge station was located at the end of the Alliance Tunnel on the mine's 500 foot level. A shaft sunk from the underground station boasted a 38 foot high gallows frame, a double drum hoist, a motor-generator plant, air compressors, skip-pockets in the shaft, and nearly everything else that one would find at a surface plant. By 1916 the entire mine was electrified, and in 1918 Merle Heitzman was hired as lease foreman, while the following year saw the return of M.J. Dailey as general manager, and Frank Stone as master mechanic. O'Neil, Heitzman, the Daileys, Stone, and Jack Tallon, mill foreman, would all be names associated with the Silver King Mine for the better part of a half century. During these same years the price of silver doubled from 50¢ to $1 an ounce, more miners were hired, and production soared. The Silver King was on its way to earning its name.

Jesse Knight, the Mormon Wizard, mining tycoon and owner of the Creole and Uintah Treasure Hill mines. - *Utah State Historical Society* -

CHAPTER 19

THE DALY MINES UNITED

During the years while Keith and Kearns were consolidating the claims on Treasure Hill into the Silver King Coalition, John Daly's Daly-Judge Mine was making a name for itself, paying its first dividend of $112,000 in February, 1908. The Daly-West, which had been closed because of the fight over its management, was reopened and before long its once steady record of dividends was resumed. The Ontario's drain tunnel drained the Daly-West's workings in 1908 and by midsummer "a real whopper of a strike" was made on the mine's 1,200-foot level.

When the water level fell below the 1,700 foot level another large ore body was found and a second shift had to be put on at the mill to handle the increased production. In November, 1909, the Daly-West's shaft reached 1,900 feet in depth and in January; 1911, it was bottomed at the 2,100-foot level. The same great ore body that had been found on the 1,700-foot level was still being followed on the 2,100-foot level.

In 1908 mine manager George Lambourne had 95 miners digging first class carbonate ore on the Daly-Judge's 1,200-foot level and was having the entire mine electrified for faster ore haulage. The value of zinc ore being shipped to the Grassillia plant became so great that regular dividends were being paid and the company's stock jumped from $3.70 to $4.50 per share. On Oct. 30,1909, a 1,000 gallon-per-minute water flow was struck in the depths of the Daly-Judge and some of the mines best ore had to be abandoned in the face of its advance. The water problem was solved when a tunnel was hurriedly driven into the Daly-West, channeling the flow into the Ontario's drain tunnel. The Daly-Judge was beginning to encounter the same water problems that had flooded the Daly-West and which plagued the Ontario 30 years earlier.

In March, 1910, the Daly-Judge owners decided to run a long tunnel to drain its workings just as the Ontario had done years before. The Daly-Judge's tunnel, to be called the Snake Creek Tunnel, would be driven from near the head of Snake Creek west of the Heber Valley. It was planned to be three miles long and although it would not connect with the shafts of either the Daly-Judge or the Daly-West as the Ontario's had done it would be deep enough to provide a drainage course for the great underground lake of water that plagued the workings of both mines.

The Snake Creek Tunnel was started in March, 1910, and progressed rapidly at first but soon encountered the same problems of bad ground and almost unbelievable water flows that the Ontario's miners had to contend with. The driving of the Snake Creek Tunnel was awarded to lessees, the first contract going to the Taylor Free Company.

Heavy ground and the necessity of cementing the tunnel to keep it from caving soon bankrupted the Taylor Free Company. In May, 1912, J.A. Mcllwee and Company of Denver, Colo., took over the job. The McIlwee Company continued the job until May of 1913 when a water flow of 5,000 gallons per minute drove their men from the workings. The Williams Leasing Company then took over the project, driving the tunnel past the 6,000-foot point. The tunnel was 7 feet high, 9 feet 4 inches wide, and had a water flume 4 feet wide and 3 feet, 6 inches deep. The McIlwee Company succeeded the Williams Company with a bid of $500,000 to extend the tunnel an additional 1,000 feet. The tunnel progressed more than 8 feet per shift while the water flow increased by an additional 2,000 gallons per minute. The McIlwee Company obtained additional contracts, sometimes progressing as far as 14 feet per day, until October, 1915, when the tunnel reached

10,000 feet in length.

In March, 1916, the Snake Creek Tunnel reached its planned goal of 14,000 feet and was turned over to the Daly-Judge Company. Its water flow was then 8,600 gallons per minute, water that would otherwise have found its way into the mine workings. It had been hoped that the tunnel would uncover new ore bodies in addition to draining the mine workings but other than a trace of copper ore near the tunnel's 9,600 foot point no ore of value was found.

The tunnel did accomplish its objective of lowering the mine's water level and did allow new mining areas to be opened from which a great wealth of valuable ore was taken. The cost of the tunnel had been great but its return was even greater.

J.A. McIlwee, contractor of the Snake Creek Tunnel, was only one of many names appearing during the period which would long be familiar on the Park City scene. In 1906 W.S. McFarlane became master mechanic at the Ontario and would later work for the Daly-Judge Company and its successors for nearly 50 years. In 1911, O.N. Friendly was made engineer at the Daly-Judge and when he was promoted to mine superintendent in 1914 he was replaced by George Blood, another old-timer. Two other life-long residents soon became familiar figures on the streets of Park City also. In 1911 Richard 'Dick' Hales took over operation of the Daly-Judge mill and in 1913 George Kruger became mine foreman. For over 40 years thousands of men "rustling" a job waited outside the portal of the Daly-Judge tunnel for the appearance of George Kruger in hopes of getting a job. Dick Hales, driving his big, brown Packard car, was known to the townspeople for nearly as long. The author can still recall how hard he worked as a boy, washing and waxing that big old limousine, but it was worth it, for Dick always paid well, at least a nickel, and sometimes a dime!

Only three days after Christmas in 1913, when everything looked brightest for the Daly mines, the Daly-West mill and hoisting works were destroyed by fire, putting over 300 men out of work. H.F. McMillan, then president of the Daly-West Company, announced the surface would be rebuilt as soon as possible and made every effort to help the unemployed miners. Through his efforts the married men with families were hired by the town's other mines.

Cleaning up the ruined plant began immediately and by the fall of 1914 a new steel gallows frame stood guard above the silent shaft while a new mill was rapidly taking shape nearby. Within a year after the fire over 100 miners had been rehired and the new electric hoist was working to perfection. The mill was tested and began treating 100 tons of ore each day while increasing ore reserves in the mine assured continuous operation. The Daly-West was starting to boom again but unknown to the miners digging its silver ore its days as a separate company were numbered. Its neighbor to the south, the Daly-Judge Company, was starting to take a second look at its wealth of the white metal.

The Daly-West. The Morgan Shaft at top center. Burned in 1914.

As the Snake Creek tunnel was driven ever deeper the Daly-Judge was able to open larger and ever richer ore bodies. By January, 1915, the mine was shipping 500 tons of zinc per month in addition to a huge volume of lead and silver. One raise 180 feet high was driven through solid ore all the way. The rich ore at the Daly-Judge was being produced in such a large and continuous flow that in March, 1916, the company announced that it had decided to build its own smelter instead of shipping its ore to the valley smelters. The following month work was started on a $400,000 electrolytic smelter located in Deer Valley. M.H. Kurala was placed in charge while Eric Neilson was hired as head carpenter. Financing to build the new smelter was obtained by reorganizing the company. On April 14, 1916, the Daly-Judge Company became the Judge Mining and Smelting Company with its capitalization being increased from three to five million dollars. New management took over at the same time with Otto Hanke becoming president; M.C. Fox vice president, and George Lambourne as manager.

The new company was soon listed on the Salt Lake Stock Exchange with assets of 2,000 acres of mining ground, a 1,650 foot shaft with electric hoist, and 35 miles of underground workings. Manager George Lambourne reported the company would soon be shipping more ore than ever. That was an understatement for in August, 1917, embargoes were placed on Judge ore because it was being shipped in such quantity. The mine was shipping 45 per cent zinc ore faster than either its own or the valley smelters could process it. In October, 1917, company officials announced a monthly dividend of $120,000, making a total paid of nearly $2,000,000. No doubt about it, John Daly's faith in his Empire Canyon claims had been vindicated.

In February, 1918, George Lambourne with several associates gained control of the Daly-West Company and only a year later he became president of the Judge Mining and Smelting Company. In 1920 Lambourne also obtained the old Daly Mining Company, John Daly's original property, for a reported $400,000. By then the old Daly mine had produced more than 20 million dollars worth of ore. Finally, in February, 1922, all of John Daly's mines were brought together under one company. The Park City Mining and Smelting Company was formed from the Daly, Daly-West, and Daly-Judge mines with a total capitalization of $7,500,000 in stock. George Lambourne became the company's first president as well as being treasurer and managing director, while M.C. Fox was made vice president, O.N Friendly was mine manager, and George Kruger became superintendent. Lambourne had obtained financial backing from a group of Cincinnati, Ohio, financiers on the strength that he could find the ore that the pioneer McHenry Mine had lost in the camp's early days. It didn't take him long to back up his claim. At the end of a crosscut tunnel, driven from the Ontario's drain tunnel a few years later, Lambourne discovered an ore body under the old McHenry that would add millions to the company's treasury, and in a few more years gave birth to a new mining company which would rival even the Ontario and the Silver King.

The Daly-West Mill. John Daly was told he would never find ore, but that was $30 million ago!

There were others besides the large mining companies who searched for and found the Leprechaun's treasure. The Three Kings Company located on Treasure Hill reported in February, 1917, that its miners had thrown a large amount of worthless looking brown colored limestone rock over the waste dump only to find that it assayed 3 ounces in gold, 12 ounces in silver and 25 percent lead. When that report hit the streets Three Kings stock skyrocketed. Another new company appearing on the shipping list in 1917 was the Park Utah mine, located at the lower end of McHenry Canyon, not far from old Glen Allen property.

The Glen Allen, then known as the Glencoe, was still being promoted as the coming mine but there were few people with enough faith in it to buy its stock. After the company had been unable to meet its payroll in 1909 its stock had plummeted and there were many who called it a 'white elephant'. During the following years the Glencoe owners obtained more ground, finally owning some 30 claims by 1920. But even the announcement that the company was planning a new mill failed to shake loose its reputation as a hard luck mine or to arouse much interest. One new mine that started in 1917 did arouse some interest though. Maybe it was because of its name, the Revelator, known to most Parkites as the John The Revelator.

By 1917 the Revelator, located high on a windy ridge above Brigham Hamilton's Bluebird Mine and just beyond the Bonanza Flats and Boulder Basin on the Snake Creek drainage, was shipping ten tons of high-grade silver-lead ore every month. Not much perhaps when compared to the great Silver King or the Ontario but still pretty good considering it was a "poor man's mine."

Sam Hair, a farmer from nearby Heber Valley discovered the outcrop of rich silver-lead ore that became the Revelator Mine high atop a rocky ridge that tumbled down from Mt. Majestic, one of the towering peaks which stand guard over the upper reaches of Snake Creek. Although the Revelator Mine never broke any production records it boasted steady, if small, shipments of high-grade ore for several years and proved that not all mines are found by prospectors or high-paid geologists.

The story of why Sam Hair called his claim the Revelator is of interest. Old Sam claimed that he was visited in a dream by John The Revelator, who showed him where a rich vein was located high in the mountains above, beyond Boulder Basin on the slopes of Mt. Majestic, exactly where he found it a few weeks later. Some may scoff, but those who have studied mining histories know that Sam Hair's dream was not unique. Jesse Knight, the Mormon Wizard, located his famous Humbug Mine through a "dream", John Bradshaw discovered his Cave Mine at Minersville by revelation, and nearly everyone has heard of Bishop Koyle's Dream Mine near Salem, Utah.

For several years the price of silver had been slipping and many small mines were on the verge of closing so it was with great satisfaction to the people of Park City and other western mining camps when the Walsh-Pittman Act was passed by Congress in March, 1919.

Under provisions of the bill the price of silver, which had dropped to an all-time low after the nation went on the gold standard, would be raised to $1 an ounce. Before the bill was passed there were many small mines and prospects at Park City which had closed and many of the larger mines had been forced to cut production. The effect the bill had on mining was probably best described in a Park Record editorial in April 1919, which reported a scarcity of miners, a far cry from a few months earlier when unemployed miners walked the streets and signs posted at the mines stated "No miners wanted!" Idle men were put to work and mills that had known only silence, echoed their friendly roar through the canyons again. Silver hit a high of $1.25 an ounce and lead, which had been a drug on the market, went up to 7¢ a pound. Operating mines boomed, closed mines opened, and long-forgotten, low-grade waste dumps and stockpiles were shipped. It had taken only the stroke of a pen to debunk the theory that western mining was dead.

William S. McCornick, early day banker and financier of many Park City mines.

CHAPTER 20

AUTOS, FIREBUGS & OUTLAWS

The most noticeable and immediate effect the Walsh-Pittman Act had on Park City was the start of a new mining company, one which would dominate the scene for years. In June, 1917, the Park Utah Mining Company was incorporated with Otto Hanke, head of the Judge Company, as its president. George Blood became general manager, while Paul Hunt directed affairs at the mine. Arrangements were made to use the Ontario-Daly drain tunnel to drain the mine's water and to haul ore through. By 1919 with several good ore strikes to its credit and a modern surface plant built, George Lambourne became the new company's president.

By the end of 1921 its first dividend was paid with others soon to follow. The following year Park Utah stock hit $6 per share and the company had paid $250,000 in dividends. About 150 miners were producing 200 tons of ore per day with the lowest assays showing 80 ounces of silver per ton. Near the mouth of the Ontario drain tunnel a new camp named Keetley grew up where Camp Florence had been, with homes, modern offices, a recreation hall, and a spur of the Union Pacific Railroad built to it at a cost of over $400,000.

In January, 1925, George Lambourne proposed merging the new Park Utah Company with the Park City Mining and Smelting Company and the pioneer Ontario Silver Mining Company. All concerned stockholders agreed to the merger and in June, 1925, Lambourne's proposed company started business as the Park Utah Consolidated Mining Company. Lambourne was president and general manager while company directors included M.C. Fox, Charles Lange, and Adolph Hanke. Oscar Friendly, J.W. Stoner, E.A. Hewitt, and Leonard Wilson were mining engineers while Paul Hunt, H.R. Wallace, and George Kruger were superintendents and foremen. The new company started with 925 men on its payroll of $1,500,000 per year and owned much of the richest mining ground in the district.

A "monstrous" ore body that was found on the mine's 1,800 foot level sent the new company's stock to $8 a share and an extra dividend became the first order of business. In addition at Christmas the company paid each miner a $10 bonus. Each succeeding year saw the Park Utah's production soar until soon it even made the old-time mines like the Ontario and Silver King take a back seat. The finding of new ore bodies became routine as did ever increasing monthly dividends. By 1928 Park Utah stock was $14 a share with those in the know saying it would hit $20. Park Utah Consolidated became the most active issue on the New York Stock Exchange and little wonder for that year it became the largest single silver producer in the United States.

The late 1920s were prosperous years for other Park City mines also. In February, 1929, the Keystone reopened after a long shutdown. It had produced $700,000 and paid $135,000 in dividends with no work done below the 500-foot level. In 1927 the New Quincy Company began shipping ore and the next year its stock had risen from only a few cents to over $1. Also in 1927 D.K. Konold started the Konolds Mines Corporation with an issue of stock selling at 25c that by 1929 had risen to $1. The Silver King Western, incorporated with $3,500,000 in stock, was another new mine started in 1929. Such well-known mining names as Kearns, Ivers, and Dailey were listed among its officers.

For years the old Glen Allen, started back in the early 70s, had known hard times but with the mining boom of the late 20s it also began picking up steam. The Glen Allen was destined to become the leading rags to riches story the lean years ahead would tell.

Early in 1926 the Glen Allen Mine was put up for sale to satisfy unpaid debts. On ground adjoining the Glen Allen a new company named the Park Galena was started by a group of Salt Lake City and Ogden businessmen while in the canyon just above it Charles Moore and John D. Fisher located the claims known as the Star Of Utah Mining Company. Billy Gay, foreman for the Park Galena Company, reported good ore discoveries the following year and a small concentrating mill was erected on the strength of the find.

In June, 1928, Mr. Moore purchased the Park Bingham property, consisting of some 364 acres, for $125,000 from a group in Bingham, Utah, that owned it. The Park Galena, which had been in a lawsuit with the Glen Allen Company, was being operated by J.F. Featherstone and associates. Mr. Moore was president of the Star Of Utah Company, and in 1929 incorporated it with the Park Bingham properties as the Mayflower Mines Corporation. Officials included Mr. Moore, T.L. Walden, Fraser Buck, R.A. Glenny, and Allen T. Sanford.

A tunnel was started at the new Mayflower Mine. In April, 1930 manager Billy Gay reported it was 1,500 feet deep in good ground all the way and was completely electrified. While the rest of the business world went into its worst slump in 1932 the Mayflower Mines Corporation was merged with the Star Of Utah and Park Galena mining companies to form the New Park Mining Company. Charles Moore was its president while T.L. Walden, Fraser Buck, R.C. Wilson, Clark Wilson, Robert Cranmer, and W.H.H. Cranmer were among its directors. J.F. Featherstone was secretary and treasurer. Born in the depths of a depression, the New Park Company would go on to join the Park Utah Consolidated and Silver King Coalition mines as another giant of the Park City district. The New Park was one of the few mines in the Park City District that produced commercial quantities of gold ore.

While the district's mines were recovering from the panic of 1907 and entering the boom period of the 20s Park City was moving ahead also. One of the best indications in town that the panic was over was the appearance of automobiles in ever-increasing numbers on the city streets. The horse and wagon was still the backbone of transportation, but the coming of Henry Ford's "Wonderful Model T" in 1909 ended the horse's monopoly forever. W.D. Sutton obtained the Ford dealership and built the Park Garage on lower Main Street to handle the popular "Tin Lizzies".

Several of the town belles look over a shipment of new Ford tin lizzies.

The cars were shipped into town in railroad boxcars and old-timers still chuckle when they recall the time that a single car was received. It seems that in shipment the autos brakes released and all across the country it rolled back and forth in the boxcar. When it arrived at Park City both ends were badly smashed and the speedometer registered 45 miles!

There had been a few autos in town before the Model T. One of the first that old-timers can recall was W.D. Sutton's E-M-F. The E-M-F was really a model of the popular Studebaker but most drivers called them the "Every Morning Fixum" or "Every Mechanical Failure." Sherman Fargo had an early Buick, while W.S. McFarlane drove a chain drive Thomas Flyer, then considered to be the finest auto built. Melville Dingle owned another early chain drive named the Metz. The road up Parley's Canyon was so bad that Dingle had to drive the Metz to Park City on the old Utah Central Railroad grade, even crossing the high trestle at Lambs Canyon on the ties. Wintons, Pierce-Arrows, Reos, and many others, long since forgotten, were also popular. The coming of the Model T Ford priced the auto within the reach of nearly everyone and before long the streets were busy with the chugging, wheezing "Tin Lizzies".

In 1908 the Dewey Theatre and the new Electric Theatre began showing the strange new "moving pictures" although stage shows were still popular. C.W. Hodgson, the jeweler, bought out the stock of L.E. Hubbard's jewelry store and moved into the Hubbard Building. John Held's famous Saltair Orchestra gave concerts at the Maple Hall, while the Society Hall was used mostly for lodge meetings and the Golden Rule store had come to town.

Park City's reservoir in 1898. Note the rutted wagon road, Empire Canyon.

In February, 1909, Fred Hauder, who carried the mail over the high passes to Brighton, reported that storms in the high country were the worst he'd ever seen, with drifts 40 feet deep in some places. The train to Salt Lake City was buried in deep drifts for 20 hours with snow reportedly higher than the engine's smokestack. Skiing for sport was becoming popular. The editor of the Record claimed that skiers came down Treasure Hill so fast it made him gasp to watch them.

In 1909 Henry Spriggs started the Commercial Club in rooms over his Oak Saloon and for many years its members were numbered among the town's leading businessmen and its activities benefited the entire town.

A $50,000 bond was approved by the citizens for a new reservoir and water system in September, 1909, and the Silver King Company donated a site for the reservoir with right of way to it and promised a steady supply of water from the Alliance Tunnel. The water was needed sooner than planned for on the morning of Dec. 12,1909, the famous old Maple Hall burned. It was a three-story building with what was considered to be one of the finest dance halls in the west on its lower floor and a first-class rooming house upstairs. The building also contained several businesses including a jewelry store and drug store.

The fire spread from the building's basement into the Gem and the Miners and Muckers saloons and then into the nearby Center Saloon and to the J.C. Hayes rooming house above. Hayes waited too long before leaving and had to jump from an upper window, breaking his leg in the fall. Bob Hanley, Pat Sullivan, and Bill Collins also received minor injuries. E.L. Talbot, superintendent at the Daly-West Mine, called his crew from work to fight the fire lest another disaster like the great fire of '98 occur again. Luckily the flames were confined to the big building without spreading further but the Maple Hall was a complete loss including the jewelry and drug stores as well as the Center, Gem, and Miners and Muckers saloons. The north roof of the Jefford store was burned but the big Kopp and Hales stables and barn at the building's rear were saved.

In February, 1910, Jack Creen, locator of the Naildriver Mine, died at age 80. He left his entire fortune to the Salt Lake orphans' home. In March the city's new whiteway lighting system on Main Street was turned on. But the bright lights didn't send all the outlaws hurrying for dark alleys because the next month Kid Parker robbed the Oak Saloon. The Record reported that at 12:30 on Friday night a man walked into the Oak Cafe adjoining the saloon and asked for a cup of coffee, drank about half of it, then pulled a six-shooter on counterman Jack Sullivan and ordered him to get his hands up. He then marched Sullivan into the bar where upon his entry a waiting accomplice also drew a six-shooter and ordered bartender Bill Berry to get his hands up also. There were about 25 men lined up at the brass rail including Henry Spriggs, the owner.

The first outlaw then said, "I'm Kid Parker, if you want to live put up your hands and be fast about it." He then went down the line of miners taking all their valuables and then proceeded to take the gold and silver coin from the Roulette and Faro tables putting it into a sack with the other loot. "Why isn't there more gold?" he demanded, "Gold is what we want. We don't like this and we will call on you again in six months." With that they backed out the swinging doors and had disappeared by the time the angry miners rushed out onto the street after them.

The time when the holdup took place was when Butch Cassidy, whose real name was George Parker, was still an outlaw hero. Cassidy was often known as Kid Parker to his friends and many would-be toughs adopted the name in a feeling of bravado. Henry Spriggs wasn't taking a chance on Kid Parker or anyone else pulling the same stunt again though. He had a large steel 'birdcage' suspended from the saloon's ceiling where a man could crawl into it from the floor above. For a long time afterwards he kept a shotgun guard in the 'birdcage' to watch over the gambling tables below but Kid Parker must have gotten the word for he never made another visit to the Oak.

Henry Spriggs lost another $100 a month later in almost as strange a way. For some reason, perhaps because someone made an unkind comment on his 60 years, Spriggs bet $100 he could walk from the Oak to the Rio Grande depot in Salt Lake City in only seven hours. He either figured his time just a little too close or else misjudged his age for he was still a mile and a half from the depot when the time ran out.

In November, 1910, the newly elected city officials made their first act the abolishment of gambling. It wasn't a happy decision for either the saloon owners or for the miners who liked to "buck the tiger" but newly installed Sheriff J.C. Coffey vowed to keep the gambling halls closed.

Congress was petitioned for a new Post Office building in April, 1911, and the city was assured the funds would soon be made available. The building is probably a classic in the history of government red tape. At first the powers in Washington didn't like the site chosen for the new building, and the sites they did approve of cost far more than the funds appropriated.

Park City overview.

It took five long years before a site could be agreed upon and construction was just about to begin when the administration in Washington changed and another four years passed with no progress. It wasn't until 1921, ten years after Park City was told it would soon have a new Post Office, that construction actually started on the new building that some called a monument to red tape.

July, 1911, saw Park City's two telephone companies, the Bell and the Independent, merge with the Mountain States Telephone and Telegraph Company. The 4th of July celebration in 1912 was called the best ever with building fronts all decorated and floats entered by all the leading stores. Represented among the floats were stores like Paul Brothers and Wilson, Frankels, Smith and Brim, Welsh, Driscoll, and Buck, Blyth-Fargos, and dozens of others. All the lodges were represented including the Fraternal Brotherhood, the Hibernians, the Moose, Elks, Odd Fellows, Knights of Pythias, and all the rest. The Park City Military Band furnished the march music.

Only three days after the celebration another of the city's well-known landmarks was lost to fire. The old Park City Hotel burned with almost total loss. W.H. Miller owned the building while Mrs. Marie O'Keefe owned the furnishings. Only two weeks later both the Haran and Heenan Saloon and the Corner Saloon were destroyed by fires. The city's new high pressure water system was credited with preventing

Single-Jack miners working by candle-light in the old Ontario Mine.

the fires from spreading to adjacent buildings and leading to a major conflagration.

The old Park City Heat, Light, & Power Company had been only an auxiliary to the Ontario Company's more modern power plant at the mouth of the drain tunnel so when the city's power plant was damaged by fire late in 1910 it wasn't rebuilt. Instead, whenever additional power was needed it was obtained from the Telluride Company's power plant near Provo. Not long after the fire at the city's plant all of its equipment was sold to a new company which began operating as the Utah Power & Light Company with O.C. Lockhart as the manager.

Another business long familiar to Park City got its start in March, 1913. Members of Henry Sprigg's Commercial Club met and decided to try to raise $20,000 for a new hotel to replace the old Park City Hotel which had burned a year earlier. A committee began soliciting funds and were so successful that only two months later clean-up of the site of the old hotel began. The fine new brick building, paid for and built by Park City people, quickly rose under direction of J.H. Marshal, contractor. Henry Brain and his crew of plasterers put the finishing touches on the third floor and on Nov. 3, 1913, Mrs. Marie O'Keefe opened the new hotel for business. It had cost $22,455 to build and since the old hotel had been known as the old Park Hotel, what better name was there for the new one than the New Park Hotel?

In July, 1913, the Commercial Club began planning for an auto road to connect Park City with Heber Valley. The mail contract to Brighton had been lost only a few years earlier because no road to Brighton existed and the club members didn't want a Park City horse to lose out to a valley auto again. Also in July George Quinn and Frank Collins began building a new theatre then known as the Quinn but which was later called the American. The following summer Mr. and Mrs. Brand took over the Golden Rule store and A.R. Haustein started a bakery.

Not all of the news was quite so tame though. In October, 1913, J.A. McIlwee, who had contracted the Snake Creek Tunnel and later the Silver King Consolidated shaft, got into an argument with his foreman, J.D. Matheson. Matheson's father-in-law, W.C. Clark, was nearby and decided to take a part in the argument. McIlwee pulled a pistol and tried to scare Clark by firing a shot in his direction. He had intended the shot to be only a warning to stay out of the argument but the bullet hit Clark in the leg and he had to be taken to Salt Lake City for treatment. Foreman Matheson had McIlwee arrested but he was released on $500 bond pending trial. Just before the trail the matter was settled between the two men and the charges were dropped. Times were getting modern in Park City but sometimes a fast six-gun would still end an argument faster than words.

Mine cages inside the Ontario shaft house.

CHAPTER 21

WAR & THE GREAT EXPERIMENT

The year 1914 saw the price of metals, long at a low ebb, begin a slow rise. The increase was attributed to the war in far-away Europe, a war Park City residents weren't too concerned with. The price rise was welcome for it meant more jobs for miners and a boost for business. Since more men were being hired at the mines and there were ever increasing numbers of autos, improving the city's streets became a first order of business. Main Street, and its extension up Empire Canyon to the Judge Mine, became a state road and was graded for autos. The same year also saw the beginning of regular auto stage service between Park City and Salt Lake. At least it was regular in the summer time. During the winter months it was called a tri-weekly stage. It made a trip to Salt Lake if the snow wasn't too deep, and then tried to get back before the end of the week!.

By 1916 two rival auto stage lines were competing for the Park City-to-Salt Lake business. John Sweatfield and Robert Kimball owned the S&K Stage Line, while Howard Hout's high-wheeled Daisy Stages were making the trip four times each day.

A new mail route was started from Park City to Silver Lake at Brighton with six deliveries each week in the summer and one delivery per week during the winter, the winter delivery being made on skis. The mail carriers took their chances when winter came to the high country for men still were lost in snowslides that roared down from the high ridges without warning. An issue of the Record in March, 1916, reported that Alma Kimball was killed in a slide near Rocky Point. Deep snows also claimed isolated mine buildings and sometimes city businesses as well. Park City's famed Dewey Theatre was one victim of the heavy snows.

On the night the Dewey Theatre caved in from the weight of heavy snow piled high on its roof a particularly fine movie was being shown. The house was packed with over 300 people but though the show was a good one the patrons weren't happy. The film was being shown so fast that people didn't have time to read the descriptive captions flashed across the screen and the piano player couldn't keep up with the plot. Occasionally a loud snap or pop could be heard by the audience but its meaning was lost in their attempt to follow the movie's theme. Many irate customers yelled at the projectionist to slow the film but unknown to them his orders from the manager had been to show the movie so fast that people would get mad and leave. That was just what happened.

By the time the movie ended only a few customers remained and just as soon as they were out of the building the manager sighed with relief. Unknown to them while the movie played he had been high in the building's attic bracing sagging and snapping timbers. At first he had thought of sounding the alarm to evacuate the building but reconsidered when he realized that in the hurried exit someone might get trampled, or worse yet, the sudden rush might shake the already strained timbers and cause their collapse.

When everyone was finally out, a hurried inspection showed the roof and ceiling timbers were breaking under the weight of the heavy wet snow above. Since there was little that could be done before morning and since everyone had gotten out of the building safely the manager closed and locked the theatre for the night. He had hardly gotten home when a loud crash roared through the winter night. Hurrying back downtown he joined the first amazed spectators gathering in front of the great pile of ruins that had been the famed theatre only a few hours earlier. Only a cloud of dust slowly settling over the broken and twisted timber marked the building's site. It was snowing lightly and that small additional weight of snow had literally become the straw that broke the camel's back. The four walls of the building had bowed outward under the great weight from above and allowed the roof and ceiling to drop straight downward. The rows of seats which had been filled with customers only a few hours earlier had taken the force of the falling timber and were crushed flat against the floor. Probably a few of the on-lookers wondered at the smile of thankfulness on the manager's face that night.

In April, 1916, a new theatre was built on lower Main Street by Frank Knotts and W.J. Mahan. It was named the Orpheum and was welcomed by people living in the town's lower end who up to that time had had to walk all the way uptown to see a show. In December, 1916 James Ivers, director of the Silver King Company, died in Salt Lake City. He had started his career at Park City by working as a blacksmith at the old Daly Mine and had later driven an ore wagon. He obtained an interest in the Silver King Mine when it was only a hole in the ground and made his fortune from it. A few days later Barney Riley, well known partner in Riley & Towey's saloon and gambling hall, also died. In January, 1917, Dr. R.V. Barta first hung out his shingle in Park City and the same month a new bank known as the State Bank of Park City opened its doors. In February the Oak Rooming House was started above the Oak Saloon and the Adams Express Company succeeded the well-known Wells Fargo Company.

The far away war in Europe suddenly came home with a boom to Park City. On May 25, 1917, registration for the draft began. All men between the ages of 21 and 31 were required to register with no exceptions regardless of status. There were 109 eligible men registered in Park City with a total of 1,109 in Summit County. The first call of 25 men from Park City was made in September but some didn't wait that long. In July, Keith Buck, Tom Birkbeck, William Harding, and Lester Hamilton enlisted and were soon followed by others. A patriotic celebration was held on June 14 with the ramrod figure of Dr. E.P. LeCompte, the pioneer Indian fighter of Col. George Custer's command, as marshal of the day. Dr. LeCompte was a colorful figure who still owned and sometimes carried the heavy old .44 Colt single action revolver he used in the cavalry. In later years he gave that famous old pistol to City Judge George Crossman who in turn gave it to the author who now counts it among his most prized possessions.

Prohibition's over. The boys line up for a drink at Sam DeAngelo's Saloon.

An imposing electrically lighted 100-foot flagpole that weighed 2,500 pounds and had a gold ball on its top was erected and dedicated. The Red Cross asked for $5,000 in donations from Park City but by the end of June over $12,000 had been raised. The war had been far away only until Park City's own boys were called to fight and then it became Park City's war.

On Aug. 1, 1917, Park City joined with the rest of Utah in "The Great Experiment." It was prohibition. Since the first time that miners had come to the slopes of the Treasure Mountains 'booze' couldn't be bought in Park City. The law took effect at midnight, after which time possessing liquor was illegal and drunkenness was punishable by a $50 fine. As the final night of legal liquor wore on the saloons kept dropping the price of their drinks. As the deadline neared liquor that couldn't be sold in time was 'on the house'. As the midnight hour neared every saloon in town was sold out of liquor except W.J. Kappas's Gold Label where eight bartenders were kept busy serving the boistrous miners right to the last minute. Those who weren't served fast enough helped themselves and as the last minutes passed there were as many bottles stolen from the bar as were sold.

Then exactly at the stroke of midnight the "grave diggers bell", rung by City Sexton W.A. Gidley, the happy grave digger himself, echoed its mournful toll

An early photo of the Oak Saloon. - *Utah State Historical Society* -

through the hills giving Park City and Utah a two-year head start on the rest of the nation in the "Great Experiment". It had been a wild night but at midnight Park City's 20 saloons closed their doors as scheduled. It didn't take long though to discover it was easier to pass the prohibition law than it was to enforce it.

Bootleggers built stills in secret places in the hills wherever a spring could be found while peddlers carried the illegal 'moonshine' into town. Law officers were kept busy searching for the stills and hunting for caches of hidden "white lightning."

Two saloon owners, Art Murray and Dewey Porter, hired a southern moonshiner to make whiskey for them, and a still was set up by a small spring high on the north side of McHenry Canyon, in a rocky gulch across from the Wasatch Tunnel. Emmett Sproule and Bob Durismore used a horse to pack the heavy loads of "mountain dew" to town. With a little search that old "moonshine trail" can still be followed from near the Constellation Shaft and high above Lake Flat across a bare ridge and down into McHenry Canyon. It's not hard to find, for Emmett and Bob carved their initials on just about every aspen along the way.

On May 31, 1918, 227 gallons of whiskey were found in autos coming from Evanston, Wyo., and fines of $1,200 were levied against the captured bootleggers. The worst part was, according to the thirsty miners, that the confiscated whiskey was poured on the ground. Cars with secret floor wells and concealed panels were rigged to fool the lawmen and raids on homes where stills were concealed in attics, under floors, between the walls, and in hidden caves became daily affairs. The bootleggers used all sorts of ingenious ways to conceal their stills and move their moonshine.

One sheriff and his deputies were busy searching autos coming into town one day when a funeral procession was seen approaching. In respect the lawmen stood aside while the funeral coach and mourners' cars passed by. It was only later that they learned to their chagrin that the late departed inside the shiny black coffin was named John Barleycorn.

One "raid" was described in a Salt Lake City newspaper. "The Park City Purity Squad consisting of Marshal Tommy St. Jeor and deputies Bill Moulding, W.R. Jefford and Bud Johnson went gunning Friday night. When the officers entered the Vienna Pool Room, Officer Moulding made haste to get behind the bar. The bartender, Joe Solo, attempted to stop him, but the muzzle of a six-shooter against his stomach promptly quieted him. A pitcher of booze was found under the bar, and Solo was given his choice of being placed under a $300 bond or serve 4 months at "hard labor". Solo paid the fine.

The New Grand Rooming House opened for business in July, 1917, and the Orpheum Theatre was showing such popular actors as William S. Hart, Dusty Farnum, Theda Bara, and Fatty Arbuckle.

J.W. Poponoe was starting an ice cream parlor in the Hurlbut Building; J.E. Jenkins had established a photography studio, and Dr. J.A. Hatch, a chiropractor, moved to town. Fare on Howard Hout's Daisy Stages was $2 to Salt Lake or $3 round trip.

In 1918 Park City lost two of its most prominent citizens and favorite sons. On April 15 David Keith, builder of the famed Silver King Mine, died in Salt

Lake City's Hotel Utah. Keith was one of the most outstanding pioneer mining men in the west. Before coming to Park City he had sunk several shafts, including the well-known Sutro Tunnel at Nevada's Comstock Lode. He had been foreman at the Ontario, superintendent at the Anchor, and long-time president of the Silver King Company. He was succeeded by his life-long friend and associate, Thomas Kearns. Kearns' time as head of the company was destined to be short however for on October 10th, 1918 he was struck by an auto at the corner of Main and South Temple and died on October 18th.

Like Keith, Kearns had been born in Canada and had made his way to Nevada's Comstock. He worked as a miner at the Ontario and after shift prospected and studied geology. He obtained part interest in the Mayflower Lease which became the Silver King Mine. He was associated with many other mining ventures and businesses as well as being U.S. Senator from Utah. Both Keith and Kearns were giants in western mining and were missed by their friends in Park City.

The Old Park Tavern, later owned by Mike "The Greek" Sophanides.

Both Keith and Kearns had fine homes in Salt Lake City and were living there at the time of their deaths. Like many others they made their fortune at Park City and then moved away. The great mansion built by Kearns was particularly impressive and rivaled anything built on the coast or in the east. Built on South Temple Street, then known as Millionaire's Row because so many wealthy Park City people built fine homes there, it was the city's finest residence. It cost three quarters of a million dollars to build and that was when prices were low. It boasted 32 rooms with 10 fireplaces, all furnished in the most ornate and elaborate style, of Flemish oak and Russian mahogany paneling. There were 6 marble bathrooms with silver plated fixtures, a marble kitchen, a billiard room and three vaults for storing silverware and gold plated dishes, a grand ballroom on the upper floor and even a bowling alley in the basement.

In 1939 the mansion was presented to the state by Mrs. Jennie Judge Kearns and served as the official governor's mansion until 1956 when it became the Utah State Historical Society Building. Twenty-four years later it became the Governor's Mansion once more when Governor Scott Matheson accepted it as the official residence. No governor in any state has a more splendid home.

Kearns also built two of Salt Lake City's finest office buildings, the Kearns Building and the Salt Lake Tribune Building, both well known landmarks on the city's Main Street. He also built St. Ann Orphanage and paid for the completion of the Cathedral of the Madeleine. David Keith also had a fine mansion not far from the one built by Kearns, in addition to building the Keith and Ness buildings.

Other men who made fortunes in Park City mining and then built beautiful homes in Salt Lake City included John J. Daly, Henry Newell, and Ezra Thompson. Mrs Mary Judge, widow of John Judge, built the Judge Memorial Hospital for old and sick miners who were victims of the "miners con." Later it became the Judge Memorial School. The Judge Building on Main Street was also built with the Judge fortune. A partial list of other downtown Salt Lake City buildings built with Park City money would include the Brooks-Arcade Building, Thompson Building, Murdock Building, and the Summit Building. The list of hotels built in Salt Lake City with profits from Park City mines is equally impressive and includes the New Grand, Moxum, Semloh, the Hotel Little, and the Bransford Apartments.

Col. Ferry donated 22 acres for the site of Westminster College and built Ferry Hall on the campus. During the boom days of Park City mining and before the decline of western mining a large number of the major buildings on Salt Lake City's skyline as well as many of the great mansions along its "Millionaire's Row" were built by Park City people.

Blyth-Fargo Store on a busy shopping day.

The list of Park City people who became well known throughout Utah and the nation included many in addition to those connected with mining. In addition to Thomas Kearns who became senator from Utah, both Ezra Thompson and W. Mont Ferry were mayors of Salt Lake City. Dan B. Shields, who taught at the Ontario's little one room school, became a highly successful lawyer and finally United States attorney. Roger McDonough became a Utah State Supreme Court justice and Willis Ritter a Federal District judge. David Trevithick was appointed postmaster of Salt Lake City, and Roger Traynor became chief justice of the California Supreme Court.

And of course Mrs. Emery-Holmes, Park City's seamstress and Utah's Silver Queen, owned a number of Salt Lake City businesses and her Amelia Palace was known around the world. No other mining camp produced so many outstanding citizens or contributed so much to Utah, the west, and the nation.

The year 1918 saw the coming of masked men to the streets of Park City. It wasn't an outlaw invasion, but the great influenza epidemic. The board of health required everyone appearing on the streets or highways to wear a gauze mask, at least six layers thick, and to boil it at least twice a day. Anyone seen without a mask was subject to immediate arrest. City officials warned that people leaving town could not return unless quarantined first. To enforce the law Dr. LeCompte was placed in charge of the quarantine.

In one of the first weeks of the epidemic, nine people died in Park City but because of the strict rules that were rapidly set up, the epidemic was not as severe as in many other places. Still it was a time of trial for everyone. The end of the war in November, 1918, and the return of those who had been called away helped replace the loss of those who had died in the epidemic. Not all who went to war returned however. The Record listed those who had been lost in battle. Among them were Frank E. Peterson, Henry Smith, David Ivie, Tony Polies, Ray Peterson, and Elwood Garvin.

The end of the war saw a decline in the need for metals and a resultant drop in prices. While the mining companies were making readjustments to keep the miners working in the face of steadily declining prices, the miners union called a strike to raise wages to $5.50 a day and cut the work day to six hours. By April, 1919, all the mines were closed. In October the union-managed miners' hospital closed its doors, reportedly because of poor management. An emergency four-bed hospital was opened in the New Park Hotel and on Woodside Avenue Mrs. Margaret Clark, a nurse who had been with the hospital, opened her home as a clinic to give medical care. On May 2, 1919, 35 ex-service men got together at the Elks Hall and started one the nation's first American Legion posts. It was named the Frank E. Peterson Post in honor of one of Park City's first war dead.

In the fall of 1919, the Judge Company began buying large quantities of foodstuffs which they resold to their employees at very low prices. This was a great help for many of them had little or no income due to the strike. In July 1920, the Judge Company opened its own store named the Summit County Mercantile, on lower Main Street. Groceries, work clothes, shoes and household items could be purchased on credit at low cost. August Harmes was the store's first manager but was later succeeded by John 'Scotty' Baxter.

The Judge or Park Utah Company was always more employee oriented than the camp's other mines. Over the year school boys and home owners were given tons of nails, thousands of wedges, countless blocks of firewood and no one knows how much lumber to build tree houses, cabins or secret clubhouses. Jack Beck and Eric Joffs must have sharpened every axe or saw in town at one time or another, while there was hardly a household in town that never had a snow shovel "borrowed" from the mine. Not all of the mining companies were so civic minded. A school boy would have had a hard time getting anything from the Silver King, and at one time that company even had the manufacturer print a legend on the light globes it purchased from them, "Stolen from the Silver King!" on a ten cent light globe, no less!

Burns &Carpenters Snow Park Resort in Deer Valley.

To satisfy their employees the Silver King Company was forced to open their own store also. In November, 1920, the Silver King Company purchased the old W.H. Roy grocery store building and stocked it with goods that could be purchased on credit and deducted from the miners' pay. It was located across the street from the Dewey Theatre site and was named the Woodside Store. Jack Welsh was the store's first manager, while Bill Horan was one of the last to run it. Earl and Thelma Reseigh were also long-time managers.

In January, 1920, W.D. 'Tommy' St. Jeor was named city marshal. He had the reputation of being a tough one. Bootleggers were still a major problem for the "Great Experiment" was still going on. The Record of March, 1921, reported many stills were being raided including one found at the Nelson Queen Mine that had 200 gallons of moonshine and 16 barrels of mash. Whiskey runners from the wilds of Wyoming were a main cause of the lawmen's headaches.

An occasional killing still kept the city's police busy as the Record of March 16, 1923 noted. June St. Clair, one of the "girls" in the "red light district", was found murdered and all the evidence pointed at Pedro Cano. City officers followed the bloody trail and found Cano, still covered with blood. Mob violence was threatened but Cano was hurriedly locked up and tempers cooled. At his trial he was given the death sentence but received a last minute reprieve from Gov. George H. Dern. The reprieve was temporary, however, for in May, 1925, Cano faced a firing squad at the Utah State Prison.

The 1920s must have been the heyday of the social club at Park City for there were many whose activities were reported in the Record. The ones most frequently mentioned were the Jeffersonians, Bonnes Ames Club, Silver Bridge Club, Evening Card Club, The Jolly Dozen, Octagon Club, the Long & Short Club, Athenaeum, and several other referred to only as the D.O.E.O., the O.A.C., and the F.O.P. There was one more mentioned, but apparently it wasn't a social club. The Record reported that the Ku Klux Klan burned a fiery cross near the Ontario Mill and added that where they met or how many there were no one seemed to know.

A more legitimate sport than burning crosses became more popular in the 1920s also. Skiing, which had changed from a necessity to a pastime, was fast becoming an organized sport.

In March, 1922, the Utah Ski Club met at Park City and spent a day of ski jumping on Treasure Hill where local skiers had built a jump. Alf Engen, for years the best known name in skiing, was with the group and selected a spot near the Creole Mine where the next year's meet would be held. The following January the group met again at J.J. Fitzgerald's store. Forty-two skiers attended with each bringing a lunch and a tin cup for coffee. The group jumped at the Creole Mine jump and toured King Con Ridge above. Motion pictures taken at their 1926 meet were shown on RKO Pathe news films in many theatres and attracted wide attention to Park City skiing. Probably none of the little group or any of the townspeople watching them realized the impact that skiing would have on the city's future.

Resting on the ridge, early day cross-country skiers.

In September, 1923, a new store was opened by the Skaggs chain, Dr. Bardlsey announced he would build a new two-story brick building, and John Rugar became manager of the American Theatre. It wasn't long until Rugar headed a group that raised $50,000 to build the fine new Egyptian Theatre on the site where the old Dewey Theatre had been. It was built of brick, seated 450 people, and opened on Christmas Day, 1926. The Daisy Stage was housed in a new brick building also, just across the street from the New Park Hotel.

"Old Grover," the Chinese, died in Park City in March, 1926. For over 30 years he had been a friendly and familiar figure. Few Park City residents knew his real name was Quom Nom Low or that he signed his name Quom Nom Low de Grover. He had a wife living in China, who had never been in America, and a son known as Joe Grover. For the next 30 years Joe Grover would be just as well liked, and familiar a figure as "Old Grover" had been.

Another death in March, 1926, caused considerably more excitement than that of "Old Grover."

On March 12, while waiting to start shift at the Judge Tunnel, a miner named Herbert Crouse became involved in an argument with a Mexican miner named Pantoj. A few names were called, blows were exchanged, and then to the horror of the watching miners Pantoj suddenly pulled a knife and stabbed Crouse three times in the chest. Crouse fell dead in front of his friends and only the arrival of Sheriff Clark prevented a lynching. Miners at the Judge Mine refused to enter the mine unless all the Mexicans employed there were fired immediately.

Mine superintendent George Kruger refused the miner's ultimatum and the men walked off the job and returned to town making mob action appear imminent. City officials closed all public places to prevent trouble and county officers and deputies from the American Legion patroled the streets to maintain order. The following Sunday the miner's union called for a strike against the Judge Mine with the vote being carried 190 to 2. Company officials led by manager Paul Hunt met with the miners and agreed to most of their terms, including getting rid of the trouble makers, and the men agreed to return to work. It was a near brush with mob violence for the miners and the city.

In 1925 a new high school was proposed and a bond to raise the money was approved by the citizens late that year. Construction began in 1926 and the building was completed in February, 1928, with that year's class being the first to graduate in the new school. It was quite different from the class which attended high school in the attic of the old Lincoln School in 1898 when there were only 16 boys and 16 girls attending. Metal prices were going up again and things were looking good at the mines and for the town. The Labor Day celebration in 1926 was held near the mouth of the Spiro Tunnel with the Silver King and Park Utah companies footing the bill, which included free drinks and refreshments as well as $1,600 in prizes.

In 1927 Park City lost two old time stores and gained two new ones. On March 18 the huge Blyth-Fargo store burned to the ground. The "Big Store," as it was known, might have been saved but because of the sub-zero weather many people had been letting their water faucets run to keep them from freezing and the reservoir was nearly empty. Angered firemen were forced to stand by and watch the fine store with all of its contents burn to the ground. The following month the old Montgomery store, built in 1873, and the first store in Park City, was torn down. It had been made into a blacksmith shop in later years and along with Kimball's barn was the only building on lower Main Street to escape the great fire of '98. In April, 1927, the first advertisements for the new Safeway store appeared in the Record and the same month Zack Oblad opened his popular Quality Shop.

In 1927 two of Park City's most popular doctors started their practice. Dr. H.I. Goodwyn opened his office in July, and Dr. T.E. Clark hung out his shingle in September. Both were longtime favorites in Park City. In October, 1927, one of the greatest and best-loved of Park City's pioneer mining men died. John J Daly, who did as much as anyone to make the Park City district famous, died at his home in Los Angeles, Calif. Although he had not been active in Park City mining for many years due to ill health, he was still remembered in connection with the Daly, Daly-West, and Daly-Judge mines. It was men like R.C. Chambers in the camp's early days followed by men like John J. Daly that built Park City into the west's leading mining camp. John Judge deserved a lot of credit at the same time as foreman at the Daly Mine and partner in the beginnings of the Daly-Judge Company. E.P. Ferry stands high on the list of town greats also. He purchased the pioneer Flagstaff Mine; developed the Woodside; built the Anchor into one of the camp's best producers, and consolidated the Pinyon Ridge claims into the Crescent Mining Company. Both George Lambourne, who developed the Park Utah Consolidated, and Charlie Moore with his New Park Mining Company did much for Park City as did Keith and Kearns with the Silver King Coalition. But it was John J. Daly more than anyone else who made Park City the famed mining camp it was. At the same time he had the interests of Park City people at heart and because of that he was the most respected and best-liked of all the camp's mining leaders.

In the late 1920s Park City skiing really started attracting the professionals. Ecker Hill located just north of Snyderville drew some of the country's best ski jumpers. In 1929 Axel Andrason held the jumping distance record with 86 feet but it would be a short-lived record. In November, 1929, the leading Norwegian and American jumpers looked the various sites over and chose the Creole Hill jump used earlier by Alf Engen as the area's best. A new jump was built at Ecker Hill in 1930 to compete with it and it proved its superiority that winter when Alf Engen jumped 195 feet for an unofficial record, the jump being made just after the meet officially closed. Engen's jump the next year was official though and it was the winner at 247 feet. Other professionals at the Ecker Hill meet that year included such greats as Einar Fredbo, Sverre Engen, Ted Rex, and Kalmer Andrason. Special trains carried spectators to the famous hill to see another record set by Engen in December, 1931, when he jumped 256 feet. Even that record didn't last long.

During those years the Record reported many other city notes of interest. Some, such as the death of Henry Spriggs while attending the annual Park City picnic in Salt Lake City in August, 1930, and the death of the city's pioneer photographer, W.A. Adams, who first came to town in 1884, saddened the people. Some items told of new business houses like the Silver King Garage on lower Park Avenue and the building of Kimball's fine brick garage, the city's largest and costliest, on Park Ave.

The Record also reported with nostalgia the finding of an old-time book while cleaning out the Ontario boardinghouse. It had been used by David Keith and contained the names of Ontario miners for the year 1885. Among those listed were Matt Connelly, John Nimmo, John Dunsmore, Bartley McDonough, John Ryan, and a then little-known miner named Thomas Kearns. But probably the most important article told what happened on a Friday late in October, 1929. It was Friday the 29th, but not just any old Friday, for this day would be remembered by Park City and the rest of the nation for generations to come as "Black Friday", the day the stock market crashed!

Albion Emery bought into the Silver King with borrowed money and became a millionaire.
- Utah State Historical Society -

CHAPTER 22

DEPRESSION DAYS

The year 1929 started out as a particularly good year for Park City with signs of prosperity on every hand. New homes and businesses were being built and several newly formed mining companies were listed on the Salt Lake City exchange. The population was over 4,200, metal prices were up, and "prosperity was just around the corner." But all that was before "Black Friday." Just before the stock market crash Silver King stock was selling at $12.87; Park Utah at $6.40; Park Con at $2, and New Quincy at $2.50. One year later Silver King was $6.50, Park Utah $1.50, Par Con 27¢, and New Quincy 7¢.!

Though metal prices slipped and stocks plummeted most of Park City's mines kept working. The huge American Smelting & Refining Company took over the East Utah in January, 1930, and the American Flag, by then reorganized by lessees as the Central Park, was working the mine's rich 1,100-foot level. In February, 1930, most of the mines were forced to cut miners' wages 50¢ a day due to steadily lowering metal prices. The cut was soon felt in town, for most of the movie houses advertised that they would be closed two days a week due to poor attendance. Silver had reached its highest price in 1919 when it sold for $1.12 an ounce.

In 1930 it had dropped to 38¢ an ounce and in February, 1931, it hit an all time low at only 25¢. Lead, which had been 7¢ a pound at the time of the crash, fell to 2¢ by mid-1932. In May, 1931, the mines were forced to cut wages another 25¢ per day while many of the smaller companies were beginning to close down. The Silver King Mine kept a crew of 500 men working until 1932 even though it meant a financial loss to the company. Other companies suspended dividends and cut every unnecessary expense in order to keep as many men as possible on the payroll.

Even with the larger mines operating as best they could there were still more and more unemployed men in town. The Record reflected that "even with good times just around the corner things were so bad that a soup kitchen had to be set up to feed the hungry!." A civic relief committee was organized and reported that by January, 1932, 42 families were on the relief roles while many single men were receiving two meals a day at the "Hoover Cafe." By March the number of needy families increased to 86 but over $7,000 had been raised in town to help the relief committee care for them.

New York Governor Franklin Roosevelt defeated President Hoover in 1932, and in Park City, as elsewhere, people were singing, Happy Days Are Here Again. Roosevelt made many sweeping changes, but to the miners at Park City his repeal of prohibition was without doubt the most welcome. Legal booze returned and miners with a thirst built up over more than a dozen years went on a roaring binge. Brewery beer with names like Fishers, Beckers and American Beauty took the place of "home brew", while bonded bourbon replaced "white lightning" and "bathtub gin".

Saloons like the old-time Oak, the only bar in town that never sold "moonshine", put on a night long party. They are all gone now, but old-timers will still remember Les Roach and Bill Neil at the Oak, the Black Label at the bottom of Main Street, the White Front next to the Senate Cafe, Black Sam's by the Central Hotel, Art Murray and Dell Raddon's Mint, Dunivans just above Frankles Store, the Palm owned by Art Murray and Dewey Porter, the Club across from the Post Office, run by Louie Dunn and later Heinie Hernan and a whole host of others, up and down both sides of the street.

Saloon owners whose bars had been closed for

years brushed the cobwebs off once polished oak bars, took the covers off long unused pool tables, dusted off the old Dewey machines and were ready for business. As far as Park City miners were concerned, happy days were here again.

Things began looking up by mid-1933 with both metal and stock prices starting to rise and some companies opening their closed mines again. In 1934 Charlie Moore of the New Park Mine hired a crew of men and started work on opening the old shaft at the Flagstaff, the first mine in Park ever to ship ore. Early in 1935 the price of silver jumped from less than 40¢ to 50¢ and then to 65¢. The price of gold was raised from its long time price of $20 an ounce to $35, greatly helping companies like the American Flag which had high gold content in its ore.

The rising metal prices resulted in the opening of the Park Con Mine and the old Naildriver as well as marking the start of a new project known as the Thayne's shaft. It was sunk by the Silver King Company near the head of Thayne's Canyon just below the old California-Comstock Mine.

While conditions were slowly improving in Park City mining changes were taking place in town also. Government organizations such as the WPA and the PWA were taking men off the relief roles and giving them jobs. Over 200 of Park City's unemployed miners were working on the "make work" projects by 1934. In 1934 the city's First National Bank joined the First Security Bank system with Robert Guy as manager. Almost unnoticed at first a new miners' union known as Local 99 of the Mine, Mill & Smelter Workers was organized late in 1933. It proposed that the miners must take a more militant stand on the questions of shorter hours and higher wages. During 1935 the Park Con company notified its employees they would be put on a seven-day week. Immediately the new union objected stating that the union's objectives were a shorter work week, not a longer one.

Another conflict between union and management occurred early in 1936 when the Silver King Company wouldn't agree to a "closed shop" or to "time and a half" for overtime work. Negotiations between the new union and the mining companies continued but agreement couldn't be reached and on Oct. 16, 1936, 1,000 Park City miners walked off their jobs at the Silver King, Park Utah, Park Con, New Park, and several other smaller mines. The strike spread to most of the other mining camps in Utah also, eventually

Early morning shadows on a deserted Main Street.

putting over 2,500 men out of work and idling all of the state's major underground mines.

The Deseret News of Salt Lake City reported that "Mines which produced $20,000,000 in 1935 are shut down and producing nothing. The entire payroll of Park City, the greatest silver-lead district in the nation, is shut off by the strike."

By the end of October, 1936, Park City business was off 50% and hundreds of miners were anxious to get back to work. The union still demanded a 50¢ per day wage increase and an eight-hour shift starting from the time the men entered the mine until the time they left it. The mine operators offered 25¢ an hour and neither side would compromise. Rumors were heard that the companies were hiring professional strike breakers but nothing came of it and the rumors were forgotten. Finally the miners learned that the "valley men," those miners who worked at Park City's mines but lived in the small farming towns of the Kamas and Heber valleys, were going to the mines en masse to accept the company's offer. By early morning on the day they were supposed to come into town 400 angry miners waited where the road from the lower valley comes into town and shortly after noon 124 cars traveling in close convoy could be seen approaching town. The two groups met at the bottom of Main Street where the Park City miners were so closely packed that the out-of-town autos couldn't get through. Within minutes autos were being rocked back and forth and the "valley men" were being pulled from them to meet flying rocks and smashing fists. Women threw hot water on the outsiders from upper floor windows and for 20 minutes it was a glorious free-for-all.

Finally Sheriff Adamson and his deputies gained control and the' "valley men" turned their autos around and left town, having had their fill of crossing Park City's union miners.

In mid-December the union and the mining companies agreed on a settlement and the men returned to work. As was usually the case in strikes nobody won anything but it was finally over and the city began a return to normalcy. In March, 1936, the Veterans of Foreign Wars was organized by Eric Joffs, Joe Pezeley, Bill Horan, Percy Aubrey, Harry Derry, and several other veterans. July saw the old Woodside Store, started in 1923 by the Silver King Company for its employees, close its doors.

September of that year found a crew of WPA workers from Park City excavating for a lodge to be built at Brimhall Lake on Bonanza Flat. Around $13,000 had been appropriated to build a cobble stone and polished log lodge for the Girl Scouts of America at the 9,500-foot high lake and the Park Utah Mining Company donated a 15-acre site to build it on. The scout camp was first called Camp Pine Air but was later named Camp Cloud Rim when Mrs. Herbert Hoover, national vice-president of the Girl Scouts of America, visited the camp in August, 1938, to dedicate it. Many thousands of Girl Scouts from Utah as well as many other states have spent happy and memorable vacations at the camp since its completion.

Star Hotel on upper Main Street in the winter of 1948, the worst ever.

Winter sports were becoming more popular all the time also. In December, 1936, the Denver & Rio Grande Western railroad ran a special train to carry skiers from Salt Lake City to the slopes just above the Park Con Mine in Deer Valley. The idea was so popular that it was repeated the following year with an additional train coming from Ogden. In 1939 a nine-coach train brought hundreds of skiers to the steep slopes above Deer Valley while at Ecker Hill a crowd of over 5,000 watched some of the most spectacular ski jumping ever seen.

In town a new grade school named the Marsac was opened in November, 1936, on the site where the old Marsac Mill had crushed millions of dollars worth of silver ore years earlier. In 1937 a new cooperative store owned by the miner's union was started and the Senate restaurant closed its doors, not from lack of business but because Charlie Chong, its owner, left to take an out-of-state business opportunity. The Senate had been a favorite meeting place for Parkites since 1913.

During the mid-30s plans were being made for another new building to be known as the War Veterans Memorial Building. The Memorial Building was first considered right after the World War in 1919 when the newly organized American Legion planned it as a place to hold their meetings but plans and finances couldn't seem to be brought together at that time. Finally with the help of County Commissioners Ed J. McPolin, Lysle Lemmon, and John M. Stevens, a tax assessment of one mill was levied and with the cooperation of the government's PWA the long-delayed plans became a reality. In January, 1938, the site of the old Blyth-Fargo Store on Main Street was purchased by the county and cleaning up the burned ruins began. In April, 1939, Park City Legionaires laid the building's cornerstone and in January, 1940, the new building was dedicated. Commissioners McPolin, Lemmon, and Stevens and American Legion Commander Carl Winters officiated with Gov. Henry H. Blood and two ex-Park City boys, Utah Supreme Court Justice Roger McDonough, and U.S. Attorney Dan B. Shields, as well as city officials in attendance. The new Memorial Building was built with an auditorium, lounge, dining room and kitchen, bowling alley, game and pool rooms, as well as meeting rooms for lodges and organizations; all available to people of the entire county upon request.

In July, 1938, the Park City Utah Mining Company, originally located as the Liberty Mine in lower McHenry Canyon, announced the opening of the old Wasatch Tunnel on Bald Mountain and the sinking of an incline shaft from it to connect with the Star of Utah workings. A crew was hired and work went along without incident until January, 1939, when a cave-in trapped eight miners for nine hours. They were all rescued and after getting a second wind went back to work again. Such was the life of a miner.

Ore from the Wasatch Tunnel was hauled by truck on the old wagon road up McHenry Canyon, across Lake Flat and down Ontario Canyon to the Judge Loading Station. Joe Hylton of Heber City, the driver, always had lots of company, for all of the kids in Ontario Canyon took turns riding with him. Of course that was long before OSHA was heard of.

By 1941 the Park City Utah Company was working on a two-shift basis with of crew of 75 men. At about the same time, in October, 1938, the Park Con Company began a somewhat unusual way to pump water from its lower workings. On the mine's 1,050-foot level a 24" hole was drilled 520 feet and a submersible pump lowered to its bottom. The pump raised water to the 900-foot level and drained the mine workings without interfering with work in the nearby shaft. More labor unrest and shutdowns were starting to be seen in town because of actions taken in Washington. In January, 1938, President Roosevelt ordered the price of silver cut from 77¢ to 64¢ and as a result the Silver King Mine was forced to cut its work force by 150 men with the Park Utah Company announcing a similar cut. In April the Silver King shut down its operations "indefinitely", putting 450 men out of work. Soon all the Park City mines were forced to do the same and were followed by the mines in Idaho, Montana, and other mining states.

A "mancha mule" locomotive underground at the Park Con Mine, Deer Valley.

When the mining companies shut down because of the lowered silver price set by the government the miners' union renewed its demand for a six-hour work day, claiming the change would put men to work and better conditions. In order to get the mines operating again a tentative contract between the union and the mining companies was drawn up and presented to the miners. It was rejected by a vote of 683 to 68 and in the face of steadily dropping metal prices and the union's demand for a six-hour day plus a wage raise it seemed a forlorn hope that the mines would ever be reopened.

After months of forced idleness a temporary agreement coupled with the government agreeing to return the price of silver from its arbitrary price of 64¢ back to 77¢, the mines began working again on a limited scale. In October, 1939, the union accepted a 25¢ raise with the provision that if metal prices fell again wages would be cut. Things were just returning to normal once more when in May a wage cut was announced because of rapidly declining metal prices. A strike vote was immediately taken by the union but luckily the price drop was only temporary and before the strike could take effect the wage cut was cancelled and a two-year contract was signed. At long last, after four years of almost constant strikes, shut downs, unemployment, and hard times, men were working regularly again, stores were being patronized, and Park City was beginning to look like its old self.

In November, 1939, almost as if to show their thanks for their long siege of labor troubles Park City had two Thanksgivings. It was the year President Roosevelt changed the traditional holiday date and in protest most of the people joined the rest of the nation in observing both the new and the traditional dates. Earle Roseigh was elected mayor, Joe Rozzelle took over the big Kimball garage, changing its name to the Silver Town Service, and the Nevada Hotel opened in the old Park Utah Hotel building to accommodate the increasing number of new miners moving into town.

Dark war clouds were hanging ominously over Europe again and in October, 1940, the order came for men to register for the draft once more. Signing were 517 men from Park City and 1,082 from Summit County. That same night an American Legion dance was held in the newly completed Memorial Building. On Dec. 8, 1941, Congress declared war and a few weeks later the first draftees were called from Park City to be followed by additional call-ups almost weekly. Bill Mon, son of Bob Mon of Bobs Cafe, was one of the first Park City boys called.

Doctor Gordon in front of the old McGinley Drug Store during the winter of '48.

Entry into the war brought rationing with auto tires being one of the first items placed on the list. Ration Books soon made their appearance followed by sugar stamps. By early 1942 men from 45 to 65 years of age were being registered for the draft. A total of 346 from Park City and 738 from the county signed up. Amid the confusion of war and rationing life continued as near normal as possible.

'Lije' Duke renewed the Park City to Heber mail contract for the 40th year, all of the old abandoned iron hoists, pumps, and other machinery around the mines was being shipped as scrap metal to help the war effort, and Mrs. Emery-Holmes, Utah's Silver Queen, died while traveling in the east. The ex-Park City seamstress was 83 and had been married four times. Her passing brought many nostalgic memories of Park City's boom days to the town's old-timers.

Strangely enough, with the nation's demand for metals and with ever larger ore shipments from the mines, Park City mining stock took a nose dive, hitting its lowest point since 1912. Silver King, which had soared to over $80 a share in the early days before it had been reorganized as The Silver King Coalition and its stock leveled off at $12.50, dropped to only $2.55 while Park Utah was $1.50 and New Park only 28¢. With most of the city's younger men being called away to war a shortage of miners soon, developed.

To speed the flow of necessary metals many draftees considered more vital to the war effort as miners instead of soldiers were returned to western mining camps. In typical army tradition boys who were miners were kept in the service while whose who knew' nothing of mining were sent to work in the mines. In September, 1943, 37 of the new draftee-miners arrived to work in the mines at Park City. Many of them had worked in the coal fields of the east and proved to be quite poor metal miners since coal mining in no way resembled metal mining. However, most of them tried hard and a few learned the trade and stayed at Park City after the war was over. Gold mines, which were considered non-essential, were ordered closed so gold miners could be diverted to producing strategic metals. In mid-1943 the Ontario Mine drained its long flooded lower levels to get at the rich bodies of zinc which had been left untouched. In the early days zinc had been considered almost worthless but the war demanded great quantities of zinc and the Ontario soon became a major producer.

Because of the lack of miners' production in Park City's mines never reached the level in war time that it had in pre-war days. As late in the war years as February, 1945, production was figured at only 65% of pre-war production. In 1944 the Silver King and the Park Utah mines were short about 150 miners each and at the Silver King only one shift could be worked due to the shortage. Increasing water problems at depth, particularly in the Silver King's west end shaft, also slowed production. In October, 1944, when a vein of ore was blasted 60 feet below the shaft's 1,900-foot level a major water course was struck. All available pumps were installed and the water flow seemed to be checked but early the following morning an even greater flow broke into the workings, drowning out the pumps and flooding the shaft and closing all mining in that area.

To help alleviate the shortage of fresh farm crops during the war years and at the same time channel needed produce into military supply agencies, the Park City Victory Gardens were started in the spring of 1943. The Silver King Mine donated fields of good farm land on the old Ferry Ranch near the mouth of the Spiro Tunnel and furnished irrigation water, something the King Mine had plenty of. By mid-summer there were many fine gardens producing not only fresh produce but also varieties of fruits and vegetables not easily obtained at the city's stores. In 1944 the city received authorization to purchase a much-needed fire truck. The old 1923 Graham Brothers-Dodge fire truck had been patched together about as much as it could be so everyone in town sighed with relief when a shiny new Mack truck with all the modern equipment arrived in town. That autumn a fire which nearly got out of control burned the Nevada Hotel and a half block of vacant saloons and boarded-up buildings. Everything on the east side of upper Main Street from the Silver Spot Saloon to the O'Hara house was lost. It was the most spectacular fire in Park City in many years.

On April 12, 1945, President Roosevelt died at Warm Springs, Georgia, just four months before the surrender of Japan on Aug. 14, 1945. Park City went wild when news of the war's end came. Horns honked, sirens screamed, and the saloons did a "land-office" business. The next day all the mines shut down and all business houses closed (except the saloons!) for a day of celebration. A parade was held during the day and a dance was held that night. The Labor Day celebration a few weeks later, always Park City's biggest holiday, was an especially gala and carefree one. The long war was over, the boys were coming home, the mines were all working, and at last Park City could turn its attention to planning for the future and keeping the town in its role as Utah's leading "hardrock" camp.

The Utah Central arriving on time, in spite of winter.

CHAPTER 23

HARD TIMES

When the war was over the normal life of the city began returning. Kendall Webb and Murri Hari opened a new photography shop named the Valley Studio and the Ford garage was showing the first post-war models. Park City's first ski lift, the Snow Park, was built in Deer Valley by Bob Burns and Otto Carpenter, not far from where the ski trains of ten years earlier had brought skiers to the slopes above the Park Con Mine. The new lift was promoted by the local ski club and featured a rustic 1,400-foot lift built of pines poles cut right from the ski runs, a jumping hill, and a warming hut where hot coffee and sandwiches could be purchased.

Back then Burns & Carpenter would have been amazed had anyone even suggested the fantastic $50 million dollar investment now being made in Deer Valley skiing, although even then most Parkites knew that Deer Valley, Lake Flat and Bald Mountain were the best ski areas. But in those days it was for fun, not for profit.

Not all the business at Park City was prosperous though, for at least one wanted to call it quits. In May, 1946, the Denver& Rio Grande Railroad petitioned the Interstate Commerce Commission for permission to abandon its Parley's Canyon route into town. The D&RGW and its predecessor, the old Utah Central, had a total of more than 50 years of service to Park City. The route was a difficult one, especially in the winter time, and couldn't compete with modern motor buses for the passenger business and according to its petition there wasn't enough freight business for both it and the Union Pacific. Besides the loss of the D&RGW two familiar faces were lost from the Park City scene also for in 1946 Norman Neil, known nationwide as "Coffee John", sold his well-known roadhouse and moved to Salt Lake City. There probably wasn't a cross country trucker who didn't know Coffee John before the highway was changed. Everyone used to stop there just to listen to his Scotsman jokes.

In July, Thomas 'Tom' Paul died. He had operated the Paul Brothers & Wilson general store with Archie Wilson for 48 years and was a favorite of every kid in town thanks to the big old-fashioned jars of penny candy he always kept on hand for them.

In February, 1946, the Newmont Mining Company began operating the East Utah Mine located near the New Park Mine. A tunnel was driven for nearly 4,000 feet with several cross cuts but three years later the operation was abandoned after $400,000 had been spent without an ore body of shipping size being found.

In July, 1946, the editor of the Richfield Reaper, a Southern Utah newspaper, described Park City's Park Con Mine as one of the west's forgotten mines. The editorial stated that from 1929 to 1939 the Park City Consolidated had been one of the state's leading mines, having produced nearly $4,000,000 in vital metals, and that during a time when metal prices were at an all-time low. Nearly all of the company's income had been reinvested in the mine and it was finally forced to shut down during the city's period of low metal prices and union labor troubles. The Reaper article added that even though metal prices were rising the mine remained closed and therefore "it is today one of the west's forgotten mines."

In addition to its property at Park City the Park Con Company owned several other mines, including one in Colorado and one in Missouri. About a year later, in October, 1947, the Park Con was reported to be on the verge of opening and the rumor seemed to be bolstered when the company paid a $68,000 dividend in February, 1948, and another of the same amount in

August but still the great mine sat idle and as the Reaper editor said "was a forgotten mine."

The winter of 1948 was probably the worst ever witnessed in Park City. It was the year when deer and elk wandered through the suburbs of Salt Lake City eating rose bushes and shrubbery while herds of sheep and cattle starved and froze in pastures buried under snow drifts. Buildings in Park City were literally buried, and only the city's main streets could be plowed and often even they were closed for days at a time. Many times the roads to the mines where snowed-in forcing miners to walk from town to the shafts and tunnels in the canyons above. Snowslides began occurring in places where they hadn't been seen for years. While coming down Empire Canyon from the Judge Mine, Herbert Savage was caught and killed in a slide which narrowly missed several other men. High on the steep slopes of Scott's Pass two telephone linemen, Alden Winchester and Ernie Anderson, were hit by a slide which roared down on them without warning. Winchester was buried, but Anderson was able to dig himself out and go to Thayne's Shaft for help. When the rescuers returned to search for Winchester's body they found him still half buried where he had managed to dig his way to air. A few days later they were both back on the job patroling the lines again but keeping a little closer watch on the silent slopes above.

The contract between the Mine, Mill, & Smelter Workers Union and the Park City mining companies expired in June, 1949, and was not renewed, resulting in a loss of over 800 jobs. The cause of the disagreement between the mining companies and the union was not completely one of wages and hours but also one of politics. The Mine-Mill Union had been branded as a Communist-led organization by the government only a short time before as a result of a nation-wide crackdown on Communism taking place at that time.

Soon after the mines closed, the union membership severed their long-time ties with the Mine-Mill union and affiliated with a new union known as the Progressive Metalworkers. For several months there was separate bargaining with each company resulting in the New Park Mine starting operations again while the others remained closed. Then in the midst of the confusion the union's membership voted to leave the Progressive Metalworkers Union since it hadn't been progressive enough and join the United Steel Workers of America. Many of the old-time miners wondered what silver miners were doing in a steel workers union.

Remains of the First National Bank after the great fire. - *Courtesy of Ken Webb* -

Months passed with no progress and many of the unemployed miners began leaving town to find steadier jobs and more certain futures. The Pacific Bridge Company which had been operating a large mill to rework the great pile of mill tailings accumulated below town closed its operation adding further to the number of men out of work. In April, 1950, after 54 years of service, Frankels clothing store closed its doors for the last time and not long afterwards the fine New Park Hotel went out of business. Its board covered windows seemed to prove that another western ghost town was in the making.

Though their town had come on hard times and looked the worst it ever had Park City residents still kept up the spirit that only people who have been raised together in a small town and who have been through hard times together before can know. One source of pride never lost by the townspeople was their schools, always among the state's best, and their high school band that had won honors throughout the state and beyond, rivaling and beating in contests bands from the state's largest cities. The band's greatest triumph and the highest honor paid to Mr. Jones and Park City came in December, 1950, when the Park City High School band was chosen to be the feature band performing at half time at the famed Shriners East-West All-Star Football Game at San Francisco's Kezar Stadium.

The invitation came just when the people needed a boost in morale, but in 1950 the mines were shut down and the city coffers were empty. Parkites went all out to raise the necessary money so the band could attend the famous pageant. Mr. Jones made the band's desperate condition known and within days contributions from Chicago to California began pouring in. Money came from strangers who had never been in Park City but who knew of the band's fine record and wanted to see it attend the pageant. In only several weeks over $4,000 had been received from townspeople, former residents, and from anonymous well wishers, assuring the band's attendance and success at the great pageant.

The band went from Park City to San Francisco's Sir Francis Drake Hotel where the members had their pictures taken and were interviewed by radio, television, and news media. Two concerts were given at the Shrine Hospital where the mayor of San Francisco personally congratulated the players.

On the big day the Park City band marched tall and proud into the great stadium while the television and radio announcers called "Here comes the high-stepping band from Utah, the Park City High School Band!" When the band played again at half time 67,000 persons seated in the stands rose to give them the biggest ovation ever given anyone in the stadium's history. The director of the pageant gave them the greatest tribute of all when he announced the performance was the most outstanding band demonstration ever presented in any pageant. If the reports that Park City was a ghost town were correct then there were some pretty lively ghosts still left!

Only a snow-thrower could keep Main Street clear of snow in the winter of 1948.

In spite of the success of its band things weren't getting any better for business or people in Park City. Metal prices dropped daily and the mines still running were operating at a loss. About the only ray of hope was a $321,000 exploration loan made to the Silver King Mine by the federal government to search for new ore bodies. It wasn't lack of ore that had the mines shut down but rather the price they received for the ore they produced and a loan to search for new ore wouldn't cure that. In December, 1954, Welsh, Driscoll, & Buck, a Park City institution since 1896, closed after its last day of business. U.S. Highway 40 was rerouted, leaving Park City six miles off the main highway, and finally, almost as a last indignity, Park City lost the Park Record. In January, 1956, LePage Raddon who had managed the pioneer paper through the town's lean years died and for the first time in 70 years left the paper without a Raddon at its helm. He had been associated with the Record since he was 10 years old and had been a partner in its ownership for more than 30 years. Lynx Langford, lifelong employee at the Record office, kept the paper going for the next few months until H.C. McConaughy purchased it as well as Coalville's Summit County Bee and Morgan City's Morgan County News. In the interests of economy all three papers were published in one plant which was located at Morgan and then sent by mail to Coalville and Park City.

Although the pioneer newspaper's 80 years of steady publication hadn't been interrupted its out of town plant just wasn't the same as being able to stop at the cluttered little office on Main Street to chat with

Lee Raddon or Lynx Langford. But even though the Record wasn't quite the same it still carried on the tradition of reporting local news and mining matters started three-quarters of a century earlier by Sam Raddon. The bleak picture presented by Park City's declining population and business might have looked like the end of the line to outsiders but Parkites, used to the ups and downs of a mining camp, kept their spirits Lip and looked to the future.

Over the years hundreds of two and three-man prospects and numerous small mining companies had merged together or had been absorbed by the larger companies until only a few large companies remained. No one was particularly surprised then when in 1953 two of Park City's oldest and largest mines merged their resources under one name. The Silver King Coalition which included the old Woodside, Keith & Kearns, Creole, Crescent, Alliance, Uintah Treasure Hill, and a whole host of lesser mines joined the Park Utah Consolidated, made up of the Park Utah, Ontario, Daly, Daly-West, Daly-Judge, and all the other properties it had acquired, to form the United Park City Mining Company. The giant merger brought nearly all of Park City's mining, except for the New Park Company, under one management, cutting a great deal of overhead costs and expenses as well as allowing the new company to mine undeveloped ground between them whose ownership had never been established. What was more important for Park City though was the new company's name, United Park City, for at last the mines and the people were about to get together to build a united Park City. The pendulum of fortune had turned and although its movement was hardly noticeable the beginning of a bigger and better Park City was in the making.

The merger of the Silver King and the Park Utah resulted in the closing of the Silver King shaft and mill while the shops at the Judge Mine and the hoist at the Daly-West became the new company's surface plants and the Park Utah tunnel became the mine's main access and ore haulage route. All through the interconnected workings exploration for new and unknown ore bodies went on with several new discoveries being made, one of the best finds being on the 1,900-foot level of the Daly-West. Although the costs of developing new ore bodies was great and resulted in losses to the company still it was cheaper in the long run to keep operating and hope for better times than it was to close down and allow the tunnels and shafts to cave in. In the meantime new ore reserves that could be sold when metal prices rose were being found. Several old-timers long associated with the mine's early development died while the new United Park Company was being formed.

Simon Bamberger, who had succeeded John Daly as manager of the Daly-West, died in January, 1958. Only a few months later he was followed in death by Paul Hunt and Harry Wallace, both former superintendents at the Park Utah.

In 1956 while the new United Park City company was exploring the depths of its mines for new ore bodies the independent New Park Mining Company made an unusual discovery on its 1,755-foot level. In the mine's Pearl Fissure ore-containing up to seven ounces of gold and 45 ounces of silver was found in bedded ore, the finest ever found in the mine. More important however was the ore's gold content for the New Park had been chiefly a lead, zinc, and silver producer with little gold in its ore.

At its 1957 stockholders meeting, W.H.H. Cranmer, company president, announced that the New Park was joining the Lucky Mac Mining Company in building a $7,500,000 uranium mill in Wyoming. But even though the New Park had high gold content in its ore as well as interests in other companies it too was finding it ever harder to operate with metal prices at a long time low and was finally forced by mounting losses to announce the closing of the famous old mine.

The shutdown of the New Park was of short duration, however, for a few months after its closing the miners formerly employed by the company proposed a novel plan to keep the mine working. The miners suggested that the company lease the mine to them with their wages depending upon the quantity and quality of ore mined and shipped. Although the leaders of the miner's union protested, the lease was made and by the following spring nearly 100 miners who would otherwise have been out of work were operating the mine at a profit, both for themselves and the company. What was important was that the mine was kept open for all too often it was found that when a mine was temporarily closed its tunnels and shafts caved until no amount of work would reopen it. The story of many western ghost towns had their start when their mines shut down, just "temporarily," until times got better. Often "temporary" became quite permanent.

CHAPTER 24

A CAMP REBORN

While the new United Park City Mining Company was getting its feet on the ground and the New Park Mine was being operated by lessees Park City itself presented a grim picture to strangers. The city's population dropped at the rate of 500 each year until there weren't much more than 1000 residents left. Almost daily, families left town for there were no jobs at the mines and families have to eat. Doctor and dentist services were no longer available and the town's last barber left for greener pastures. George Hoover's meat market, long a Park City favorite, went out of business and the Palace Grocery's long-time service ended. Julius Frankel, the pioneer clothier who started his store in 1896, died on Sept. 5, 1957, followed only a week later by Ed J. McPolin, one of Park City's best-liked citizens. McPolin had been instrumental in obtaining the War Veterans Memorial Building for Park City as well as serving on the city council as county commissioner, and state representative.

The following January Mrs. Marie O'Keefe, another longtime resident, also died. Mrs. O'Keefe had been manager of the early hotel located in the Maple Hall and later the old Park City Hotel. When it burned in 1912 she was placed in charge of the well-known New Park Hotel and operated it until 1952.

After the Park Record was moved out of town the old Record Building was left abandoned and neglected. Early in the spring of 1958 when winter's snow weighed heavily on its roof passersby could see its walls bulging and hear its ancient timbers creaking. To prevent a dangerous cave-in such as the one when the Dewey Theatre collapsed Mrs. Maie Raddon, the building's owner, had it torn down. It was one of the first buildings erected after the fire of '98 and its vacant lot was a silent reminder of another landmark lost. Still another landmark was lost later that year when the house, barns, and livery stables of John Sweatfield's pioneer freight business and stage line were burned.

Almost as if disclaiming some poor country cousin, Summit County inflicted a not-soon-to-be-forgotten insult on the failing camp. In an expensive advertisement which appeared in the Salt Lake Tribune in June, 1959, boosting the beauties and advantages of living in Summit County there was no mention made of Park City. It was not even shown on the accompanying map and even the road leading into town was missing! After having paid more taxes than the rest of the county combined and producing hundreds of million of dollars Park City had been erased from the map as though it had never existed. Perhaps the county was ashamed of the boarded-up buildings that lined Main Street and the rows of empty houses whose broken windows, like empty eye sockets in a bleached skull, stared at its deserted streets. Little wonder that Salt Lake City newspapers were calling Park City a ghost town.

The Sunday feature writers were a bit hasty though when they called Park City a ghost town for as Rhea Hurley, wife of pioneer mining man Andy Hurley and life-long resident of Park City said, "We've got some damn lively ghosts here!" And all the ghosts weren't die-hard miners either for weekends were beginning to see lines of out-of-town cars parked along Main Street. Modern highways had brought Park City within only minutes of the Salt Lake and Provo valleys and people from there were beginning to discover the old mining camp's delightful summer climate and authentic western atmosphere. At first it looked like the out-of-towners were only driving through, taking pictures of the long-cold smokestacks and deserted mine buildings, and then leaving for good. But they came back, often bringing friends with them, and besides just taking pictures sidewalk artists began painting striking pictures of the quaint old houses with the quiet pines and shadows of Treasure Hill in the background. And then one day businessmen began to report increased sales of film, gasoline, and antiques, and even the town's people could see the cafes and saloons were a little more lively and a little more crowded. And the new faces weren't ghosts either. Not in Park City. The treasure house of the Wasatch was on its way back up again.

The High School Band on parade. Note the Park Garage in the background.

At first the signs were hardly noticeable, a few more cars on weekends, a few more strange faces, and maybe a tourist asking questions about the old camp's past. And then somebody sold a house. It was the first one sold in years for with rows of empty houses that could be rented for almost nothing who would want to buy one? The rumor was that someone from Salt Lake City had bought it for a summer home, "Just to escape the valley's heat" it was said, and a few Parkites began asking themselves if other people from the lower valleys might not also be interested in trading the heat and noise of the big cities for the cool and quiet of Park City. After all, they could live in Park City and drive to their jobs in the valley in only minutes. Their question was answered in August, 1956, when a new mountain townsite of 200 lots named Summit Park was laid out just under the brow of Parleys Summit, not far from where the rails of the old Utah Central had crossed the rocky pass 70 years before.

Summit Park was so successful that it was enlarged to 800 acres having 1,600 lots which sold from $1,250 to $3,000 each. Paved roads snaked their way through the pines and aspens and before the leaves turned scarlet in the fall several fine homes were nestled in the shadows under the ridge. Summit Park was built in Summit County, closer to Park City than to Salt Lake City, and proved that people were interested in living in the mountains if they could have the conveniences they were used to in the city.

Perhaps the interest in summer homes and year-round residences was contagious for before long several more Park City houses were sold and homes and businesses that hadn't known a fresh coat of paint in years blossomed out in gay new colors. Hoses of the fire department were used to wash building fronts whose only washing in years had been from the rains and women pitched in to scrub windows long covered with cobwebs. Weathered building fronts were sprayed with donated paint and even the power and light poles weren't overlooked. The people of Park City had always banded together to help each other during hard times and now they joined together in a common effort to rebuild their town and disprove once and for all the myth of ghost town status.

Their efforts didn't go unnoticed either for in the summer of 1958 Park City was chosen by Walt Disney Studios for the filming of a short movie named "Rusty And The Falcon." A few townspeople were used as extras and though it wasn't a feature-length film it was seen by millions of television viewers and attracted still more attention to the reviving town.

Because of its sheltered location, nestled in deep canyons between Bald Mountain and Iron Peak, Park City was unable to get television reception when Salt Lake City stations first began broadcasting. Early efforts resulted in good sound reception but no picture could be obtained. It didn't take long, however, to discover that the higher the antennas were placed on the mountain sides the better picture reception became. Evans Smith, who lived in Ontario Canyon, discovered through experimentation that by placing an antenna atop Rossie Hill and running bare copper wire to it a fine picture could be had. Although the manufacturer's instructions stated that antennas couldn't be placed more than 70 feet from the sets soon lines several miles long were being run from all over town to the hill's crest and before another year was over the top of Rossie Hill had sprouted a bumper crop of television antennas in assorted shapes and sizes. Often deer grazing on the mountain side would knock poles over or get the lines tangled in their antlers so that sometimes long after dark men with flashlights could be seen high on the mountainside making emergency repairs so that some favorite program could be seen. Several years later a community owned receiver-reflector station was built on the exact spot where the first antenna had stood and made the running of separate lines to the mountain top unnecessary as well as bringing television to all who wanted it.

In 1959 a group of citizens met at the Memorial Building to discuss the possibility of promoting the tourist and recreational potential of Park City. A tentative plan to rejuvenate the town's sagging economy was agreed on with one of the first orders of business being the construction of an auto road to connect with the resort areas at Brighton. The road plans were achieved sooner than expected when engineering battalions of the Utah National Guard agreed to build the road as part of the summer training program. Though rough and rocky at first it wasn't long before sightseers were coming into town over the 10,000 foot Guardsman Pass, following the trail of '68 taken by Col. Connors soldier-prospectors. The Bonanza Flats are a place of beauty in the summer and a riot of color in the fall and many of the newcomers were university art students who painted scenes of the pine-covered slopes above town as well as pictures of the town's old buildings and winding streets. Many of their paintings were later shown at art displays and at state and county fairs where they created more interest in Park City.

The Kimball Hotel and Overland Stage Station, Snyderville.

The new tourists who visited the old camp weren't disappointed after they arrived for they found a gold mine of interesting people and places. Old-timers like Lawrence Berry showed them the 'dungeon', three small dark and windowless cells below the city hall where outlaws had been imprisoned in the camp's boom days. Built of stone with iron doors hand-made by Mr. Berry's father, they remind one of some medieval dungeon, complete even to the balls and chains with which the prisoners were manacled. One of the cells still has wrist and ankle irons fastened to its cold, stone wall. It and the prison at Yuma, Arizona are the last of the old territorial prisons.

Other old-timers like Joe Streets and Albert Carlson could be found on sunny days sitting in front of the old Salt Lake House or the Oak Saloon, eager to answer questions about the town's past or tell tales (sometimes tall) of its mining history. Before long even the store windows began to take on a different look with all sorts of unusual and valuable antiques on display.

Early-day photos of mining and city life along with ore specimens sparked the viewers interest while sun-colored bottles, high button shoes, antique clocks, and 100-year-old furniture caught the eye of all who saw them. A city park built at the north end of town where tourists could stop for lunch and where children could play was an added inducement for people to spend a few hours visiting in town. And the people's efforts to rebuild their town began to pay off in other ways for business houses that had been on the verge of closing remained open and people who had decided to move out of town changed their minds and stayed.

As though in sympathy with the people's efforts metal prices began to climb and mines that had worked with only a skeleton crew began advertising for miners. The United Park City Company began sinking a new incline shaft from the Ontario's 1,800-foot level to develop new ore bodies and add to the mine's ore reserves. New-found ore added to the mine's production and luckily no great amount of water was encountered to hinder operations. A government loan of $81,000 matched by an equal amount from the company was obtained in 1964 to explore for new ore bodies in the Daly-West Mine with several promising leads soon being uncovered. From depths below the historic ore-producing zones a 6-foot vein of high-grade ore was found in the Daly Judge Mine resulting in greater production and, even more importantly, to a more stable economy for the town.

Meanwhile the lessees at the New Park continued to operate that mine successfully. Its workings were sunk below the 2,000-foot depth with ever-increasing amounts of gold being found in the ore. Over a ton of ore was blocked out in reserve for every ton being mined, assuring a steady operation. In 1961 Charles Steen, millionaire king of Utah's uranium mining industry, acquired a substantial part of the New Park stock and became executive vice president of the company. The following year he succeeded W.H.H. Cranmer as president of the company. While Cranmer was still the company's president a contract had been made in which the giant Hecla Mining Company took over the New Park Mine and agreed to sink its shaft past the 2,400-foot mark, run 15,000 feet of new drifts and cross cuts in a major ore exploration effort, and build a 400-ton per day mill to process the known reserves of 275,000 tons of silver, lead, zinc, copper, and gold ores the mine had.

The mill, the first new mill built in Park City in years, cost $650,000 and was built to reduce free-milling ore, the gold freely separating from the country rock with the use of cyanide. The mill's waste tailings were pumped back into the mine where they were used to re-fill worked out areas and at the same time reduce the need for costly timbering as well as eliminating the waste dumps and stream contamination that were common to milling operations. Over $2,000,000 was spent by the Hecla Company and 90 men were employed. That the new operation was successful was proven when the first six months of 1961 showed a profit of $657,000, the entire cost of the new mill.

The New Park Mine's total production since its humble beginning as the Glen Allen claims 90 years earlier passed the $37,000,000 mark. It was no longer the hard-luck mine known to Col. Shaugnessy as the Glencoe and later to Charlie Moore as the Mayflower. It now ranked among the leading mines of the west. With mines like the New Park and the United Park and with people with spirits that couldn't be broken Park City had retained its title of Utah's leading hardrock camp and was fast becoming a popular tourist mecca.

The Crescent Tram Narrow Gauge, elkhorns on the engine.

CHAPTER 25

THE NEW BONANZA

In 1957 when Park City was at its lowest ebb its Mormon Church members demonstrated their faith in the town when they voted to build a new chapel at a cost of $114,000. Some people thought such a large expense in a ghost town was unwarranted but apparently the ghosts didn't know they were dead for in only five years the new chapel was completely paid for. Its dedication in December, 1962, was a tribute to the faith of Park City's Mormon population. Back in the camp's early days opposition to the Mormons were very strong. In 1886 an organization known as the "Loyalty Legion" wrecked the home of a Mr. Davis, then leader of the city's "Saints", and encouraged the mining companies not to hire Mormon miners. For seven years the ban against hiring Mormon miners remained in effect but finally in 1894 church leaders prevailed upon the mining companies to give their members fair treatment. After the ban was lifted Church membership grew rapidly until there were 300 members who held their meetings at Roy's grocery store on Main Street. A new chapel which they built on Park Avenue was lost in the great fire of '98 and the "Saints" were again without a meeting place until 1904 when Church President Joseph F. Smith dedicated their second chapel, also built on Park Avenue.

While the new Mormon chapel was being built during the late 1950s some of the first new homes built in town in many years made their appearance. Modern siding and fresh paint gave many of the older homes and business houses a face lifting. The arrival of Dr. John Cook in 1960 ended the city's no doctor status and the opening of the old Central Drug store, later renamed the Poison Creek Drug, was welcome news for everyone. Two well-known old-time buildings were torn down in 1961 to give birth to a new business house The Utah Coal Company building, one of the first erected after the great fire and the Jefferson School, built in 1891, were both torn down. Blaine Jolly and Mason Smith, two of Park City's favorite young men, used the bricks from the old school house to build the town's first drive-in where the pioneer coal company had been. The new business, named the Snow Palace, opened for business in May, 1962. While the two old landmarks were falling before the wreckers hammer two others were lost to fire. John & Olga Aimo's City Cash Market was completely destroyed by fire in below zero temperatures in March, 1960 while John Mitchell's home at the head of Main Street, a particularly impressive and well-landscaped old home, burned in November, 1962. The same week that the City Cash Market burned an old-time store owner from the camp's early days died at Denver's Brown Palace Hotel. Mrs. Belle Brand, owner of the old Golden Rule Store, died and left a large estate to relatives and friends as well as a fortune to Utah's Shriner's Hospital.

Many people were puzzled at the spiraling land values of Park City real estate during the late 1950s and early 60s. The United Park City Mining Company began buying up a lot of unused land and old buildings while out-of-town people were paying prices unheard of before for vacant lots and empty houses. Realty companies were advertising Park City property for sale in Salt Lake City newspapers while land agents were offering to buy business properties for unknown buyers. For several years residents had been hearing vague and often mysterious rumors that a giant year-around vacation and recreation complex was being planned for the area but no one seemed to be able to learn anything definite. Then in May, 1961, an unexpected announcement made by the United Park City Mining Company put an end to speculation and verified the long heard rumors. The Park City Land & Development Company, a newly formed subsidiary of United Park, was organized with the mining company officials as its officers. The new recreation company was formed as a result of a 1959 stockholders meeting which proposed that the mining company turn all of its surface rights, some 10,000 acres, over to the new company to develop a year-around vacation center and recreation complex.

Early in 1962 the new recreation company applied to the federal government's Area Redevelopment Administration for a million-dollar loan to start an ambitious long-range plan which would make Park City a center for summer and winter sports and outdoor activities. The mining district was officially a depressed business area and if it could be shown that the loan would result in the creation of a substantial number of new jobs the loan would be made, providing the mining company could put up funds to match the government's money. After months of anxious waiting by Park City residents who knew they could no longer depend upon mining alone to support their town the ARA office made its decision. A loan of $1,232,000 to finance a major recreation and tourist center was announced. The mining company matched the loan with $650,000 and 10,000 acres of some of the finest and most scenic mountain country in the west. The new complex was planned to include the nation's finest ski lifts, activity center, mountain restaurants, golf course, and other outdoor facilities.

Opening night at the Grand Opera House, March 31, 1898.

At almost the same time that the recreation company received its loan the city obtained a loan of $40,000 to build new sidewalks and repave Main Street. Directors of the recreation company advised Parkites to keep and improve their homes and property and take advantage of the expected influx of tourists who would soon be visiting the area. A new bonanza even greater than the one started 100 years earlier was expected but instead of depending on silver the city's future would be built on the unchanging beauty of the Wasatch Range and its ever renewing mantle of winter snow. A feeling of excitement not seen since the camp had been a boomer was felt throughout the town and hope could be seen on people's faces once again.

In order to beat the coming winter, work was started immediately on building ski trails, laying out the path the new ski lift would take, and planning for the restaurants, hotels, riding stables, and a golf course to follow. The angry buzz of chain saws and the sharp ring of axes along with the clanging roar of bulldozers sounded from high on the slopes of Treasure Hill as trees were felled to mark the start of the new bonanza. While the government's red tape was being unsnarled the mining company put up the necessary funds to get work started. The United Park City Mining Company put up $105,000 with $200,000 coming from the recreation company, $210,000 from the American Smelting & Refining Co.; $150,000 from Anaconda Copper, and $360,000 from the sale of ten-year bonds. The gondola high-ride ski-lift cost $435,000 and was the nation's longest with over 100 fiberglass cabin cars designed to carry 800 people per hour, and was one of the first purchases made for the new complex. Two other ski lifts were also planned, the Thaynes Canyon lift costing $123,000, and the Jupiter Basin lift costing $66,000. The Summit House located high on Crescent Ridge at the gondola's upper terminal, would cost over $170,000 and offer the finest cafe and lounge services. And even more exciting plans were in the making.

While winter was fast approaching, ground was

being broken for the new ski runs. The winter of 1962 proved to be the worst since 1948 with drifts piled deep in the mountains and temperatures of 30 degrees below zero in town. Snowslides roared down into quiet canyons while motorists were snowbound on the highways. Skiers thought the deep snow was just fine though. Over in Deer Valley, Otto Carpenter's Snow Park lift was kept busy every weekend. Main Street business houses were noticing the added business also for the "ski bums," as they called themselves, were discovering the interesting shops and old-time saloons.

Remains of the Grand Opera House after the great fire of 1898. - *Courtesy of Ken Webb* -

The increase in business could also be seen in the improvements being made. New roofs, modern siding, and fresh paint brightened the New Park Emporium, Murphy's Beanery, and the Masonic Temple, while the Frantz Apartments were remodeled and the old Sutton Building was rebuilt to include a beauty salon and office space. In November, 1962, burglars cut their way into the bank from an upstairs apartment and for the first time in over 90 years Park City had a bank robbery. A hole was blasted into the vault and although the thiefs couldn't get into the safe inside the vault over $1,300 in sacked silver dollars was taken. The FBI investigated and called the job a professional one but despite their aid no progress was made in apprehending the thieves.

In December, 1962, the recreation company received a check from the ARA for $1,232,000 and its effect was soon felt throughout the town. A plan to make Park City a historic attraction of national prominence was adopted and ways of opening closed business houses and removing those too dilapidated for repair were discussed. Citizens were urged to improve their properties and a museum having historical photos, early mining equipment, and relics of the town's past was planned. In March, 1963, the old Egyptian Theatre was completely remodeled and named the Silver Wheel Theatre. The theatre wasn't reopened to show Hollywood films however, for once more it would be cheer the hero and hiss the villian! Under the direction of manager Merrill Sanchez melodrama returned to Park City and once more old-time stage plays such as "The Drunkard" and "No Mother To Guide Her" played to packed houses.

In April the Mountain Fuel Supply Company announced it was extending its lines into the Kamas and Heber valleys and that if enough people at Park City were interested in having natural gas installed a line could be run to serve the city. At one time, many years before, natural gas had been proposed for Park City but had been declined because it was thought that its use would hurt the coal mining business but now the offer was accepted with 85 per cent of the people requesting the service. A line was laid over the pass from Keetley and on Aug. 7, 1964, the first gas was tuned into the new line. No longer would Park City school children wake up in cold houses or would housewives have to kindle a fire before breakfast could be started.

On May 11, 1963, just as soon as winter's snow was gone from the foothills, ground was broken marking the start of the 2 1/2 mile gondola high ride, the longest gondola ride in North America. The ceremony began when Gov. George D. Clyde swung a silverplated pick to symbolize the beginning of Park City's second bonanza. Utah Sens. Wallace F. Bennett and Frank E. Moss attended the Bonanza Days parade and celebration which featured bands and floats from both Salt Lake and Summit counties. The Cannon Construction Company was awarded the contract to build the city's new recreation complex and work started immediately. Great towers to support the gondola, some over

100-feet high, were erected along the trail that had been cut through the forest and by late summer the heavy 1 1/4 inch cable to support it was being stretched along the steep 12,800-foot course. Just as soon as the molded fibreglass gondola cabins began arriving from Salt Lake City's Fibron Company they were placed on the cable and by early December testing the new lift began. Bags of sand weighing 800 pounds each were placed in each cabin and sent on the 2 1/2 mile trip. On Dec. 26, 1963, Mayor William Sullivan cut a ribbon marking the opening of the Treasure Mountain Recreation Center. John M. Wallace, president of the United Park City Mining Company, and other officials joined the grand opening and the wives of all of Utah's congressional members added their special wishes for success of the new venture.

While the gondola lift was being built and tested, other ski lifts necessary to completion of the complex were also being built. The Thayne's Canyon lift, named the Prospector Lift, would return skiers to the gondolas upper terminus after they had skied down into Thayne's Canyon. It was designed as a 174-passenger double chair lift which presented a breath-taking mile-plus ride over its 24 high towers. The 4,200-foot Silver King lift at the gondolas mid-point and the Tenderfoot lift adjacent to the recreation center itself all added greatly to the complex.

The view from the nearly completed Summit House was one of the most outstanding found anywhere and from the gondola's lower terminus visitors could view the lower reaches of the first 18 miles of ski slopes and trails being completed. A foot of new snow on the center's roof was a reminder that soon the trails and slopes would be covered with 10 feet of glistening powder snow.

For those visitors who were not interested in skiing, the first phase of the Treasure Mountain Golf Course was completed in October, 1963. Mining company president John M. Wallace drove the first ball down the fairway of the nine-hole course.

Located at nearly 7,000 feet and dotted with aspen, spruce, and fir and with several sparkling lakes the new golf course was opened to the public and it wasn't long before reservations were necessary to use it. With the nation's finest ski lifts and gondola high ride and a most unique golf course to mark the start of its tourist and recreation center and with even greater plans in the making, Park City's second bonanza was promising to be even greater than its first.

The way it was done then, complete with twelve-foot skis and home-made poles.

CHAPTER 26

AN UNDERGROUND SKI LIFT

The building boom that had its start in 1963 really hit its stride in 1964. In May, plans to build a $1,000,000 condominium apartment hotel to be named the Treasure Mountain Inn were announced by a group of developers known as Treasure Mountain Inn, Inc. Built on upper Main Street where Welsh, Driscoll & Buck's pioneer store had stood it was without doubt the most impressive building ever erected in Park City and was the equal of the best hotels in Salt Lake City.

Daily, sidewalk engineers supervised its building, from groundbreaking through construction, and as the 58-unit hotel approached completion they were the first to admit that it beat anything ever seen in town before. The finished building was opened to visitors in February, 1965, with nearly 4,000 people taking advantage of its grand opening to view the apartments which sold from $13,000 to $19,000 each as well as to see the Roaring Lion Lounge, the Ontario Room, and the beautiful lobby with its mural painted by artist Joseph Pumphrey which depicted scenes from Park City's past. The new Treasure Mountain Inn, as fine as any apartment hotel in the state, was visual proof that Park City was on its way again.

In September, 1964, well-known Parkite Lloyd Offret and Kenneth Holt of Santa Ana, Calif., applied to the city under the name of Ana-Park Inc., for a permit to build a three-story resort lodge on lower Norfolk Avenue. The permit was granted and with a long-time lease on the ground obtained from the United Park City Mining Company work on a new lodge began. Named the Chateau Apres, the new lodge had 32 private rooms as well as both men's and women's dormitories. Designed in the style of a Swiss Chalet and located near the bottom of the gondola ski lift it became a mecca for skiers when winter's snow came again. At the same time the Chateau Apres Lodge was being built, ground on Nelson Hill near the old Miner's Hospital was broken for still another fine hotel to be known as the Silver King Lodge. Three stories high and having 28 beautifully furnished units built around a center lounge it soon became an outstanding addition to the city's new tourist accommodations. Built by William Blonquist adjacent to the Treasure Mountain Recreation Center at a cost of $250,000 and located at the edge of the new golf course many thought it the city's most beautifully situated resort hotel.

While new hotels and lodges were blossoming forth all around the foot of Treasure Hill the fine old New Park Hotel on lower Main Street had been standing empty and deserted. That is until 1964 when it was purchased by Mr. and Mrs. Vaughn Johnson of Wyoming. Everyone was happy to see the boarded-up windows and doors of the landmark hotel opened once more. The new owners began completely remodeling the old hotel and by the time it was opened for public inspection over $270,000 had been spent, more than ten times what it had cost to build back in 1913. At its opening Parkites discovered that rooms throughout the hotel had been modernized while a steak pit, lounge, and dance floor had been built in the basement. The hotel featured two exciting bars, the Golden Sleigh Room which had a real old-time red and gold gilded horse-drawn cutter from the town's boom days, and the Forge Room which was built around the original blacksmith forge, complete with soot blackened bonnet, from the old Silver King Mine blacksmith shop.

Hotels weren't the only new buildings going up at Park City for in June, 1964, ground was broken for a new telephone company business and office center. The center's new equipment included the first "Touch Tone" system installed in Utah as well as both local and long-distance direct dialing. An open house was held the next spring allowing residents to see $17,000,000 worth of the most modern electronic equipment. Old-timers couldn't help but agree that telephone service had come a long way from the days of the Independent Telephone Company when the Record reported that "talking to Salt Lake City is just like talking to someone three feet away!"

Not all of the new businesses being started in Park City were as costly as the telephone company's but they were equally welcome. David's Restaurant, opened by David Brown in the basement of the old Frankel building on upper Main Street featured everything from trout to lobster while on lower Park Avenue the Christopher, a beautiful Italian-style restaurant housed in the continental style building, was built by Mr. and Mrs. Plott.

Gordon Despain started the Timberhaus in the Foster Building as a sport shop featuring a full line of ski and sporting equipment. Even the post office was remodeled. Several hundred of the old boxes installed back in 1888 were taken out to make room for new ones and plans were made to remodel the entire building in the style of the 1880s. Many families had used the same post office box for generations; the Park Record had used the same box for 85 years.

Two well liked Parkites died in 1964. J.B. Pezeley, owner of the New Deal Market and known to everyone in town as "Si" died in Salt Lake City. Merle G. Heitzman, long time superintendent of the Silver King Mine, also died in Salt Lake City. In August, 1964, Lady Bird Johnson, the "first lady" toured Park City's new business district and recreation center. Apparently she was inpressed with the warm reception given her and the exciting ride on the gondola high-ride for after her return to Washington letters of thanks were received by Mayor William Sullivan and Mark Jolly of the mining company.

"The Curse Of An Aching Heart" was being performed on the stage of the Silver Wheel Theatre, but "The Great Robbery" would have been more appropriate for at the Treasure Mountain Recreation Center burglars were busy blowing open the office safe and making off with the receipts of $5,800!

In a race to be ready for the 1964-65 winter season the world's most unique ski left was being readied. At the edge of the golf course and not far from the lower terminus of the gondola high ride the white limestone and quartz waste dump of the old Spiro Tunnel stood out in sharp contrast against the dark green of the wooded mountain front beyond. The Spiro Tunnel had been driven at the foot of Treasure Hill years earlier to drain the Silver King Consolidated Mine workings but had been little used in recent years. The old tunnel was the scene of feverish activity late in 1964 for crews of miners were busy putting in new timber and relaying mine car rails. The tunnel wasn't being reopened because of any new silver strike, however, but as part of the world's most unique ski lift.

Picturesque old-time wagons carried skiers from the recreation center to the tunnel entrance where specially built enclosed passenger cars pulled by a mine locomotive whisked them deep into the heart of the mountain to where the tunnel connected with the bottom of Thayne's Shaft, sunk from high in the steep, snow-covered recesses of Thaynes Canyon above. There the skiers took their skis from the mine train ride and got into the waiting cage to be hoisted up the shaft to the surface 1,700 feet higher in elevation and two and a half miles from there they had entered the Spiro Tunnel. Once on the surface the skiers rode a double chair life 2,760 feet for a vertical rise of 887 feet to the Summit House high atop Crescent Ridge at the upper terminus of the gondola lift. Below them lay miles of outstanding ski runs down the slopes of Treasure Hill and those who weren't skiers could ride the gondola cars back to their starting point. The unique and novel underground ski lift was hardly completed before winter's first snow covered the face of Treasure Hill with its blanket of white and skiers and winter sports enthusiasts began arriving.

By November new snow covered the mountain's upper reaches and on the 21st of the month the new ski season officially opened. A month later four feet of snow was measured at the Summit House and in January there was eight feet of the finest powder snow on the slopes. The new mine train ride and Thayne's Canyon chair lift were operating in addition to the gondola high-ride and two smaller lifts. Skiers from far and wide came to try the slopes of Treasure Mountain, including world and Olympic champions. All agreed the runs were among the finest anywhere and predicted a great future for the new center. High on Crescent Ridge where the gondola and chair lifts met, skiers gathered at the unique Summit House with its restaurant and lunch room to enjoy one of the most beautiful winter views to be found anywhere. With everything shiny and new including ski lifts, recreation center, the nation's longest gondola ride, and only underground mine tunnel ski train ride in the world, and the novel Summit House high above the clouds in addition to the million-dollar Treasure Mountain Inn and the other fine hotels and lodges all newly completed, Park City was unrivaled as the country's most outstanding new sports and recreation area. And it was only the beginning for even greater plans were in the making.

CHAPTER 27

THE NEW DAWN

Back at the turn of the century there had been no library at Park City so the ladies of the Congregational Church decided to do something about it. Book cabinets were ordered and placed in a room in the basement of the Church and as funds became available books of interest to all were purchased. Although the little library was operated by the ladies of the church it was open to all who wanted to use it. In time obsolete and unpopular books were removed and were replaced by those in demand so that in a few years a first-class library resulted. When the city opened its own library a few years later the books and furnishings of the church library were donated to it. The city's library was established in a building adjoining the city hall and eventually grew until there were over 5,000 volumes on hand in addition to all the popular magazines and periodicals. Volunteers from the women's Antheneum and other civic organizations aided the librarians, including Mrs. Frida Consoni, the long-time librarian presently in charge, in keeping the books bound and in repair, making the library a place to be enjoyed.

S.L. Raddon, Editor of the Park Record.
- Courtesy of Mrs. Maie Raddon -

In 1965 Park City boasted a new art gallery where the many artists who had been painting scenes of the old camp could display their work. Once the university students discovered the wealth of subject material and scenery the area presented, many well-known artists began visiting the town to capture its charm on canvas. When the new art display center opened it was named The Hanging Gallery, appropriately reminiscent of Park City's often wild and turbulent past. Among the better-known artists who had their work shown at the new center were Francis Sellers, Barbara Goggen, June Sorenson, and Joseph Pumphrey.

On the golf course players could be seen from early morning until near dark. From the time that winter's snow left the greens in April until they returned again in November there was seldom a time when reservations weren't needed to play. At the United Park City Mines Company James Ivers Jr. was elected company president, succeeding John M. Wallace. Ivers studied mining at the University of Utah and had worked at the Silver King Mine from 1950 until 1955 as well as having been a mine superintendent in Michigan's iron mining district. He was well-liked by Parkites, being considered almost a local boy since his grandfather had started working at Park City as a teamster and blacksmith back in the camp's earliest days and had worked his way up to director of the Silver King Mine.

In town new building continued on a grand scale

with ground breaking for larger and more lavish hotels all the time. In May, 1965, Salt Lake City businessman James Pappas announced the start of the city's newest hotel. Named the C'est Bon, it was built on lower Empire Avenue within easy walking distance of the Treasure Mountain Recreation Center. When it was completed a year later the $720,000 building was unequaled anywhere. With 56 beautifully furnished first class rooms in addition to an underground garage, beauty salon, sauna bath and steam room, plus a fine bar and package liquor agency as well as a variety of shops, it soon became the convention headquarters of the intermountain area, hosting business meetings and conventions of all the better known firms as well as fraternal and government organizations. In November, 1965, the city commission approved the building of a second condominium apartment hotel to be built on lower Woodside Avenue, only a block from the new C'est Bon Hotel. Named the Eidelweiss Haus, its completion added still another fine building to Park City.

A Sullivan air compressor at the Silver King Mine.

Three new auto service stations, all with the most attractive styling and modern equipment, began serving Parkites and the ever increasing tourist trade. A Standard Oil Station was built on Park Avenue at a cost of over $50,000 while at the highway intersection just below town an American Oil Station as modern in appearance as any fine home made its debut. Bud Gasparic, the American Oil dealer, was in charge while the Standard Station became a sub-agency for the Ford line of autos. Not to be out-done the Conoco Service, operated by Cliff and Clyde Streets, soon opened the most complete and best equipped station in the area. With lifts, tire changers, and repair facilities adequate for even the large ore haulage trucks of the McFarland & Hullinger Company, the $80,000 station was a far cry from the little Conoco gas station operated on nearly the same spot for so many years by Art Lefler and Tommy St. Jeor.

Thanksgiving week marked the start of the 1965-66 ski season. There were 300 skiers in town for the sports carnival marking the start of the winter season and the new hotels and lodges were filled with capacity crowds. Skiers and winter sports enthusiasts from all the leading resort areas and clubs visited Park City during the season including many well known the world over. Lowell Thomas, famed news broadcaster, sportsman, and world traveler, lent his name to the contests held that year, making the beginning of the first annual Lowell Thomas Classic. Another famous visitor that year was Miss Lynda Byrd Johnson, daughter of the president. Miss Johnson took her first skiing lessons in December and afterwards made a tour of the recreation area and mine tunnel ride. Many visitors came to town aboard the "Hootspa Special", the first passenger train to serve Park City in 15 years. Through the cooperation of the Union Pacific Railroad, 322 tourists and sightseers from the Salt Lake City and Ogden areas as well as from out of state came to Park City via the Weber Canyon and Silver Creek route. The "Hootspa Special" was reminiscent of the ski trains Of the 1930s and was an innovation acquainting many more people with the new resort area and boosted both Park City and Utah skiing.

In February, 1966, the 3rd annual dog sled races were held at Flinders Mountain Meadow Ranch near Snyderville. Dog sled teams of all descriptions competed for $1,000 awarded in prize money. The races lasted three days with prizes going to the teams making the best time in the 15 to 20-mile races held each day. Over 1,500 spectators watched the races and enjoyed the hospitality of Park City's new hotels, restaurants, and gay 90s saloons. On Washington's birthday weekend skiers of all ages, visitors and sightseeing groups, and tourists from as far away as the Pacific coast, crowded into town to enjoy the sports and just bask in the clear winter sunshine, high above the crowded valley's smoke and fog. With its new hotels and cafes catering to record crowds and its honky-tonk bars packed to over-flowing, it looked just like old times again at Park City.

Early Park City ski bunnies. Note the length of their skis.

Even with its shiny new ski lifts and modern equipment skiers found they still had to approach the mountain on its own terms. On the afternoon of Dec. 21, 1966, a snow slide unexpectedly raced down from a high ridge just above the old Silver King Mine boarding house and swept across the ski slopes below. Three Skiers, Theodore Berg, his son Bruce, and T.J. Jones were carried along by the slide. Young Bruce Berg managed to stay on top of the swirling mass of white while Mr. Jones grabbed a broken tree branch with which he poked an air hole to the surface when the slide finally stopped. A rescue group quickly gathered together but found Mr. Berg too late to save his life. Once again the mountain showed that it was neither tamed nor conquered.

Antiques were fast becoming one of the most fascinating attractions at Park City business houses with some of the best being found at Ed Grose's Antique Floral Shop and at Wilcox's Emporium. In May, 1966, Kendall Webb remodeled his Valley Studio photo shop and built an addition where Dr. John Lambert, a much-needed dentist, opened his office. Later that summer Park City lost a well-known landmark which was also being remodeled. Pop Jenks popular cafe burned in September while it was closed for alterations. Located on the highway just below town it had been a favorite with tourists as well as Park City people for 30 years. Almost all of Park City's old time saloons were also being remodeled to conform with the image tourists expected to find in an old western mining camp. Most of them were already as authentic as they could be, being virtually unchanged since the camp's boom days, but they weren't like the saloons viewers watched on television westerns.

The old Oak Saloon, built by Henry Spriggs and operated for 45 years by "Cappy" Roach, became Bessie's Garter. The Drift Tavern, located in the old Hurlbut Drug Building, became the Gold Digger Saloon while Frankels clothing store was completely renovated and named the Silver Palace. The huge barn-like Grill Saloon became the Handlebar after extensive remodeling and Mike Sophanide's Park Tavern was refinished in early mining camp style and christened the Red Banjo. Bob Murphy turned the old Independent Telephone Building into the Alamo, a bar so filled with western mining camp relics that it was more of a museum than a saloon. Only Heinie Hernans Club and Hugh Steel's Cozy remained unchanged.

For awhile people were beginning to think that winter would never come in 1966 but then in December snow started falling and within days there was over three feet of white powder on the slopes. With a ski season under way once more and the hotels reporting record numbers of reservations Park City began to boom again. In February, 1967, the 3rd annual Lowell Thomas Classic was held with skiers attending from Aspen, Sun Valley, Jackson Hole, Lake Tahoe, the Air Force Academy, and other areas. The contests were close with a few of the local lads making a good showing. On Washington's birthday weekend another "Hootspa Special" ski train steamed into town bringing 350 skiers to join the hundreds who had come by auto and bus.

A new idea called ski-bobbing, in which the skier can either sit or stand and can turn at will, made its appearance on the slopes while motorized snow sleds raced across the sidehills and along the snowpacked streets. The new gas-powered sleds and ski lifts whisked skiers to the top of Crescent Ridge in only minutes, making the days of 40 years before when men like Fred Hauder climbed and skied all day to carry the mail to Brighton seem like an awfully long time ago.

That Park City was becoming more attractive to people from the lower valley communities became more evident all the time judging from the number of families who purchased long vacant houses or built new homes and from the increasing number of people doing business in town. Summit Park atop Parleys Canyon was closer to Park City than to Salt Lake City and even nearer were Sunrise Hills and Silver Creek Estates, two newly started sub-divisions. In May, 1967, another year-round home area was announced. Appropriately named the Treasure Hills, it was located near the base of Quarry Hill, only a few minutes from the center of town. Modern homes and a shopping center were included in the plans, all to add greatly to the stability and economy of the area.

At almost the same time that the new housing development was announced Dave Loeritscher reported that he had disposed of his ranch located midway between Park City and Snyderville. The property was planned to be developed into a whole new ski area and recreation complex by a California company known as Park City West. As part of the continuing expansion of Park City's sports and tourist potential the Treasure Mountain Complex announced the opening of the West's most interesting and unique mining museum. Located in a huge underground chamber two and a half miles from the mouth of the Spiro Tunnel it soon contained everything in the way of early mining relics and machinery. A second museum was also planned for a location near the tunnel's entrance. By the arrival of the 1967-68 ski season Park City had become a summer fun area as well as a winter sports center with plenty to do and see no matter what the season.

As 1968 dawns over the Treasure Mountains 100 years of Park City history is drawing to a close. A century has passed since that day when a handful of weary soldier-prospectors climbed the dividing ridge from Big Cottonwood Canyon and looked out across the Bonanza Flats to the Treasure Mountains. A century of discovery, exploration, and growth that transformed a quiet canyon visited by only an occasional band of wandering Indians into first a tent and board shack boom town of rowdy miners and then into a first class city of respected and substantial citizens.

Tourists are now carried to the top of the peaks in only minutes inside comfortable gondola cabins high above the rugged slopes where bearded and booted prospectors once hiked for hours. Their ride takes them by the old Woodside Mine where a poor miner named Tom Kearns dug for silver and past the Mayflower Mine where the strange actions of R.C. Chambers and his lawsuit created a silver queen. From the retreat of a warm cafe the viewer can look down on the famous old Silver King Mine where over $100,000,000 in silver was dug from the bowels of the earth and beyond to where other great mines and mills added to the camp's total production of a half billion dollars and more.

With the bottom of the treasure chest not yet in sight and modern means available to allow ever deeper mining Park City's second century promises a brighter future than ever. And with a proposed Arts and Sciences Center as well as a fresh-water lake for water skiing and skating planned for Deer Valley and a golf course double its present size its destiny of becoming the west's leading fun and recreation center is assured. Already ground work is progressing for a whole new complex of ski lifts and resort facilities at the edge of town and all within only minutes of the areas population centers. New subdivisions are in the making and high on the Bonanza Flats summer homes are being built.

With an exciting and colorful past unrivaled by any mining camp behind it and the future bright with promise of even greater things to come it is little wonder that as a new century dawns over the Wasatch Park City folks are justified in being proud of their Treasure Mountain Home.

The Dewey Theatre on upper Main Street, long a Park City favorite.

ABOUT THE AUTHORS:

George Thompson was born and raised in Park City, a descendant of one of the pioneer families of 1847. He was employed by several of the old Park City mining companies, including the Silver King and the Park Utah. Long a student of western history, he has more than 100 published articles to his credit. Much of the material in this book was drawn from his extensive collection of Park City memorabilia. He is the author of five western history books including the best-selling *Some Dreams Die: Utah's Ghost Towns and Lost Treasures.*

Fraser Buck was born in Nova Scotia and came to Park City in 1894. In 1910 he became manager of the pioneer Welsh, Driscoll & Buck general store. He served as city councilman and as director of the New Park Mining Company. His life long collection of Park City historical material and his careful editing of it helped make this book possible. Mr. Buck died on April 25th, 1979.

INDEX

GORLINSKI'S GENERAL MAP OF

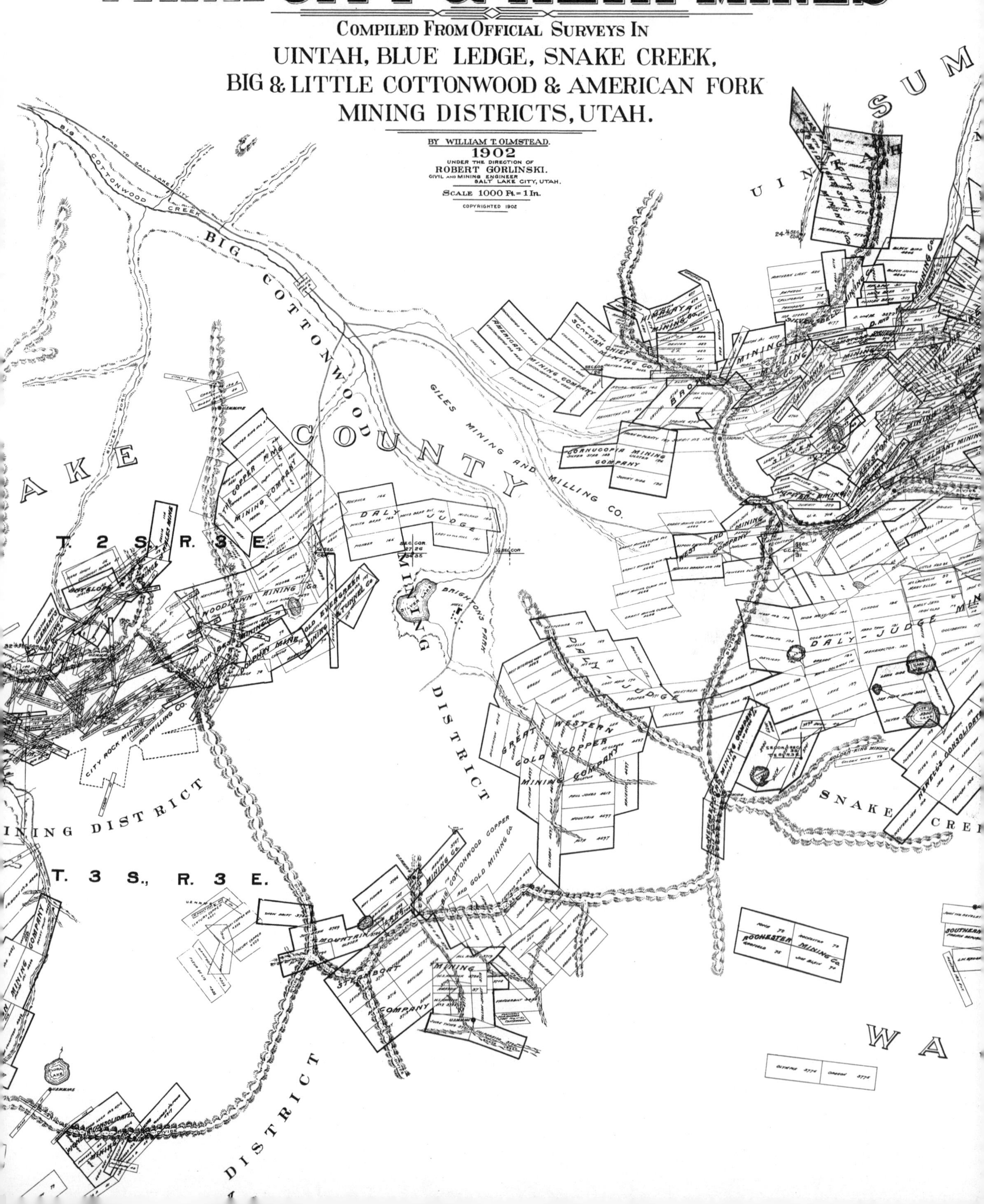